"**Guyana: History and Literature** *illuminates the troubled history of the author's native country through essays and reviews whose erudite, balanced and humane critiques confirm the creativity as well as tragedy of contemporary Guyana.*"

Bridget Brereton
Emeritus Professor of History
University of the West Indies, Trinidad and Tobago

"*The author's interest in history and expertise in literary analysis inform this fine work which rescues from obscurity many works relevant to an understanding of Guyanese literature and contemporary society.*"

Peter Fraser
Senior Research Fellow
Institute of Commonwealth Studies, University of London

"*While the sixty-four book reviews in* **Guyana: History and Literature** *cover much of the country's history, from Amerindians to the present time, they also acknowledge efforts of Guyanese to shape their lives in positive directions.*"

Brinsley Samaroo
Emeritus Professor of History
University of the West Indies, Trinidad and Tobago

Guyana: History and Literature

Frank Birbalsingh

Published to coincide with the
50th Anniversary of Guyana's Independence 1966-2016

First published in Great Britain by Hansib Publications in 2016

Hansib Publications Limited
P.O. Box 226, Hertford, SG14 3WY

info@hansibpublications.com
www.hansibpublications.com

ISBN 978-1-910553-31-2

A CIP catalogue record for this book
is available from the British Library

Production by Hansib Publications Limited
Printed in Great Britain

CONTENTS

CONTENTS

PART THREE

PREFACE

Guyana is the only English-speaking nation on the mainland of South America. As a former British colony, it might be compared with Belize (formerly British Honduras), the only English-speaking nation in Central America, except that Belize has strong and historic relations with Spanish-speaking neighbours. Guyana, meanwhile, has one foot – its North-Eastern, Atlantic coast – that dips in the Caribbean sea, and the other buried deep into the Amazon forest, which seals the territory off from neighbours such as Venezuela in the West, Brazil in the South, and Suriname in the East. There is no doubt of Guyana's strong, creole, cultural links to English-speaking Caribbean islands like Jamaica and Barbados, with similar populations mainly of African descent; but its South American location, between a huge forest and a wide sea, also suggests a continental component within its national profile.

Slavery and indenture were the chief colonising tools of European explorers and adventurers who established plantations, in Guyana, growing coffee, cotton and local produce, before switching to more profitable, large scale cultivation of sugar on plantations that required workers as slaves, brought from Africa, and as indentured immigrants mainly from India, but also from China, Madeira and other places. Guyanese place names, for instance, Uitvlugt and Soesdyke from Holland, Le Repentir and Chateau Margot from France, and Hampton Court and Wales from Britain, give away the country's domination by European, colonial rulers, for three and a half centuries, the Dutch from the beginning of the seventeenth century to the early nineteenth, the French during brief periods mixed with Dutch and British rule, and the British continuously from the early nineteenth century to Guyana's independence in 1966.

Whether under Dutch, French or British rule, the naked inhumanity of slavery and the dehumanising horrors of the Atlantic slave trade were well known. Suffice to say that, for two and a half centuries, from around 1600 to 1838, with African slaves as the main workers, Blacks formed a clear majority of the Guyanese population that also consisted of much smaller numbers of Whites serving as administrators, merchants or plantation officials, and equally small numbers of brown, mixed blood African/Europeans. But hundreds of thousands of Indian indentured workers were brought between 1838 and the end of indenture in 1917, and although Africans remained a majority until about the end of the nineteenth century, by 1911, Indians had taken over majority status in Guyana's population, which they retain to the present day. The joint effect of an Indian majority and a South American location account for Guyana's unique position in the Caribbean. (Of Caribbean islands only Trinidad & Tobago has a large Indian population, although not a majority.)

Inevitably, three hundred and fifty years of colonial rule have left an imprint on Guyanese society the basic formation of which, during slavery, was regulated by values of race, class and colour, with Whites as the ruling class, brown or mixed blood Euro-Africans in the middle, and Blacks as the lowest class. When they first arrived, Indians occupied the lowest rank within the plantation structure, below Blacks. But largely through economic enterprise, Indians not only rapidly rose to higher social levels but, through their newly acquired numerical majority in the population, had a decisive impact on democratic, post-colonial elections, based principally on ethnic preference.

While plantation manners and population changes are crucial factors in the growth of Guyanese society, they omit an important aspect of Guyanese social development: as already mentioned, whether voluntarily or through compulsion, Guyana was settled by succeeding populations of Europeans, Africans, Indians, Chinese, Madeirans and others; but all these were preceded by the first settlers - Amerindians, indigenous to the Americas - for instance, the Arecuna, Arawak, Akawaio, Carib, Macusi, Patamona, Warrau, Wapisiana and Waiwai who, especially during the colonial period, lived in virtual seclusion, within the Amazon forest, insulated from their fellow countrymen who, living on the Atlantic coast, derisively dismissed them as mere "bucks."

Such biased attitudes have changed since independence, and Amerindians whose own languages, legends, folktales and culture have now been recognized, appear as characters principally in the fiction of Wilson Harris. Review #36, in *Guyana: History and Literature*, also comments on Roy Heath's novel *Orealla* which considers the fate of a Macusi character named Carl who is alienated by contemporary, Guyanese culture. An even more positive sign of growth of a more inclusive, Guyanese nationality is seen in recently concluded national elections, when Amerindian voters were hotly canvassed by major political parties, and may have played an important role in the final result. While creolization remains a continuing process of cultural change in the whole Caribbean basin, unique elements in Guyana, including increasing closeness to Brazil, one of the BRIC nations, point to evolution of a more multicultural, Guyanese nationality, at least partially reflecting its South American character.

ACKNOWLEDGEMENTS

Thanks to the British Library for use of research materials over many years. Thanks also to Harry Ramkhelawan and his paper *Indo-Caribbean World* in which most of the reviews in *Guyana: History and Literature* first appeared. I am most grateful to Katharine Birbalsingh and Christine Birbalsingh for help with word processing, and to Arif Ali and Alan Cross of Hansib for publication.

INTRODUCTION

Part One of *Guyana: History and Literature* opens with three essays - "Degraded by Usages of Slavery," "Here Were Blacks, Yellows and Tawnies," and "The Colony was not Regarded as Home," each on an historical text written respectively by Dr. George Pinckard, Henry Bolingbroke, and Henry Dalton. These essays introduce sixty-four book reviews that form the prime focus of *Guyana: History and Literature*.

The sixty-four reviews in Part Two consider books, mostly novels about Guyana, including books on other subjects such as Guyanese history and politics, or six volumes of poetry by Guyanese. The reviews follow a rough chronology that opens with writing on Guyana by visitors, then narratives reflecting on African slavery or its aftermath. Next are reviews of books about indenture and the plantation experience, mainly of Indians, as well as reviews of volumes on the two most important Guyanese politicians of the twentieth century – Dr. Cheddi Jagan and Mr. Forbes Burnham. Other pieces follow on writing by Guyanese in the diaspora and the six volumes of poetry.

Part Three of *Guyana: History and Literature* consists of a longer essay and an interview: the essay "He [Burnham] put Fat Black People to Work in Sugar and Rice Factories" discusses a fictional portrait of Forbes Burnham's Presidency by five authors, one Indian-Trinidadian, and the others Indian-Guyanese, while the interview with Wilton Angoy, "Fear of Indian-Guyanese Domination," puts its finger on perhaps the root cause of political turmoil in Guyana. The aim of the short, historical essays, book reviews, and longer essay and interview is to create a general impression of the interdependence between recurring themes in Guyanese history and literature.

Subjects in *Guyana: History and Literature* are chosen randomly to produce an informal rather than systematic, academic study. For instance, there is no commentary on Amerindian legends or folktales which have been translated into English, and while there is no review of novels by Edgar Mittelholzer, Guyana's most gifted novelist, references to Mittelholzer's work creep in regularly, and insinuate a feeling of Mittelholzer's spirit haunting the entire volume. Also, although Walter Rodney's seminal work - *A History of the Guyanese Working People 1881-1905* - is not formally discussed, its celebration of interdependence and cooperation between Guyana's two major ethnic groups, meshes into a spirit of national cooperation with which most items in *Guyana: History and Literature* are imbued.

If there is no formal examination of fiction by Rooplall Monar, we do not miss references to familiar idioms of Guyanese, plantation speech of which Monar is the acknowledged master. As for Wilson Harris, *éminence grise* of Guyanese literature, his name appears often enough, even if his books are not individually analysed. Work by every important Guyanese writer may not be covered in *Guyana: History and Literature,* but the volume creates a reliable impression of main themes of Guyanese history and literature.

The territory of Guyana was inhabited by Amerindians for centuries before its recorded history, written by Europeans, took shape in the late sixteenth century. At first, the territory was named "The Wild Coast," a section of the North Eastern edge of South America that would later be subdivided into British Guiana, (B.G.) Dutch Guiana (Suriname) and French Guiana (Guyane). As part of a continuous struggle among

European nations for possessions and power in the New World, and frequent trading of possessions with each other, as dictated by fortunes of war, contacts were made by the Spanish, Portuguese, English, French and Dutch in what is today Guyana; but it was the English explorer, Sir Walter Raleigh who, in 1596, wrote the first book-length description of Guyana - *The Discoverie of the Large, Rich and Beauwtiful Empyre of Guiana with a Relation of the Great and Golden Citie of Manoa which the Spanyards call El Dorado.*

Greed for gold, in the form of a legendary, golden city of Manoa, lured most European adventurers to Guyana's shores; and by the early nineteenth century, out of all competitors, the Dutch held adjoining colonies of Essequibo, Demerara and Berbice for the longest, continuous periods. In 1803, after much colonial horse trading, all three colonies passed finally into British hands. Not until 1831 was the previously amalgamated colony of Demerara-Essequibo united with Berbice to form the single colony of British Guiana, (B.G.) that remained as such until 1966 when the colony gained freedom and became the independent nation of "Guyana." To avoid repetition, whether events take place before 1966, in colonial B.G., or after 1966 in independent Guyana, the country will mostly be referred to as "Guyana" throughout *Guyana: History and Liter*ature.

After more than three centuries of European rule in Guyana, African slavery and Indian indenture left the most enduring influences, in the African case, of ingrained hatred of servitude, and in the Indian, of bitter memories of exploitation. Slavery ended in 1838 when indenture began, mainly with Indians, but including smaller groups of Madeiran Portuguese, Chinese from Hong Kong, and others. While Africans were brought to work as slaves on British-owned plantations, Indian labourers later worked on the same plantations after emancipation, when they occupied identical logies (dwelling quarters) vacated by the emancipated Africans.

But a dilemma arose after Africans had begun arriving from around the early sixteenth century, and formed a majority of the population of Guyana up to the middle of the nineteenth century: as more and more indentured Indians arrived, between 1838 and 1917, their growing numbers overtook those of the Africans who had preceded them. This reversal in the proportion of African/Indian numbers is what created a mathematical enigma in democratic elections when universal, adult suffrage was introduced in the 1950s; for in free and fair elections, where votes were cast on a basis of ethnic preference, the more numerous Indians consistently emerged victorious over the longer-resident African-Guyanese.

Although, in 1953, all ethnic groups in Guyana supported one united party, the People's Progressive Party (PPP) led by Dr Cheddi Jagan, African-Guyanese later came to be represented by the People's National Congress, (PNC) a political party led by Forbes Burnham, which won fewer seats than the Indian-Guyanese party – a revamped People's Progressive Party, still led by Dr. Cheddi Jagan - in three consecutive elections in 1957, 1961 and 1964. These majority PPP victories in 1957, 1961, and 1964 confirmed that, so long as ethnic voting prevailed, an African-Guyanese party could not win a majority of votes, in free and fair elections, by defeating the more numerous Indian-Guyanese who had arrived in Guyana more than two centuries after them.

Whether openly expressed or not, this perception of unfairness, built into the electoral infrascture of Guyana, developed into an abiding conviction among African-Guyanese that what they saw as their righteous claim to political supremacy must be asserted on a basis of their prior arrival in the country. As introduced by Forbes Burnham, leader of the PNC, in elections, in 1968, this assertion relied on a variety of unfair or illegal electoral practices to secure a majority of votes for his party through repeated rigging of elections, from 1968 to 1985. Although Burnham died in August, 1985, elections held in December, later the same year, were staged by Desmond Hoyte, the new PNC leader, who employed even more rigorous rigging than Burnham to achieve victory.

If it is unacceptable for an African-Guyanese minority to be out-voted by an Indian-Guyanese majority, in free and fair elections, during the colonial period, 1957-1964, it is equally unacceptable for an Indian-Guyanese majority to be disenfranchised by illegally manipulated elections between 1968 and 1985, since Indian-Guyanese did not gain numerical ascendancy over African-Guyanese through pre-conceived planning: the discrepancy is clearly an accident of history created by British imperial rulers, whose guiding star was consistent economic profit, or increased self-enrichment, totally unmindful of any sociological fall out. Greedy economics of empire nurtured Guyana's tangled sociology by bringing Africans, Indians and other, smaller ethnic groups from foreign lands and lumping them, unceremoniously together, in barely livable conditions, in Guyana.

Imperial greed, however, is not the only explanation of Guyana's persistent, ethnic dilemma: political collusion too, through cynical, colonial neglect also plays a part. Long before the 1950s, (in 1929) when a British emissary, Rev. C.F. Andrews, was sent from India by Mahatma Gandhi, to observe conditions of Indian immigrants in Guyana, his "Impressions of B.G. 1930: An Emissary's Report" [p. 97] recognised a potential for friction between Indian- and African-Guyanese: "I wondered more than once whether some rise in psychological temperature might not produce a racial clash between East Indians and Africans of a very painful nature." [p. 60] At that distance in time, on a mere visit, Andrews foresaw the problem: "Negroes [Africans] and coloured people… whose forefathers actually made B.G. so fruitful… are never likely to do more than patiently tolerate, in a friendly spirit, the East Indians who came into their country." [p. 60]

Much later, similar insight is shown by Eusi Kwayana and his wife Tchaiko Kwayana in their book *Scars of Bondage: A First Study of the Slave Colonial Experience of Africans in Guyana* [p. 85] where they argue that foundations of civil society in Guyana were first laid by African-Guyanese. This is the crux of the matter that highlights the conundrum of resolving a colonial-made dilemma: in elections requiring fairly sophisticated and rational or, at least, objective consideration of issues and policies, all that joint survivors of slavery and indenture, in Guyana, can so far muster is spontaneous, automatic, emotional or tribal gestures of preference, stemming directly from ethnic loyalty.

Ethnic voting is one of many aberrations arising out of colonialism in the Caribbean, through a mix of fractures, divisions, dislocations and discontinuities, embedded in issues of race, class, colour, and a continuing need of Guyanese or West Indians to replace feelings of deracination from their lands of origin, with a practical degree of adaptation to the native Amerindian culture of their new homeland. Amerindians not only preceded Africans and Indians as migrants in the region, but suffered genocide from Europeans in Caribbean islands, and exile in the Guyana forest. Yet Amerindian literature, as hinted earlier, is almost completely neglected.

Roy Heath's novel *Orealla* exposes a yawning chasm between Africans and Indians living on the Guyanese coast, and the interior (inland) culture of Carl, an Amerindian Macusi, whose village, Orealla, provides him with: "the security of the womb [away from] the terrors and beauty of this [coastal] world… [while] Carl and his clan were holding out against the advance of an alien way of life with the dead hand of its justice sanctifying a crime of appalling enormity." [p. 153] Heath suggests nothing less than a redefinition of a (colonial) concept of creolisation to include, not only indigenisation to the Caribbean environment but, in some degree, adaptation at least to aspects of the culture of first migrants to the region – Amerindians – our First Nations or indigenes.

Part One

"DEGRADED BY USAGES OF SLAVERY"

George Pinckard
Notes on the West Indies Including Observations Relative to the Creoles and Slaves of the Western Colonies and the Indians of South America. 2nd. Edition.
London, Baldwin, Cradock Joy, Paternoster Row & L.E.Seeley, Fleet Street. 1816. Two Volumes

George Pinckard (1768-1835) studied medicine first at St. Thomas and Guys Hospitals in London, then at Edinburgh, before he graduated, in 1792, in Leyden. He was appointed as physician to the forces, and served under the command of Sir Ralph Abercromby during his expedition to the West Indies in 1795. Pinckard's *Notes on the West Indies* gives candid, day-to-day impressions of the West Indies, and Guianese colonies off the coast of South America, in the last decade of the eighteenth century. *Notes* also includes reflections on medical matters, for example, the treatment of yellow fever, a fearsome scourge at the time, and on the author's views as a passionate advocate of the abolition of slavery when anti-slavery opinion was gathering steam.

Coming directly from Barbados, Pinckard lands in Demerara-Essequibo on 21st April, 1796, and is immediately struck by the Dutch appearance of the chief town, Stabroek. Demerara-Essequibo, after all, had been in Dutch hands for much of the previous two centuries of turbulent warfare between European colonizers. Instantly, following up on what he had recently seen in Barbados, another slave colony, Pinckard seizes an opportunity to take up the cudgels against slavery: "Divested of every right, a slave has no redress, not even against the bitterest wrongs; however oppressed, however injured, he has no resource - no means of relief! Not having the power of changing his home, he has no escape from ill usage or cruelty; but is condemned to travel the long journey of life in hopeless discontent." [pp. 342-343]. Hopeless discontent! How closely observed, exact, and seemingly deeply felt is Pinckard's eloquent denunciation of the inherent inhumanity of slavery!

Harping back to Barbados which he recalls as something of a sub-metropolis, and source of world news to neighbouring islands, remote from the European centre of the world, Pinckard cannot miss the same all-pervasive aura of slavery around him in Demerara-Essequibo: first a slave begs him to buy her; then a white woman takes delight merely upon hearing the cries of a slave being beaten; and he witnesses a slave being flogged by two drivers who spread their victim on the street, with arms outstretched and tied to stakes, while his feet are splayed on the street in the form of a 'Y' and also tied. Stung enough to introduce a note of vitriol into his normally precise views and controlled writing, Pinckard defines drivers as: "Slaves so termed from being promoted to the distinguished office of following their comrades, upon all occasions, with a whip at their backs, as an English carter attends his horses." [p. 348].

On a visit to Mr. Osbourn, a planter, Pinckard is rowed by slaves six miles up the Demerara river, after which his boat is pulled a further two miles up a creek, before he reaches Arcadia, Osbourn's coffee plantation. A neighbour, Mr. Dougan, owns a sugar estate that also grows coffee and fruits - oranges, shaddocks, forbidden fruit, limes, lemons, cherries, custard apples, avagata pears, grenadilloes, water lemons, mangoes. While there is nothing extraordinary in such tropical productivity and variety, what is certainly unusual is Dougan's apparently affectionate relationship with his slaves, to some of whom he assigns property that they are responsible for upkeeping. Although Dougan claims his slaves are happy, and do not need to be emancipated, he does not oppose emancipation.

Dougan's happy slaves, however, are miles apart from Pinckard's description of a slave market, where slaves are inspected and handled like merchandise, being made to jump, bend, spread their arms or open their mouths in order to be examined, before one of them is selected, and a piece of string or coloured tape is tied around his or her neck. Among Dutch proprietors, the scene consists of a long table at one end of which sits the auctioneer or vendue master, while at the other end the slave on sale stands on a chair. Slaves parade along the table and are viewed by potential buyers on either side. It is like cattle in Smithfield market, as Pinckard observes. Nothing could be more objectifying, degrading or dehumanizing; and it says something of the coarseness of plantation culture on the whole that the market is attended both by women and children.

For all that, Pinckard's eloquently professed sympathy for slaves will probably fall on deaf ears among readers nowadays. He does not argue against slavery on grounds of human equality, or on what we now see as universal principles of indivisible human rights for all, advocated, for example, by international organizations like the United Nations. His argument is based on personal belief in the inhumanity and injustice of slavery. For him, Africans belong to an ethnic group that is less developed than Europeans but, rather than exploit this difference, he recommends that Europeans should treat Africans - natural underdogs - with kindness and humanity. Slavery undoubtedly violates this personal code of morality, and naturally elicits the persuasive catalogue of cruelty and injustice suffered by slaves.

On a visit to Berbice where travel between plantations is by river, Pinckard is impressed by the strength of negro/slave oarsmen who row the boat: "That even negroes could support so many hours of heavy and incessant labour in such a climate was past our conjecture. The only relief they required was to rest, occasionally, for a few minutes upon their oars." [p. 418] Again, it is the difference of the African underdog and his physical prowess that Pinckard notices. Essentially, his is a liberal/paternalistic view that enjoins just reward for hard work or faithful service from a humane master.

The hospitality that the author receives from his Dutch hosts in Berbice is generous and lavish. He also meets Amerindians whom he regards as: "ignorant of the comforts and conveniences of civilization." [p. 503]. As a fresh culture emerging out of a so-called European civilising mission in the new world of the Americas and the Caribbean, Pinckard's impression of British Caribbean colonial society is hardly admiring. He relates that, at night, his Dutch hosts wished him and his fellow guests good night by accompanying them to their bedroom, and saying in French, that if they needed anything else, they only had to ask a slave; it was none of their business: "This was genuine West Indian complaisance; it offered a lamentable proof of the absence of moral principle in a country degraded by the usages of slavery." [p. 537]. Despite his own unnoticed moral failings, Pinckard is still correct in pinning everything on slavery as a degrading yet defining factor of national development in British Guianese, colonial society.

"HERE WERE BLACKS, YELLOWS AND TAWNIES"

Henry Bolingbroke
A Voyage to the Demerary, Containing a Statistical Account of the Settlements there, and of those on the Essequibo, the Berbice and other Contiguous Rivers of Guyana.
London, Richard Phillips, Stevenson and Matchett, Printers, Norwich, 1807.

Born in Norwich, England, Henry Bolingbroke (1785-1865) worked in Demerara-Essequibo as vendue master or auctioneer in a slave market, from 1798 to 1808, after which he served as vendue master in Suriname, before retiring home to England in 1813. His *A Voyage to Demerary* consists chiefly of letters about his experience in Demerara-Essequibo, which he wrote home to his family. He arrived shortly after the British capture of Demerara-Essequibo and Berbice in 1796, when there was an orgy of colony-swapping between Britain, Holland and France, until a final take-over of these colonies by Britain, in September, 1803.

Bolingbroke's first impression of Stabroek, (Georgetown), catches an atmosphere of vigorous jostling and juggling among a nondescript, polyglot crowd of Africans: "Here were blacks, yellows and tawnies, bawling and vociferating in a wretched jargon, half Dutch and half English, whether he had anything to sell, each trying to hitch himself closer than his neighbour." [p. 24] No one was native Caribbean, and each vied for survival in a frenzied melée, within an environment unfamiliar to them all, Africans as well as Europeans, whether slave or free.

One year later, by the author's estimate, the population of Stabroek consisted of 5,000 negroes (Blacks), 2,000 free Coloureds, and 1,500 Whites. Of the Whites two-thirds were English, while the remainder were divided among a nondescript commingling of Dutch, Germans, Prussians, Russians, Swedes, Danes, Spaniards, French and Americans. In 1774 its superior harbour, and better developed estates clinched selection of Stabroek as capital city of Demerara-Essequibo.

Upon Bolingbroke's arrival, the principal streets in Stabroek ran in a straight direction with Middle Street, for example, beginning at King's Stelling, the main wharf on the East bank of the Demerara river, and running directly East. Middle street was paved with bricks, and carried lamps along either side. The colony's Governor and Chief Secretary had their houses in Stabroek. There was also a court, and Sunday services were held, in one church building, by a Dutch priest from 10.00 - 11.00 am, and an English priest from 11.00 am - 12.00 noon. Such were the marks of early Guianese urbanisation!

The wider, regional picture was one of power and prosperity shifting from longer-cultivated, more prosperous Caribbean, island colonies to Demerara-Essequibo. In 1796, for example, Demerara-Essequibo yielded more wealth than all the Anglophone islands together, except Jamaica, which, to the author's regret, confirmed: "the declining state of our own islands." [p. 327] One reason for greater productivity in Demerara-Essequibo was the superior enterprise of English settlers over the Dutch, who neglected the coastland for fear of flooding, while English settlers built dykes, began distilling rum, and growing cotton on the coast. In 1796, Bolingbroke writes, 6,000 bales of cotton were imported by Liverpool (the English port) from Demerara-Essequibo whereas, in 1804, only seven years after the British take-over, 24,970 bales were imported.

Bolingbroke sees some dissimilarity between Dutch and British colonists: "They [British and Dutch] naturally both go out with a view of making money; but the one [the Dutch] with an intention of ending his days abroad, and the other of returning to his native country." [pp. 304-5] He also notes that a British colonist will be content with a simple cottage, while his Dutch counterpart will invest in a large house, garden, and pleasure boat with trained negro sailors. In spite of his Anglo-centric partisanship, Bolingbroke acknowledges a somewhat hands-off approach in British colonists, who are well known as absentee owners of Caribbean plantations, and display: "restless pursuit of riches to be displayed in old age among new acquaintance, and in another hemisphere." [p. 385]

During his six years in Demerara-Essequibo, Bolingbroke observes that North American theatre companies toured the region twice, and comments: "In an illiterate community, which can only learn through the ear, the drama is an important engine of instruction, and might be rendered essentially conducive to historic and moral information and even to the civilization of the vulgar and indisciplined." [p. 43] To his credit, the author perceives a heightened sense of orality in local culture, although not without betraying his dismissive disdain of the culture itself.

Bolingbroke believes most negroes [Blacks] were already slaves in Africa, before arriving in the Caribbean where they were not only better fed, but treated with: "the utmost degree of luxury and accommodation consistent with sobriety." [p. 112] By the author's account "seasoned negroes" can rear domestic animals, plant gardens or work as tradesmen and keep retail shops, accumulating enough money to buy their freedom. While he regards enslavement of free Blacks as "a detestable oppression" [p. 111] the author claims that many negroes told him they considered being brought to the Caribbean "a real service." [p. 111] He also reports that Blacks who owned slaves were reputed to deal more harshly with them than white owners, while white owners themselves would often threaten to sell their slaves to a black owner if they misbehaved.

Unlike Pinckard, Bolingbroke stoutly defends the African slave trade, arguing that the African slave in the Caribbean is better regarded as a vassal because: "he has climbed a step in humanity." [p. 124] To him the slave trade: "redeems slaves to exalt them into vassals," [p. 130] and its continuance: "is of value to the whole negro race." [p. 130] He openly sneers at Wilberforce and other abolitionists, and is certain that if Blacks who had lived for a long time in the Caribbean: "were sent over to Africa to enlist voluntary recruits only, they, would, I doubt not, be followed back by whole nations [of Africans] of their own accord." [p. 130]

Bolingbroke's preposterous views on slavery imply that he is locked into the blindness of seeing imperialism as a civilising mission. In a society where white slave masters routinely exercised "droit de seigneur" rights over powerless, female slaves, he asserts: "The number of negroes may apparently decrease, and yet the collective population may be on the increase; for many negro girls cohabit with white overseers, and spend the years of child-bearing in producing mulatto progeny." [p. 127] Since female slaves are powerless, there can be no better example of blaming the victim.

Yet, Bolingbroke, identifies important elements in the evolution of Guyanese society. Demerara-Essequibo, for instance, is seen as a beneficiary of Caribbean islands, notably Barbados, that accomplished their: "appointed task in the civilization of the world," [p. 369] through "the cultivation of sugar in small islands, where African labourers could not run away; [without which] there would have been no possibility of rearing and training a creole peasantry adapted for the coasts of the West Indian archipelago" [p. 369] Demerara-Essequibo also had advantages in sugar production over the islands: there was less danger from hurricanes and drought, and punts rather than mules could be used, making the transportation of canes cheaper, and helping to reduce production costs over all.

Despite limitations in his attitudes to race, from his initial impression of a bewildering kaleidoscope of races and colours when he first enters Stabroek, Bolingbroke at least hints at, even if he does not fully recognise, the fundamental importance of ethnicity in Caribbean society. If he dwells too much on relations between ruling Whites and powerless Blacks, it is because slavery was the dominant institution of his time; but he was also aware of ethnic feelings and burgeoning ethnic loyalties. His reference to: "the civilization of the vulgar and indisciplined," or to differences between black owners and the slaves whom they ill-treated, suggest a subtle insinuation of class as a bedfellow of race, while his distinction between slaves who are either black, tawny, mulatto, or mestee confirms awareness of shades of colour as another divisive factor of ethnicity, especially when buying a housekeeper: "who will do all that a wife does except preside at table." [p. 43]

Although Bolingbroke depicts Amerindians mostly as a hostile presence on the fringe of society, for example, in his report that, toward the end of the 1763 slave rebellion, Dutch troops drove defeated slaves into the forest where they were killed by Amerindians, he does not ignore the latter. Amerindians were enough of a factor for him to observe: "The Indians [Amerindians] have a sincere dislike and contempt for the blacks, considering them apparently as an inferior race, born, like cattle, to labour for the service of their betters." (p. 196) Bolingbroke's picture is one in which, ethnic variety and mixing has a distinct potential for friction woven into the fabric of local society.

"THE COLONY WAS NOT REGARDED AS HOME"

Henry G. Dalton
The History of British Guiana. (Two Volumes)
London, Brown, Green & Longman, 1855.

Henry Gibbs Dalton (1818-1874) was the son of Edward Dalton, former sugar planter, and Postmaster of British Guiana. Henry studied in Brussels and London, before practising briefly as a Visiting Surgeon at two Guyanese estates. He also gained a M.D. from the University of Philadelphia. His two volumes of *The History of British Guiana* are packed with information about all aspects of Guyanese history, including statistics and details such as the name "Essequibo" being given by Juan Essequibel, an officer of Diego Columbus, and an estate in Guyana being owned, in 1841, by Henry Barkly, less than a decade before he became Governor from 1849 to 1852.

Like Bolingbroke, Dalton recognises the commitment and dedication of the Dutch as New World settlers, willing to live with Amerindians, and build permanent structures such as bridges and canals, or institute fresh laws and policies in a new land. The daily routine of a typical Dutch planter, according to Dalton, is for him to rise in the morning, take coffee and drinks, and consult with overseers and assistants, before leaving on horseback for an inspection of his estate, with a boy carrying tobacco and a gin flask, running beside his horse. After giving orders to his workers, he returns home for breakfast that may consist of fish, hams, sausages, pepper pot and cheese. He then has a siesta, visits neighbours, looks over buildings and machinery, or attends to correspondence. Lunch follows with soups, fish, fowl or meat accompanied by beer and wine, while Amerindian servants beat mosquitoes away with branches; and the day concludes with drinking and smoking.

Unlike Pinckard and Bolingbroke, Dalton stresses the unusually powerful role of the plantation owner in creole society, making him sound suspiciously like a feudal lord in medieval times. Firstly, since the owner's slaves are bought by him, they are "human property" totally at his command and mercy; tradesmen who probably come from more developed Caribbean islands are beholden to him for both employment and pay; merchants sell him goods and need his patronage; professional men cannot prosper without his influence; and government officers need his hospitality to carry out their public functions. In all these respects there is little to distinguish the Caribbean plantation owner from a medieval lord of the manor. As Dalton predicts, though, such unlimited, power, influence and wealth would later suffer reversals from economic and other changes.

Dalton falls into line with a common nineteenth century, Darwinist, European view of Africans virtually as a less developed species, who are ignorant and unfortunate victims of more highly developed and civilised Europeans. Besides, in his opinion, Africans are callous, idle, obstinate, cunning, artful, helpless, ignorant, brutal, timid, abject, debased. In his case, it must take more than a touch of hypocrisy or self-contradiction, for Dalton to denounce the plantation system and slavery for exploiting Africans.

So far as daily estate routine goes, work for slaves who lived collectively in long ranges, began at dawn when they were divided into gangs and led by a driver. They worked until 8.00 am, when they took breakfast and a rest. They next worked till noon, had dinner, and worked yet again till 5.00 or 6.00 pm, before going home. Some slaves had small plots of land which they cultivated with crops such as bananas, plantains, yams and eddoes to earn money; they also kept pigs and poultry. For punishment slaves were whipped and put in the stocks, while a worse (unmentioned) punishment was reserved for murder.

Dalton's view of the slave market tallies with Pinckard's: "Delicacy, pity, generosity never interfered with the mercenary considerations which regulated these proceedings." [p. 165] Slaves who escaped into the Guyana forest were called bush negroes, and were regarded as criminals or terrorists. Slave owners were helped by Amerindians in capturing bush negroes; and offered a bounty for the right hand of a bush negro. If such brutality seems to be an outcome of excessive power, it fits in with his notion of its inherently corrupting effect which Dalton sees as the inevitable result of the planter's already mentioned, limitless power: "Unrestrained by the presence of refined or virtuous women, and enjoying a perfect impunity of power over all surrounding associations, the colonists surrendered themselves to a life of unbridled depravity. Having no scandal of public opinion to encounter, being wholly liberated from all religious and social obligations, they formed intimate relations with the humblest of their slaves... gradually breaking down the barriers of honour and decency, until the whole country presented a scene of demoralisation." [p. 174]

Within such a mixed and rapidly evolving social context, Dalton reports hostility between planters and missionaries when the former accused the latter of aiding and abetting slaves who were struggling for emancipation. Dalton also reports briefly on the two most tragic slave rebellions in Guyanese history, in 1763 and in 1823. In Dalton's view: "They [missionaries] were appalled at the despotism and the hardihood exhibited by the white man; at the unlimited extent of punishment, and the means of terrible vengeance he wielded; and were dismayed at the revolting picture of moral abasement so prevalent throughout the land." [p. 288] But the discontinuation of the slave trade by Britain in

1807 reinvigorated movement toward total abolition and, by the 1820s, the writing was on the wall.

By the time of Sir Benjamin D'Urban's installation as Governor in April, 1824: "The condition of the negroes was altered. They were no longer insensate, stolid, and incapable of combination and unanimity. They were already rising in the social scale; some were promoted to situations of trust and confidence, and others had in their turn become masters, and actually owned slaves." [p. 362] Dalton identifies different ways in which Blacks developed wealth and skills as tradesmen, coopers, carpenters, masons, boatmen, or even as hucksters: "employed as vendors of different articles for household uses." [p. 363]

On 21st July, 1831, the three colonies of Demerara-Essequibo and Berbice were united into the colony of British Guiana, and on 12th June, 1833, the British House of Commons passed the bill for Emancipation to take place on 1st August, 1834. Despite resentment over the Apprenticeship Act that required ex-slaves to work until 1838 while being paid, the rejoicing on 1st August, 1834 was universal:" Universal rejoicing commemorated the day. The churches were opened and hundreds flocked to its altars to offer up a prayer of thanksgiving and praise. The militia troops formed a procession in the most public places, where a proclamation and address was read by His Excellency... The negroes in their gayest apparel, paraded the streets and roads." [p. 396]

Although Dalton recognises Emancipation as the most important event in the development of Guyanese society up to that time, he does not ignore insidious flaws lurking within an environment created out of centuries of psychological coercion and physical compulsion. Planter depravity and social debasement have already been noted. More insidious ills lurked, for example, among the Free Coloured who: "aimed at rivalling the Whites in their fashions. Turning away from the advantages which might have resulted from agricultural pursuits, and seeking rather the means of livelihood in the towns, they let several opportunities pass by of advancing as a class... they consequently became much reduced in means and position, and eventually were the worst off in a community where, at one time, they held a middle rank." [p. 255]

In a society rampant with legacies of inequality, whether of race, colour or class, between white and black, or among Blacks themselves, no group felt fully secure from taint or threat. Despite their privilege, even the white creole was vulnerable. He: "is surrounded by dependants and flatterers, and no one restricts his inclinations or corrects his judgment. Under the impression that he is the exclusive lord of the soil to which he is born, he awaits the approach of fortune without making any efforts to seek it... he never rouses himself to compete with more energetic dispositions; hence he is invariably outstripped in the race of life." [p. 314]

Nor did the race for life become easier, after 1838, when Apprenticeship ended, and indentured immigration began. Dalton firmly believes that immigration saved the country from anarchy and dissolution. For all that, when indentured immigrants, whether from the West Indies, India, Madeira, China, or elsewhere began to arrive and stir the population pot, the social mix became so complicated that even planters themselves who, from the beginning, were reluctant settlers, now felt even less at home: "The colony [B.G.] was not regarded as a home, as an adopted country, a field sufficiently worthy of their occupancy but rather as a purgatory, through which they [planters] must pass to obtain the Elysium of their desires. Their exertions to gain wealth and depart were incessant, their anxiety about their success intolerable." [pp. 435-436] History had come full circle to complicate clear distinctions between victimiser and victim. If it was no longer a contest between master and slave, there were still distinctions separating Guyanese from each other in a continuing struggle for equal treatment, harmony and justice.

Part Two

Part Two

TIMELINES OF GUYANESE HISTORY

Lal Balkaran
Timelines of Guyanese History: A Chronological Guide to More than 2000 Key Events in 23 Categories Since 1498. - pp.219. New York, Seaburn Publishing Group, 2012, (Second Edition). ISBN 1-59232-357-X

Timelines of Guyanese History: A Chronological Guide to More Than 2000 Key Events is a handbook rather than treatise on Guyanese history. Its author Lal Balkaran has already produced two photographic documentaries, one on Guyana, and the other on Guyanese Amerindians of whose culture he has first hand experience. A brief Introduction describes *Timelines* as: "a unique and comprehensive reference [work] showcasing a range of issues that helped to shape Guyana and Guyanese." Twenty-three Chapters discuss different aspects of Guyanese history, culture, politics, economics, religions and education.

Chapters in *Timelines* range mostly from three or four to thirteen or fourteen pages in length, the longest – on politics – being forty-two pages long. The first Chapter "Amerindian Issues" sets a pattern of particular years or historical periods being listed chronologically on the left hand side of each page, and commentaries on those years or periods on the right hand side, for example: "1580 – The Dutch make contact with Caribs and attempt a settlement on the Pomeroon," [p. 10] or "1957 – In the August General elections, Stephen Campbell...

becomes the first Amerindian to enter the Legislative Assembly." [p. 17]

What a challenge to classify five hundred years of history into only twenty-three categories! Not simply the scale of the research itself, but anxiety over possible duplication: every topic must not only be related to Guyana, it must also be differentiated enough to appear in Chapters with differing titles. Overlap is inevitable. For instance, issues in Chapters such as "Diplomatic Events," "Political Issues" or "Events Related to Trade Unions" are closely related to each other, as are details in "Business History" "Economic History" and "Mining History." Other Chapters are more discrete, for example, "Amerindian Issues," "Architectural Issues," "History of the Capital City – Georgetown," or "Issues of Slavery." but Balkaran succeeds in giving a plausible overview of Guyanese history.

He succeeds through consistent use of chronology to record facts, events, or topics. For instance, the two entries from "Amerindian Issues" already mentioned about initial Dutch contact with Amerindians, and the much later achievement of Stephen Campbell as the first Amerindian-Guyanese legislator would appear less significant if they were not attached to specific years; and these years 1580 in the first case, and 1957 in the other, remind us of the growth and development of Amerindian society in Guyana from the time of European settlement to the present day. It is well known that Amerindians were virtually excluded from Guyanese coastal society, and not until the twentieth century was their rightful claim to full citizenship accepted in Guyana.

This capacity of visually reproducing the movement of Guyanese history is most prominent in "Political Issues" where chronological listing captures the turbulence of Guyanese history, through Balkaran's consistent notation of swift changes, from one European colonial administration to the other, for example, from Dutch to French to British, and again from French to Dutch and finally British. Equally important is the suggestion that because the Dutch ruled longest in the early period of settlement in the seventeenth and eighteenth centuries, it is to them that Guyana owes the foundation on which its present structure and management of water supply for agriculture, the lifeblood of the nation, is built.

Balkaran captures similar turmoil in a more modern period, during the 1960s, when violence, mayhem and destruction were partly produced by interference from foreign or colonial powers (chiefly the US and Britain) in Guyanese affairs. Although *Timelines* offers neither the extended analysis of an academic treatise, nor the alphabetical organisation of an encyclopedia, it achieves the author's claim in his Introduction of helping Guyanese to: "broaden their knowledge of the country [Guyana.]"

Whether it is used in the home or library, *Timelines* contains a rich miscellany of information which can prevent us from seeing the forest – Guyana - because of the trees – plethora of facts, figures, dates and details. This is inherent in the genre itself of a handbook where an overload of information can reduce seriousness and risk devaluation as mere trivia. The Introduction rules out any such possibility. On page thirty-seven we learn that as early as 1639, Jews arrived in Berbice after fleeing persecution in Brazil; then in 1942 fifty Jewish refugees from Spain are housed in the Mazaruni Penal Settlement. But we don't discover if these two events are linked in the formation of a Jewish minority in Guyana.

DEDICATED EMPIRE BUILDER

Michael Bennett, Ed.
V. Roth, A life in Guyana, Vol. 1, A Young Man's Journey, 1889-1923. pp.346.
Leeds, Peepal Tree, 2003.
ISBN 1-9007-15-54-6

A Life in Guyana, Vol. 2, The Later Years, 1923-1935. pp.302.
Leeds, Peepal Tree, 2003.
ISBN 1-9007-15-55-4

The Roths were an English family with an interest in colonial administration. Vincent (1889-1967) was born in Australia, and in 1907, joined his father Walter (1861-1933) in British Guiana. Two volumes of memoirs, *A Life in Guyana,* were originally written as journals by Vincent Roth, mostly from 1918 to 1935, during his years working for the Lands and Mines Department, in frontier-like conditions, in the interior of Guyana. The journals were later revised by Roth and, after his death, edited by his son-in-law Michael Bennett.

The Roths, father and son, were adventurers, colonial administrators and naturalists, with a zeal for collecting specimens and organising projects. Apart from his work in the Interior, Walter is remembered for his own writings, pioneering contributions to the establishment of the British Guiana Museum, and for his translation into English of *Travels in British Guiana 1840-1844* by the German-born explorer Sir Richard Schomburgk. Vincent, meanwhile, following in his father's footsteps, traversed the length and breadth of Guyana, from the North West District that borders Venezuela to the Corentyne river that forms Guyana's Eastern border with Suriname, much of the time, living among labourers, gold and diamond miners (porknockers) and aboriginal forest dwellers.

Astonishingly, in the midst of all this, Roth finds time to read, write, and record his daily routine of work, the social habits and events around him, and his observations of fruits, trees, insects, flora and fauna, the dangers of travelling up rivers, often at night, and steering over rapids and cataracts. At one stage, Roth serves as warden of a reformatory, and at another as a magistrate, all the time remaining a government officer or administrator.

But Roth's is no narrative for animal rights activists! Animals, often of exotic variety, are regularly killed, skinned and eaten by him and his workers. A dog is killed and its skin used as a rug; fried peccari brain is treated as a delicacy; an armadillo is captured in an exceptionally cruel way, and its meat described approvingly as "menu of the bush". In such circumstances, over the years, it is not surprising that the author falls ill several times, and has to be brought out to hospital in Georgetown, for treatment. Roth's memoirs provide a clinical record of life in the Interior and, through eye-witness accounts, an oral history of interesting or important events.

We learn that public celebrations were held on twenty-first July, 1931 to celebrate the hundredth anniversary of the union of individual colonies, Demerara-Essequibo and Berbice, into the single political entity of British Guiana, and that an indentured Indian, Barossa, told Roth that his mother bequeathed the family's inheritance to him while they were still in India, and caused the rest of the family to hate him, thus forcing him (Barossa) and his wife to secretly abscond and indenture themselves to Guyana. Most interesting of all is Roth's first hand description of the Great Georgetown Fire on Friday, 23rd February, 1945: "Where a few hours ago had stood the business heart of the city [Georgetown] now spread several acres of black and smoking débris picked out by numerous flashing points of light." [Vol. 2, p. 284].

Roth's memoirs could not be more different from Evelyn Waugh's *Ninety-Two Days* (1934), a travelogue also set in Guyana. The difference is that Roth writes from an insider's point of view that reflects genuine interest in Guyanese people, places and customs. His matter-of-fact usage of local words, names and expressions strengthens the authenticity and conviction of his account, for example, "pimplers" (thorns), "bateau" (boat), "ballahoo" (boat), "nara" (stomach pain), "bundari" crab, " quake" (fish basket), "curri-curri" (type of bird), "cuirass" (type of fish), "guglet" (clay goblet for storing drinking water). In particular, the persistent use of "breakfast" as lunch is quintessentially Caribbean.

Although the primary value of Roth's memoirs is their rare and rich cornucopia of information, about every aspect of life in Guyana, during the first half of the twentieth century, the author's self portrait is almost as eye-catching. In addition to his memoirs, Roth edited "Timehri" the Journal of the Royal Agricultural and Commercial Society; wrote *Who is Who in British Guiana 1935-6* (1936); *Where is it? A Gazetteer of British Guiana* (1938); and produced many other invaluable publications. In 1943 he was nominated by the Governor as a member of the colony's Legislative Council; and in 1951 he was made an Officer of the British Empire (OBE) for his services to British Guiana. As we may guess, he brought up a family while he was civil servant, legislator, librarian, journalist and second editor of the *Daily Chronicle*. He was also secretary of the Royal Agricultural and Commercial Society, and helped to set up the British Guiana zoo. Extraordinary!

On the surface, Roth seems like a tireless empire builder. As a member of the white ruling élite in a British Caribbean colony, in the early twentieth century, he enjoyed opportunities unavailable to the majority of ordinary Guyanese. But he used these advantages for the common good. He was not like Evelyn Waugh who writes with lofty condescension and haughty disdain of his: "fascination with distant and barbarous places." Roth fits more into the mould of indigenised, white, colonial families like the Grants of Trinidad, who distinguished themselves as missionaries, businessmen and sportsmen, or the Goddards of Barbados, who excelled in commerce and sport. Whether we call him an empire builder or not, we can deny neither Roth's priceless, pioneering services in early twentieth century Guyana, nor their lasting contribution to the country's social, economic and cultural development.

"WE ARE A SUPERIOR RACE"

Beryl Gilroy
Inkle and Yarico.
Leeds, Peepal Tree Press Ltd. 1996.
ISBN 0-948833-98-X

Inkle and Yarico, by Guyanese Beryl Gilroy (1924), is based on a
story from Richard Ligon's *A True and Exact History of the Island
of Barbados* (1657) about an Englishman, Thomas Inkle, who is
shipwrecked on a small island while on his way to his family
plantations in Barbados. Gilroy (née Answick) was trained as a
teacher in Guyana and, in 1951, migrated to England where she
did further studies, married, and continued her teaching career,
in London, becoming the first black Head-teacher in England.
Gilroy's writing career began with *Black Teacher* (1976), a record
of her experience as a teacher in London. Afterwards, she wrote
novels of which *Frangipani House* (1986) - about residents in a
Guyanese retirement home - is the first, and *Green Grass Tango*
(2001) the last. Gilroy is also the author of a volume of poems -
Echoes and Voices (1991).

In *Inkle and Yarico,* her seventh novel, Gilroy dramatises
Ligon's story of Thomas Inkle using Inkle's own words. After
his shipwreck, Inkle's crew is slaughtered by native Caribs
and he is saved by Yarico, daughter of the chief - Tomo. But
after cohabiting with Yarico for seven years, not to mention
having relationships with two other women, Zeze 'my youthful
delight' [p. 113), and Delvina 'my indiscretion' [p. 113] Inkle

accompanies Yarico on a vessel to Barbados, where he abruptly sells her to a merchant. Events in Ligon's story probably take place during the 17th or 18th century, but discussions in *Inkle and Yarico* about the abolition of slavery, and about contemporary activities of abolitionist Thomas Clarkson, place Gilroy's narrative in the early 1800s, shortly before slavery was fully abolished in 1838.

Debate about the abolition of slavery was as heated in the 1830s as the controversy between American capitalism and Russian communism in the 1960s and 70s; and it sustains much of its drama in the second half of *Inkle and Yarico*, while helping to advance the action into the early 1830s. On one side are plantation owners like Inkle, and on the other are Inkle's former fiancée Alice and her husband Dr. John Clarkson, nephew of Thomas Clarkson. Alice explains that she only got married after believing that her fiancé, Inkle, had died in the shipwreck. She and her husband who is a physician as well as a plantation owner are avowed abolitionists who: "gather information attesting to the cruelties endured by the slaves," [p. 126] which they send to Members of Parliament in London to help in the parliamentary battle for abolition. One can see why abolition was a vexed question when it provokes such fanatical support and fierce hostility among plantation owners themselves.

At first, Inkle claims to be neutral in the debate; but he is soon telling Alice: "We are a superior race. We need others lower than ourselves. Irish, Jews, slaves. In Barbados Jews are forbidden to employ Irish servants. Irish folk work only in their own fields." [p. 126] He is also very blunt in admitting the raw hatred of his fellow planters for abolitionists who could be seen as threatening Britain's rich income from her Caribbean colonies: "among them [Inkle's planter friends] were men whose raw hatred of those who sought to change their lucrative lives knew no bounds." [p. 127]

As narrator and chief character, Inkle steals the limelight; much of the novel's success depends on the consistency and conviction of his portrait. His ill-treatment not only of Yarico, but of Zeze and Delvina is repugnant. For example, while he is at pains to explain to Alice that it was only after he failed to find her, following a most rigorous search, that he began his association with Yarico, he airily dismisses his sexual exploitation of female Carib partners by: "the gulf of civilisation that existed between us. We understood nothing in the same way: friendship, love, kindness all meant different things to each if us." [p. 39] This is no doubt why Inkle can treat Yarico as mere merchandise, and sell her without batting an eye. But somehow Inkle's justification of these racist attitudes seems too coldly bloodless and matter-of-fact, unaccompanied by plausible emotional reactions.

In explaining why he could not imagine fathering children by Yarico, Inkle again coldly confesses: "I simply could not imagine some creature like those around me being my son." [p. 38] In addition, one of his most cruel actions is to confine the son of his most faithful slave in a cage, and hang the boy when his father remonstrates. Inkle does make an attempt to understand his Carib hosts, sometimes described as black Caribs, because they also have African blood. Early on Inkle describes Yarico as "an Eve in Eden," [p. 17] and later admits that: "The forest had a voice of its own... which could be understood by those who loved it." [p. 57] His muddled attitude toward Caribs derives simply from the ignorance and racism of Europeans during that period of history.

As a pioneering novelist exploring early West Indian history, Gilroy illuminates the role of slavery in credible terms. In addition to *Inkle and Yarico*, her earlier novel *Stedman and Joanna: A Love in Bondage* (1992) draws on the account of a British-Dutch soldier John Gabriel Stedman who describes his experience in Suriname in *Narrative of a Five*

Years Expedition Against the Revolted Negroes of Surinam (1790). Gilroy is particularly illuminating in exploring the role of women in slavery. Her female characters – Yarico, Zeze , Delvina and Alice - are far more sturdy, assertive and believable than their male counterparts in *Inkle and Yarico,* and many times more memorable.

"I HAD AS MUCH RIGHT TO FEEL GUYANESE AS ANYONE"

Patricia Wendy Dathan
Bauxite, Sugar and Mud: Memories of Living in Colonial Guyana 1928-1944. pp.220.
St-Anne-de-Bellevue, Quebec, Shoreline, 2006.
ISBN 1-896754-45-7

Wendy Dathan's *Bauxite, Sugar and Mud: Memories of living in Colonial Guyana 1928-1944* is a memoir of her family's expatriate community in Linden, Guyana, during the six years mentioned in the title. Joshua Whalley, Wendy's father, left England in 1928 to work as an accountant for a bauxite company in McKenzie (re-named Linden), in Guyana, well known for its sugar industry and muddy rivers. Linden was then a remote outpost sixty-five miles up the Demerara river and accessible from Georgetown, only by boat. Joshua's wife Gladys joined him in 1929 and Wendy, their first child, was born in 1934. Today, not only have many names been changed in Guyana, but the country is no longer a British colony, the bauxite company Wendy Dathan (née Whalley) knew has been nationalised, and her white expatriate community, named "Watooka" after a nearby creek, completely dispersed in mists of time.

Demand for bauxite during World War One is what first led to serious geological exploration for the ore in Guyana. The Demerara Bauxite Company (DEMBA), a subsidiary of the Aluminium Company of America (ALCOA) was incorporated in 1916, and their first shipment of bauxite made in 1917; but when ALCOA shifted its interest to the US market, the Montreal-based Canadian Aluminium Limited (ALCAN) that employed Joshua Whalley took over mining operations at Linden. ALCAN made a crucial contribution to World War Two: "almost all Canada's military aircraft built between 1940 and 1945, 16,000 of them, were built of aluminium supplied by ALCAN," [p. 145] and Dathan's account of German U-Boat attacks on Allied shipping in the Caribbean catches the drama of a now forgotten saga of sinking ships and tragic loss of life as well as (bauxite) cargoes during the war.

These well-researched details are matched by conviction in an insider's first hand report on Guyanese living conditions, and the culture shock faced by the author's parents when showering with brown-coloured water from the Demerara river, or waging constant warfare against an army of insects such as ants, scorpions, moths, cockroaches, and every variety of snake from the over-sized water camoodie or boa constrictor, to the smaller but poisonous "fer de lance" and labaria, or the deadly Bushmaster, Guyana's answer to the Indian cobra. No wonder the Watooka rule of thumb was: "if it moves kill it;" [p. 54] and when all of this is added to standard provocations of tropical heat, humidity, and mildew, not to mention threat of malaria and yellow fever, it is not hard to understand why Dathan's mother, who left a sleepy English provincial town for a place literally crawling with tropical exotica, never ceased to regard Guyana as "That Awful Place." [p. 13]

Despite the historical value of such information, and many nostalgic details about Guyana's bauxite industry, the Botanic Gardens, an overland trip to Kaieteur Falls, acquaintances such as the Italian Dr. Giglioli, eradicator of malaria from Guyana, and his French-Canadian wife, even about familiar British imports such as Eno's Fruit Salts, Ovaltine and Reckitt's Blue, the outstanding achievement of *Bauxite, Sugar and Mud* is its analysis of "white mores" [p. 31] in the colony, and its sensitive reconstruction of the author's childhood in Linden. For this Dathan relies on sources such as an unpublished journal written by her mother, and the diary of an American friend Carolyn Harder who also lived in Watooka; and to enlarge the scope of her analysis, Dathan throughout compares her observations to those in books about colonial societies, for instance, Michael Swan's *British Guiana: The Land of Six Peoples* (1957), Raymond Smith's *British Guiana* (1962), Evelyn Waugh's travelogue *Ninety-Two Days* (1934) and novel *A Handful of Dust (1934).*

The larger context of her research makes *Bauxite, Sugar and Mud* relevant not only to Guyana but to British colonies in general, for instance, when Dathan writes: "in the Guiana of 1929 the colour bar was complete, making most Whites treated as superior beings, irrespective of rank, job or background, class, education or personality." [p. 31] Racial segregation may be voluntary rather than legislated, but it still gives an impression of Watooka as an apartheid community. Dathan notes, for instance, that: "the [black] servants are not allowed even to reproach the white children," [p. 130] and Watooka children are taught only by white teachers.

Besides: "there were no local books that told us things that were rooted in what we could see and understand around us, and no one told us that this was really home because it was where we were really living." [p. 166] This hits the nail squarely on the head; for the imposition of a foreign culture and its language, values and education system on a colonised population inevitably creates a crisis of identity in those who are colonized. Dathan had one foot in Guyana through her birth, and the other in the colonising culture through her parents. The ambivalence explains the poignancy of her "cri de coeur" when she pleads: "I had as much right to feel as Guyanese as anyone ... even with my alien white skin and overlord political inheritance. Yet I was never allowed... I belonged nowhere." [p. 166]

Dathan's plea/complaint is moving partly because of her childhood aura of earnest, confessional integrity in *Bauxite, Sugar and Mud,* for example, when she speaks of unforgettable affection for nurses who: "rocked us [white Watooka babies] to sleep in their warm brown arms" [p. 119] or with envy of: "the music and rhythm and mystery and romance" [p. 119] in their [her nurses'] lives. But now living in Canada, and having visited Guyana as an adult, Dathan surely cannot miss the irony of hundreds of thousands of her fellow [black] Guyanese country-men and women who, being exiled in Canada or other foreign lands, for reasons exactly opposite to hers, feel weighed down by an identity-crisis of not belonging, every bit as heavy as her own.

"TREES DRAW ONE'S EYES UPWARD"

Margaret Bacon
Journey to Guyana. pp.457.
Leicester, F.A. Thorpe Publishing Ltd. 1997.
(First Published by Dobsons, Leicester, 1970)

Journey to Guyana describes a two-year visit to Guyana
in the mid-1960s by Yorkshire-born Margaret Bacon who
read history at Oxford University, and taught briefly
in England before accompanying her husband, a Civil
Engineer, who joined Bookers, then the largest sugar
company in Guyana, to help construct a Bulk Terminal.
After she returned to England, Bacon also produced
several novels about English life.

In *Journey* Bacon reports on everything from domestic life
in Georgetown, trips into Guyana's forest interior and contact
with Amerindians, to Guyanese social, economic, political and
cultural affairs; and her narrative is enlivened chiefly by a brand
of understated, English humour. After learning about Guyana's
precariously fragile sea defences, for instance, she remarks: "I was
never quite sure what stopped the Atlantic ocean from finding its
way into our Campbellville yard." [p. 80] Similarly, when she is
on a boat in the interior, and is warned against putting her hand
in the water by the boatman's story of a drunk passenger whose
flesh was bitten off his hand by pirai fish, she wryly confesses:
"Needless to say, my hand was safely out of the water before he
[the boatman] reached this grisly conclusion." [p. 168]

In hiring her own domestic staff, Bacon uncovers ethnic complexities in Guyanese society: house maids such as Lucille and Mabel are African, and her driver Jubraj and gardener Singh are Indian, indicating a population of two majority ethnic groups, Indian and African, as well as minorities of mixed blood people, Chinese, Portuguese, Europeans and Amerindians, all classified into separate geographical/economic groups. The African: "will not work on the land and speaks with contempt of the 'coolie man' who does. Instead he loves the urban areas where Africans man the Civil Service, work as clerks in offices, as policemen and postmen. The [African] women do all the domestic work as maids, cooks and washers, but the men are never gardeners." [p. 102] This historical/geographical/economic classification suggests that divisive racial politics in Guyana are partly due: "as much to differences of occupation and habitation between urban Africans and rural Indians as it was to racial feeling." [p. 126]

Her interests and insights in *Journey* separate Bacon from other expatriate Booker wives who: "are constantly harking on the superiority of all things British...and seemed to want to create a bit of suburban England in [Guyana]." [p. 122] Unlike these women, Bacon does background reading, takes interest in local manners and culture, and sympathises with Guyanese aspirations to independence. Although she comments positively on events under President Forbes Burnham until 1970, she also claims that many British people: "conceded that Dr. Jagan [the Opposition leader] was a man of real calibre who bore the stamp of leadership [and whose aim was] the devoted pursuit of his country's welfare." [p. 127]

From her privileged vantage point at the centre of an empire that colonised Guyana, Bacon's professed sympathy for Guyanese, may invite suspicion, for example, when she receives requests for help from people in abject poverty, and reacts with a seemingly sentimental question: "Who can look into the face of another human being who is hungry and not feel guilty?"[p. 255] Again, when confronted by a market woman selling fruit in a desperate effort to care for her baby she asks "What else could she [the market-woman] do? And what could I do but buy from her a pawpaw I did not want?" [p. 220] Her sympathy sounds too generalised, perhaps sentimental.

But these responses are matched by descriptions of people and places that are wholly concrete. Her evocation of the atmosphere of a lodging house in Bartica, and the service of its redoubtable manager, Miss Macatee, is a masterpiece of the macabre. In using her lodging house toilet, Bacon and her husband heard: "a mighty rush of water, and a sluicing and crashing as if of cataracts...prolonged reverberations and throbbings." [p. 177] As to Miss Macatee's tea: "The tea was very strong and some coffee seemed to have leaked into it from somewhere." [p. 181]

Miss Macatee's dismaying portrait is tempered by others like that of Teach, an energetic teacher and preacher at Santa Mission, in the upper reaches of the Demerara river, or of Granny, mother of the Captain of the Amerindian village at the mission. Granny is notable for her forest lore, self-sufficiency, sophistication authority and humility, virtues which the author believes have been debased by material comforts of modern society. Bacon is carried away by her almost religious awe over the grandeur of Guyana's interior, and tropical rainforest: "the trees draw one's eyes upward as they are by great church architecture." [p. 210]

If her admiration of Guyana's forest inspires some of Bacon's best writing, her most memorable passages appear in perceptive reflections on the psychological effects of colonialism in Guyana: "government by expatriates had perhaps fostered a curious contradiction...a meticulous attention to the manner in which things are done sometimes prevented them being done at all." [pp 438-9] Nothing proves Bacon's gift for exploration and empathy more than her identification of the plight of Guyanese who are so deeply disfigured by colonialism as to mistake shadow for substance, when they blindly mimic rather than understand the colonial habits and practices imposed on them. It reveals Bacon's sympathy for her subject which, instead of being sentimental, is both solid and genuine.

"COUPS SEEMED TO FOLLOW"

Shelagh Plunkett
The Water Here is never Blue: Intrigue and Lies from an Uncommon Childhood. pp.295.
Toronto, Penguin Canada, 2013.
ISBN 978-0670066995

Shelagh Plunkett's *The Water is Never Blue Here: Intrigue and Lies from an Uncommon Childhood* is a memoir based, firstly, on her visit to Guyana as a thirteen-year-old, from 1974 to 1976, and secondly on another stint from 1976 to 1978, mostly on the island of Timor, in Indonesia. In both cases, Shelagh accompanies her family on foreign assignments undertaken by her Canadian father. The wonder is that, despite her adolescent impressions of unfamiliar historical and social conditions or political issues recalled some forty years later, *The Water Here* captures a dramatic sense of the mysterious and tragic impact of these conditions and issues on Guyanese.

One of the first things Shelagh learns is about Guyana's strict education system requiring her to take catch-up lessons before she is admitted to St. Rose's, a seven- hundred strong, all-girl High School run by Ursuline Catholic nuns. As the only white student. Shelagh is struck by everything from the building itself which: "made me think the entire place looked like a giant chicken coop. Solid, solid like a fortress down Church Street," [p. 67] to unusual discipline that permitted caning of girls, strict enforcement of school uniform, a Latin motto "Serviam," meaning "I will serve," and a rousing school song beginning; "Storm or cloud will not dismay us. We will do and dare."[p. 73]

Some of St. Rose's practices and attitudes reflect a mood of militancy in the Burnham Cooperative Socialist Republic of the 1970s. A picture of: "Prime Minister Linden Forbes Burnham [appears] on every book that each and every student in Guyana used." [p. 9] Ideological headlines dominate daily news, for example, 'GO OUT AND SPREAD SOCIALISM,' or 'EDUCATION MUST BE A TOOL FOR SOCIALISM,' [p. 96] while, in a speech at St. Rose's, Deputy Prime Minister Ptolemy Reid urges students to accept that they are 'the people's students' or 'the people's hope' and 'Guyana's biggest hope." [p. 96] "He [Reid] said the way that things had been must be destroyed, smashed totally and replaced quick quick with something new, with something different." [p. 96]

For a thirteen year-old Canadian visitor, it is heady stuff. Headier still are rumours that Shelagh's mother Sally picks up from other expatriate wives: "about the votes all cast, [in the 1973 election] cast and far outnumbering the people who could vote." [p. 46] Sally Plunkett also hears: "it's the CIA... the MI5. The Americans and the Brits." [p. 46] Worst of all, the father of Shelagh's Indo-Guyanese school friend Farida whispers: "words like 'rape' and 'race extermination,' and claims that [through the National Service] Burnham found a way... to shift Guyana's racial balance in his favour." [p. 101] These whispers or suspicions may be compared with Shelagh's own observation: "At school we all seemed to get along, but I became aware that none of my Afro-Guyanese friends socialised with my Indo-Guyanese friends beyond the walls of St. Rose's."[p. 8] This is where, whether she realises it or not, Shelagh puts her finger on the ethnic rivalry that still bedevils Guyana's progress.

Although there are few explicit references to the Cold War in *The Water Here,* Shelagh's mere mention of rumours about the CIA and MI5 recalls the fierce, ideological battle between the USSR and the US that dominated the world during much of the second half of the twentieth century, and serves as the real cause of Shelagh's travels; for it may explain why her father, Patrick Plunkett, an expert in hydroelectricity, works in numerous countries all over the world.

Patrick's motives remain shrouded in secrecy throughout the book; but his sudden death from cancer in Shimla, India, in 1993, arouses interest about: "wherever my father went, coups seemed to follow" [p. 4] and leads Shelagh to ask frankly: "Was there a connection between my father's timing and the political upheavals in the countries he visited?" [p. 12] Although she concludes that neither her mother nor her father's friends knew the full answer, there are hints in her subtitle, and clues in Shelagh's own account suggesting that her father's frenetic travels were motivated by more than his expertise in hydroelectricity. He betrays veiled political criticism, for instance when he tells her: "That socialism talk [by Burnham's government] masked dictatorship and that would make some rich and leave the others poor."[p. 98)]

In addition, despite excessive secretiveness, it seems that Patrick is handsomely paid: he left an extensive stock portfolio, substantial savings, and numerous insurance policies. *The Water Here* opens with a Prologue that summarises Patrick's career while it implies that he covers his tracks like Hanuman, the monkey god in the Hindu epic *The Ramayana,* when he destroys Prince Rama's gift memorialising the record of his memorable service. *The Water Here* also ends with an Epilogue that describes Patrick's death in a hotel named "Dreamland" as if by design. Most of all, Patrick's former secretary remembers that he gave her a gift package to take from Vancouver to Hong

Kong, with intermediate stops, all over the world, where she was guided and fêted, without anyone knowing anything at all of the presumably precious value of the gift she was carrying. For all that, *The Water Here* is neither Patrick's biography, nor an espionage thriller, nor even a blueprint of political ideology. It is a more mongrel species, a cross between memoir and travelogue, and all the better for that.

In population statistics alone, greater atrocities occurred during Indonesia's five-year occupation of East Timor, in the 1970s, when nearly 200,000 people died. But Guyana appears as a more appetising literary subject for an author who brandishes all the authority of personal experience in reporting that 909 Americans died in "Jonestown," in Guyana's jungle, in 1978. Her paragraph evoking Guyana's tropical, water-logged landscape is also brilliantly picturesque: "Water of life, water of death. All that wet made the country leak and burst and green grew faster there than anywhere... It was magic."[p. 134]

DYNAMICS OF A BRITISH CARIBBEAN COLONY

James Rodway
The Story of Georgetown. pp.256.
"The Argosy" Company, Ltd., Printers, Demerara, 1920.

James Rodway's *The Story of Georgetown* reprints a series of articles by the author which first appeared in "The Argosy" newspaper in Guyana, in 1903. Revised and printed in book form by "The Argosy" Company Ltd. in 1920, the articles in *Georgetown* cover events from 1774 when the colony's chief town was moved from the Demerara island of Borsselen to Stabroek, at the mouth of the Demerara river. At the time, the colony was still in Dutch hands, but when the British took over in 1782, Stabroek was re-named "Georgetown;" and only in 1843 when the Parish Church of St George became a Cathedral Church and Bishop's See, was Georgetown raised to the rank of a city.

Rodway was born in England in 1848, but from 1870 to his death, in 1926, lived in Guyana where he made valuable contributions to the colony's history, literature and culture. Apart from *Georgetown* and his major work *A History of British Guiana from 1668 To The Present Time* which appeared in two parts - Volume One in 1891, and Volume Two in 1893 - he produced other writings including studies of Guyana's hinterland in *In the Guiana Forest: Studies in Nature in Relation to the Struggle for Life* (1894), and the novel *In Guiana Wilds: A study of Two Women* (1899). Rodway also helped to establish Guyanese cultural institutions such as the Royal Agricultural and Commercial Society of which he was Assistant Secretary from 1886-1888, and the British Guiana Museum of which he was the curator in 1894-1899. In addition, he edited the influential journal – *Timehri*.

Georgetown offers an historical survey of specific local conditions and physical features that influenced the formation of what is today the city of Georgetown. Unusually lengthy "Contents" pages indicate some of these features, for example, "The Beginning of a new Town," the first chapter, which reveals that the site of the new town was a "brandwagt," Dutch for "a fire watch" or guard house, sentry station or small wooden fort that was selected by Colonel Robert Kingston, whose surname still survives as the name of one of Georgetown's more affluent districts.

Other features include the construction of Water street, one of the town's important business streets which was built out of débris from fires on land reclaimed from the Demerara river; a market started by "negroes" (Africans) selling plantains; the emergence of a newspaper; issues of sanitation and epidemics, for instance, yellow fever and small pox; and because of Georgetown's climatic and geographical features, below sea level, fundamental concern over continuous water supply and drainage and irrigation. Guyanese readers will also recognise the names of familiar districts in Georgetown – La Penitence, Werk-en-Rust, Albert Town - which, in Rodway's time, were independent plantations; and Rodway mentions individuals like John Croal, Joseph Bourda, Thomas Cuming and George Lacy whose names still survive, like Kingston's, in Georgetown's streets and districts.

One of the more interesting aspects of *Georgetown* is its portrait of slavery, before and after emancipation in 1834, when the British government offered compensation to slave owners: "A great impetus was given to Georgetown through the Compensation Money on about 7,000 slaves belonging to the inhabitants." [p. 53] At fifty pounds per slave, many residents received: "handsome amounts of ready cash" [p. 54] which they used to improve their homes. This illustrates Rodway's penchant for reporting information from the point of view of white Guyanese colonists who are clearly more privileged than the slaves they owned. Not that he ignores the plight of slaves before 1834, when they were allowed out on streets or dams after 8.00 pm only if they were accompanied by their master, or carried a written pass from him, and had a lantern. Runaway slaves, if caught, were tortured with red hot pincers.

It is not the brutal inhumanity of slavery that catches Rodway's attention as much as the inconvenience caused to ordinary white residents by emancipation: "The slave emancipation was the greatest event of the Nineteenth Century...From 1834 to 1840 everything was topsy turvy. All the old laws had to be abolished." [p. 45] Although he does not ignore: "a shocking series of executions with the East Coast Insurrection [in 1823]" [p. 93] or the horror of: "a row of grizly heads were fixed on poles, and here and there along the public roads, corpses hung in chains," [p. 93] he captures the fear and panic of Whites: "At the first alarm there was a rush for the vessels in the river: ladies jumped from the stelling into the boats at the risk of their limbs if not their lives, and altogether there was a decided panic." [pp.92-93] Toward the end of *Georgetown,* in considering churches that seem attracted by evangelical or anti-slavery attitudes, Rodway does not fail to record arguments used by local Planters and Merchants in opposing the Anti-Slavery movement.

Some of the best sections of *Georgetown* deal with Rodway's practical efforts in advancing human settlement or enterprise in virgin space. His enthusiasm and energy for empire-building projects seem infinite, and his contribution to foundational services and institutions in Guyana is inestimable. Like Walter and Vincent Roth, fellow English empire builders who were his contemporaries in British Guiana, Rodway founded institutions on which others could build, for instance, the Royal Agricultural and Commercial Society, the Library, and especially the British Guiana Museum.

By his own assessment, the articles in *Georgetown*: "did not permit our dealing with every institution in anything like a comprehensive way. The main object has been to find out their beginnings."[p. 248] In the process, Rodway illuminates the internal dynamics of a typical British Caribbean colony, in which white colonists square off against a black (African) under class, both slave and free, while the Governor, who controls ultimate power through the military, hypocritically acts as referee when there is little doubt that his loyalty lies with the colonists.

"RITES OF INCIPIENT LABOUR MOVEMENT"

Juanita De Barros
Order and Place in a Colonial City: Patterns of Struggle and Resistance in Georgetown, British Guiana, 1889-1924. pp.251. Montreal and Kingston, McGill-Queen's University Press, 2002.

Although *Order and Place: Patterns of Struggle and Resistance in Georgetown, British Guiana, 1889-1924* looks like a Ph. D. thesis, its academic trappings of diligent research and meticulous scholarship transform it into a text that is both learned, in the sense of disclosing new knowledge, and accessible to the general reader. The subtitle "Patterns of Struggle and Resistance in Georgetown, British Guiana, 1889-1924" explains its subject: a study of Georgetown that reflects patterns of struggle between ordinary or poor Guyanese and their British colonial rulers, in the last decade of the nineteenth century and the first two of the twentieth. Sample chapter titles give an idea of what to expect: "Cesspool City: Sanitarianism in Colonial Georgetown", "Hucksters, Markets, and the Struggle to Control Public Space", and "Riot and Struggle to Control the Street".

Before 1834, when slavery was abolished in all British territories, the population of Georgetown consisted largely of sugar plantation owners, government officials, professionals, merchants, and their families, while the majority of Guyanese, African slaves, lived on plantations. After Emancipation, when the indenture system introduced increasing numbers of Portuguese, Chinese, Indians and others into the country, the population not only became more ethnically mixed but, for a variety of reasons, gradually began to shift more and more to the capital city. In due course, urban problems developed, involving criminals, gangs and social unrest culminating in riots. Professor De Barros concisely sums up her thesis as one which: "examines the struggle for cultural hegemony in Georgetown's public spaces - a battle over which vision would triumph... that of the city's poor or that of the local élites". [p. 4]

Two major slave rebellions, in 1763 and 1823, both cruelly repressed by the British (white) colonial government, illustrate deeply ingrained patterns of struggle and resistance in pre-Emancipation Guyanese society. So we really should not be surprised by a similar pattern in the post-Emancipation period, in 1856, when Portuguese homes and businesses in Georgetown were attacked by freed Africans who believed that their control of the petty retail trade was being taken over by newly-arrived, ex-indentured Portuguese. These attacks, known as the Angel Gabriel riots, were named after John Sayers Orr, an itinerant preacher, nicknamed Angel Gabriel.

Three other riots followed in Georgetown, in 1889, 1905 and 1924, and when they are combined with eleven riots staged in rural areas by indentured Indian workers, between 1869 and 1913, leave no doubt at all of a distinct, if incoherent pattern of struggle and resistance in Guyana, well before 1950, when the People's Progressive Party was formed, and a more coherent struggle for freedom and independence began in earnest.

Like the riot in 1856, the one in 1889 was inspired by the hostility of Africans toward Portuguese, while discontent in 1905 and 1924 expressed long-held economic grievances directed, more generally, against ruling élites. Shops and houses were attacked, and businesses in the commercial district of Water and Main Streets in Georgetown became a battle ground. Professor De Barros uncovers superabundant details, painstakingly culled from myriad sources including colonial government records and reports, parliamentary papers, statutes and newspapers, as well as from less arcane published sources such as books and articles in her discussion of these riots; and one of her main discoveries is their festive, ritual or carnivalesque nature. Crowds not only looted establishments, but ate and drank from the houses they invaded; and there were street parades: "accompanied by dancing, chanting, singing, stick wielding and drum playing". [p. 148]

Equally important is the revelation that the riots of 1905 and 1924: "drew on the rites [labour parades] of the incipient labour movement in British Guiana" [p. 146] suggesting a growing interdependence between spontaneous eruptions of public dissatisfaction and more organised trade union activity. Even more important, perhaps, is the appearance of elements of the Muslim tadjah festival, such as stick wielding and drum beating, in the riots of 1905 and 1924, implying signs, however faint, of incipient multi-ethnic nationalism.

But *Order and Place* is not simply a survey of riots or other historical examples of violence or social disturbances: the volume delves beneath the surface of events in search of common motives, patterns and practices. Racial stereotypes inherited from past slave rebellions when white masters treated black slaves little better than beasts, influenced attitudes after Emancipation, and helped create a stigma of Portuguese shopkeepers as dishonest and greedy, and of Indians as dirty scavengers and suspect milk vendors who carried disease that threatened public health. Such racial stereotypes also strengthened prejudices and inspired fear in established groups or élites as the author succinctly states: "Racial and class terror filled the colonial élites" [p. 160] or again when she refers to: "the traditional élite terror of the non-white masses". [p. 160] Inevitably, suspicion and fear among the élites were countered by resentment and hostility among the poor, driving them to acts of resistance: "manifested in festivity and play, for cultural hegemony in public places". [p. 167]

Georgetown proves to be decisive as a site of resistance because it is: "more than the hub of the colony's political, economic, and administrative world". [p. 169]. But it is not Georgetown alone; the true value of *Order and Place* is its aim: "to uncover new, urban paradigms that... reflect wider Guyanese and West Indian patterns". [p. 3] That it succeeds we can see from examples of the Jonkonnu riots in Kingston, Jamaica, in 1840 and 1841, carnival riots in Trinidad in 1881, 1883 and 1884, and the Guy Fawkes riot in St. George's, Grenada, in 1885. We should not be at all surprised by similar patterns of resistance in people who were colonised in the Caribbean: they are common victims, after all, of identical forms of subjugation, exploitation and injustice.

PLANTATION ECONOMY: INNER WORKINGS

Jack Bayley
The Mudheads.
Leeds, Peepal Tree Press, 1990.
(ISBN 0-9516167-0-6)

Main events in *The Mudheads* occur between 1936 and 1938, largely in Georgetown, Guyana, although some incidents take place on sugar estates as far away as Springlands, in the county of Berbice. The novel opens with the return of twenty-two-year-old narrator, Allan Miller, to his native country after studies in England. As son of the Assistant Colonial Secretary, Miller belongs to an élite class of Guyanese of European (chiefly British) descent who serve as government officials like his father, or as professionals, businessmen and administrative personnel on European-owned sugar estates.

From the start, when Allan's father fixes him up with a job, we cannot miss the feudalistic, class and colour ethics that prevail in British Caribbean colonies. Whether Allan realises it or not: "young white men in Demerara [Guyana] never went out in search of jobs; their father's friends found jobs for them." [p. 38] When a white expatriate is killed in an accident, riding his motor bike at breakneck speed late one night, or the Deputy Manager of a sugar estate is shot at a staff party, we also cannot miss the racially defined privilege and reckless self-gratification enjoyed by Whites in Guyana. As Allan's father candidly admits: "the drinking and high living are what they [white expatriates] come to the colonies for! They get thoroughly sick of the withering monotony and regimentation of life in England." [pp. 78-79] It turns out that the Deputy Manager is murdered, probably in revenge for his sexual orgies with estate girls, daughters of (Indian-Guyanese) sugar workers, served up to him by their own relatives, in expectation of special favours from him.

Apart from the rather lurid appeal of these revelations of corruption, bred out of racial privilege, *The Mudheads* examines the impact of the sugar industry in every corner or crevice of Guyanese society. Historically, after all, sugar is the economic *raison d'être* of the colony. Allan's friend Robert Chisholm, a fellow mudhead or native Guyanese, explains the dominance of sugar: "In the government decision-making process sugar always comes first. Whether it's drafting legislation, fixing import duties, devising new forms of taxation or planning public works, the main consideration is the benefit for the sugar industry. When sites for drainage and irrigation schemes are being chosen, for example, sugar's need for new land takes precedence over rice and other peasant crops." [p. 52]

Chisholm's role is central and tragic: he studies in England and returns to Guyana to promote reform in the sugar industry, although he ends up being murdered. Coming from a rich, plantation family who can afford to give him a fat allowance on top of what he earns as engineer in a sugar factory, his reformist intention can be seen as either exceptionally high-minded or, as the author puts it, Chisholm has allowed himself: "to become the tool of the wealthy absentee proprietors, doing their dirty work, as they pulled strings from a safe distance." [p. 7]

Whatever his motives, Chisholm's description of estate working conditions hits home: "Children work fourteen hours a day for eight cents. Factory hands are on duty eighteen out of twenty-four hours. They eat snacks on the job and catnap on the floor between work stints, all for three shillings [72 cents] a day!" [pp. 42-43] If this is not bad enough, Balram Arjune, an Indian-Guyanese and leader of the (largely Indian) sugar workers' trade union, which is supposed to defend workers' interests, has signed a secret agreement with the sugar companies to sabotage the demands of their workers. For his treachery, 'Judas' Arjune is rewarded with the princely sum of six hundred dollars each month.

Towards the end of the novel, and especially after a strike in which five sugar workers are killed by police, a new Indian-Guyanese leader Dr. Lutchmin appears as a genuine representative of the sugar workers. This incident is similar to an actual strike on the sugar estate of Enmore in 1948. There are similarities as well between the fictional Dr. Lutchmin and the historical Dr. Cheddi Jagan, leader of the People's Progressive Party, in Guyana, and between Robert Chisholm from *The Mudheads* and the late Sir Jock Campbell, chief executive of the largest sugar company in Guyana in the 1950s and 60s. These similarities suggest that Bayley shifts the activities of historical figures, Jagan and Campbell, backward to a period one dozen or more years before they actually happened, largely to synchronize anti-colonial activities in Guyana with similar agitation in other British Caribbean colonies around the late 1930s and 40s.

Not that this manipulation of chronology reduces authenticity: the novel's characters remain true-to-life, even if frequent deaths occur, often at suspiciously convenient stages of the action. Certainly, the main characters' romantic entanglements and sexual shenanigans, either among themselves or with female, estate workers, are consistent with an élite ethnic community exercising or abusing their virtually unlimited privilege. All of this comes through typical scenes and customs of domestic and social life, convincingly depicted within an ambience, quintessentially, hauntingly Guyanese.

Most haunting of all is the analysis of the sugar industry in British Guiana, and comments, for example, on: "the [louche] relationship between the major sugar companies and the extensive network of inconspicuous subsidiaries" [p. 193] or on: "such [dubious] terms as management fees, local office charges and levies, buying and selling commissions" [p. 193] which only company officials understand; for these and other revelations infer an elaborate network of interlocking, commercial activities, disingenuous accounting practices, and unusual, though not necessarily illegal, financial transactions that conceal real profit margins of sugar companies, and promote exploitation of their workers. This sealed network of exploitation is more than enough to clinch the reputation of *The Mudheads* as, probably, the most explosive, fictional account we so far have, of the inside story of Caribbean sugar plantations, in the heyday of colonial rule.

EVIL CONTRIVANCES OF EMPIRE

Selwyn R. Cudjoe
Caribbean Visionary: A.R.F. Webber and the Making of the Guyanese Nation. pp.278.
Jackson, Mississippi, The University Press of Mississippi, 2009.

As someone remembered today only by researchers like the Trinidadian scholar Selwyn Cudjoe, or by a dwindling band of Guyanese, the story of Albert Raymond Forbes Webber, (1880-1932) in *Caribbean Visionary: A.R. F. Webber and the Making of the Guyanese Nation*, fills a yawning gap in Guyanese history. In his Introduction, Professor Cudjoe makes this point: "*Caribbean Visionary* seeks to break this silence, [about Webber] recover Webber's life, and fill an important lacuna in Guyanese and Caribbean history. " [p. 12] The strange thing is that Webber was not even Guyanese by birth: he was born in Tobago and came to Guyana in 1899, although Guyana was where he remained for the rest of his life, and where he established a remarkable career as novelist, poet, historian, publicist, businessman, and most of all as journalist and politician.

Webber's father and two uncles were already in Guyana working as gold traders when he arrived. He had been invited by his uncle Ernest Forbes, and from 1899 to 1915, travelled up and down the country, in the Interior as well as coastal areas, doing a variety of jobs. Judging by his novel *Those that be in Bondage: A Tale of Indian Indentures and Sunlit Western Waters* which appeared in 1917, one job may have been as overseer on a sugar estate. While the novel betrays detailed knowledge of the daily grind of Indian sugar workers and practical hardships of white overseers, its real strength remains a magisterial survey of general administrative/economic problems of the sugar industry.

Webber came from a mixed blood (Euro/African) family which would have ranked him as "high coloured" or almost white in the colonial hierarchy of the time, and in the beginning of his career, might have encouraged him to lean toward his white side. We are told, for instance: "he [Webber] served as a spokesman for the dominant [white] capitalist class." [p. 12]. But as Professor Cudjoe also argues, Webber emerged as: "*the* major spokesman and ideologue of the working people and labouring poor of Guyana during the second and early part of the third decade of the twentieth century (1915-1932)." [p. 12]

One thing is clear: Webber was self-made, shaped by his own reading or observations, and raw experience of working in Guyana during a period of economic recession and growing resistance to colonial oppression. As a journalist and editor of the *Daily Chronicle* (1919-1925) and the *New Daily Chronicle* (1925-1930), he was in the thick of things in Georgetown, which offered a perfect opportunity for participating in anti-colonial agitation initiated by men such as Patrick Dargan, D.M. Hutson, and Ernest Forbes, and by freshly formed organisations like the British Guiana Labour Union (BGLU) led by Hubert Nathaniel Critchlow, the United Negro Improvement Association (UNIA), the Negro Progress Convention (NPC), and the British Guiana East Indian Association (BGEIA).

If Webber stands out it is through a unique combination of skills as journalist, speech maker, and untiring traveller, politician and advocate of Guyanese self-government. In 1921, for example, on a platform that included improvements for rice farming, drainage and irrigation, Webber ran for election to the Court of Policy - the colonial legislative body - and won.

In 1926, he joined with Nelson Cannon, a local White, to form the Popular Party. But when political ferment prompted the British government to revert to Crown Colony government in Guyana, in 1928, Webber lost no time in travelling to England, for a third time, to protest.

There is no mistaking Webber's most cherished goal of self-government for Guyana within a West Indian Federation. In a radio address, he spoke about: "the exciting possibilities of Guianese economic development and the prospect of inviting Caribbean persons to share in the 'vast unexplored continental inheritance in which we all have a common heritage." [p. 116] As a Tobagonian by birth, he envisaged Guyana's future firmly within a regional Caribbean context. He called for hydro-electric power and a railway from Georgetown to Brazil. At the British Commonwealth Labour conference in England in July, 1930, he and fellow Guyanese delegates demanded the right: "to exploit its [Guyana's] natural resources with equal freedom as Canada, Australia, New Zealand, or South Africa." [p. 155]

After such relentless anti-colonial agitation, Webber's sudden death from cerebral haemorrhage at the age of fifty-two appears as deeply tragic; and although Professor Cudjoe struggles to ascribe a particular political creed to him, either as a "Fabian socialist" [p. 231] or as practitioner of a: "political ideology [that] could be called a kind of socialism through parliamentarianism," [p. 231] we are left in no doubt at all about the righteousness of Webber's anti-colonialism; for, in his political activities and writing, from *Those that be in Bondage* to *A Centenary History of Guiana*, (1931) his *magnum opus*, Webber consistently deploys unerring, visionary insight into evil contrivances of empire.

Perhaps his main insight is the observation that frequent movement of officials from one colony to the other meant that: "they [the officials] were not committed to the development of [their own] society, and so an indigenous colonial stratum never really developed." [p. 199] Webber puts his finger on "divide and rule," a classic colonial contrivance which, by undermining growth of "an indigenous colonial stratum," fosters fragmentation and discontinuity that stifle the struggle for independence. This means that *Caribbean Visionary* does not simply fill a gap in Guyanese history: it rescues the deeds of one of the earliest, most articulate champions of West Indian independence, from the enforced silence that is itself a primary cause of colonial discontinuity that Webber inveighed against, with such tireless zeal and passion.

BUXTON-FRIENDSHIP

Eusi Kwayana
Buxton Friendship in Print and Memory. pp.320.
Georgetown, Guyana, Red Thread Women's Press, 1999.
ISBN 976-8157-92-5

Buxton Friendship in Print and Memory considers two
former sugar estates which were purchased and turned into
villages by freed Africans: "the people who brought the
human aspects of modern civilisation to the coastlands of
Guyana." [p. 12] Although the Act abolishing slavery was
passed in the British parliament in 1833, African slaves in
British Guiana did not gain full freedom until 1838, when
their so-called Apprenticeship period ended. Then, in April
1840, 128 freed Africans pooled wages earned during their
Apprenticeship, and jointly purchased New Orange Nassau,
a sugar estate, later re-named Buxton. The neighbouring
village of Friendship was similarly purchased in 1841.

In the 1840s, the situation in Buxton-Friendship could not
have been very different from that in other newly established
African villages such as Ann's Grove, Victoria or Lichfield.
British Guiana was a colony, and its remaining sugar estates
still continued to be: "the foundation of economic life" [p. 45]
because they were: "centres of production capital with links
to city banks, merchants and the planter government, and the
colonial Office." [p. 44] The crucial effect of the newly acquired
African villages was that because of their: "limited command

of capital and less of credit [they] had to fight for decades to influence the government." [p. 45] This fight - between the economic interests of a feudalistic, estate-centred government, and the democratic needs of free people in newly formed African villages - is what clinches Kwayana's claim that the villages: "played a part in civilising the colony in the area of economic self-reliance and social freedom." [p. 45]

10,544 new village homes had been built by 1850, but unexpected problems arose when, facing the machinations of a colonial government, the new owners found that the dice were loaded against them. For example, drainage and irrigation for their peasant farms remained a major problem up to the 1950s when: "the Drainage and Irrigation Board was headed for many years by the very man who was head of Bookers [the largest Sugar Company] which typified sugar and big business." [p. 238] With Buxton growing to a population of 2,852 and Friendship to 1,757 by 1871, population growth, bad drainage, flooding, poor sanitary conditions and increased taxation bred decline forcing villagers to seek employment elsewhere, for example, in the colony's Interior.

Far from dwelling on decline, however, *Buxton Friendship* extols the achievements of villagers in twenty chapters with a variety of local character sketches and portraits, narratives of village incidents, anecdotes and episodes, and zealously composed catalogues of names, and facts and figures designed, if not to celebrate the general success of Buxton-Friendship residents, simply to record the routine of their daily lives. Here, for instance, is the routine of a typical child above the age of five in Buxton-Friendship: "prep school at someone's bottom house, endless housework, shopping, marketing, fetching water, pig and poultry feed from nearby estates Nonpareil, Bachelor's Adventure village, Lusignan, gathering firewood from the farm bottom ground, rice planting, cane harvests, cattle minding, sheep, goats, donkeys..." and the list goes on for another couple of lines. Chapters 17 to 20 also furnish so many names and lists of schools, scholars, and scholarship winners or of Buxton-Friendship residents in so many jobs or vocations, from medicine and business to athletics, that the avalanche of details seems like history with a vengeance.

But Kwayana is not writing history, at least not what he calls "real history." He refers to himself as a "compiler" on the front cover and elsewhere, partly because *Buxton Friendship* includes contributions by others, for example, Rampersaud Tiwari's chapter on Indian-Guyanese Buxtonians, and partly because of his reliance on information mostly from oral sources. He also relies on liberal quotations from scholars who write "real history", for example, Walter Rodney in his *A History of the Guyanese Working People,* and Allan Young in his *The Approaches to Local Self-Government in British Guiana.* But Kwayana's opening words in *Buxton Friendship*: "This craziest of histories" [p. 3] and his admission that his information is: "flawed by human memory" [p. 98] and will need a second edition (presumably written by someone else) suggests that *Buxton Friendship* serves only as: "material for real history." [p. 153]

If Kwayana is disappointed in not producing history based on primary research of official documents or records, like Walter Rodney or Allan Young, it is because *Buxton Friendship* depends more on memory than print. He confesses: "Village history writing allows people to preserve the very personal qualities of men and women who have done their work among the villagers and passed on," [p. 75] The bulk of the information in *Buxton Friendship* comes from the author's personal contact with villagers.

Chapter Ten, for instance, offers historically valuable portraits of, among other villagers, Dr. Ras Makonen,

George Arlington Younge, and Nana Culley lauded as the: "most effective political activist" [p. 113] Buxton-Friendship ever produced.

Other chapters add biographical sketches that illustrate Buxton-Friendship's vital contribution to the beginnings of the People's Progressive Party, and draws attention to: "the example set by Buxton-Friendship in nation building." [p. 186] These chapters also cover specific topics such as race, ethnicity, multiculturalism, and offer insight into aspects of Guyanese customs and manners from practices in agriculture, fishing and cookery to religion, folk figures, folk medicine and superstitions.

In spite of mere reportage then, including long lists and catalogues that may prove tedious or meaningless to non-Buxtonians, Kwayana's biographical portraits and anecdotes, episodes and incidents, along with his commentaries and exposition of much arcane local lore, including special features of Buxtonian and Guyanese culture, such as the pervasive use of nicknames, or the structure and function of the domestic box oven, exhibit the imperishable value of what must finally be accepted as real history: "the public and also the inner life of the inhabitants of this joint village [Buxton-Friendship.]" [p. 205]

FOUNDATIONS LAID BY AFRICAN-GUYANESE

Eusi Kwayana and Tchaiko Kwayana
Scars of Bondage: A First Study of the Slave Colonial Experience of Africans in Guyana. pp.50.
Georgetown, Guyana, Free Press, 2002.
ISBN 976-8178-01-9 (pbk).

In the iconography of Guyanese-born political figures, Eusi Kwayana looms large as scholar, author, activist, and publicist or spokesman for a variety of causes. *Scars of Bondage: A First Study of the Slave Colonial Experience of Africans in Guyana*, written by Kwayana in collaboration with his wife Tchaiko, is a broad, slender volume, merely fifty pages long, with its pages stapled rather than bound, making it look more like a pamphlet or magazine rather than a book. The subtitle also declares that *Scars* is only a "First Study" making it appear either elementary or preparatory to something else; and the Kwayanas describe themselves as "compilers" rather than authors. Then, the volume, apparently completed in 1972, is not published until 2002, and acknowledged as: "lamentably, uninformed by recent scholarship."[p. 47] Such diffidence seems to contradict both the iconic image of Eusi Kwayana, and the importance of the volume in dealing with ethnicity, a topic that has bedevilled political progress in Guyana more than any other.

Scars contains much information about African slavery in Guyana, first under Dutch colonial masters, from the seventeenth century to 1803 when the British took over, then, under British rule until Emancipation in 1834, and the Apprenticeship Period from 1834 to 1838, a transition stage when slaves could be paid for extra work before they received full freedom. We learn a good deal about the daily routine of Africans under slavery, their major uprisings against Dutch masters in 1763, against British masters in 1823, and brutal injustices they suffered, for example, in not being able to marry and enjoy family life until the Amelioration Period, in the 1820s, when plantation owners relaxed some injustices in the hope of discouraging their slaves from rebelling.

In addition, we discover post-Emancipation struggles of the freed Africans in resisting coercion and sabotage by plantation owners to force them back to plantation work as wage labourers, and we also learn about heroic efforts by freed Africans to establish independent villages, bought with their own earnings, chiefly from the Apprenticeship Period. So called proprietary villages were established out of land bought by individual Africans, and cooperative villages bought collectively out of pooled resources by groups of Africans.

As the Kwayanas admit, the villages of the freed Africans declined under the assault of "massive pressures" [p. 24] coming from interference by plantation owners, and the arrival of destitute Indian immigrants which the authors regard as: "one of the devastating blows to the village movement." [p. 27] The Kwayanas probe the origins of a tragic ethnic rivalry, between African- and Indian-Guyanese, that would disfigure Guyanese politics in the mid-twentieth century: they draw a sharp contrast between indenture and chattel slavery, for instance, that whereas indenture allowed Indians to retain aspects of their culture such as their religion, family structure, language and food, slavery robbed Africans of a substantial part of their cultural inheritance. On top of that, the authors claim that while: "the freed indentured servant enjoyed a higher socio-economic status than the emancipated Africans," [p. 45]

Africans were never compensated for their slave labour. By reporting that indentured Indians had savings and sometimes property or capital from land awarded to them, in lieu of their return passage to India, the authors expose areas of potential unequal treatment and conflict between the two ethnic groups from their first contact with each other.

This is valuable information, even if not entirely new. Liberal references and quotations appear from the work of previous commentators, for example, Norman Cameron, H.V.P. Bronkhurst, A.R.F. Webber, Vere T. Daly, Peter Ruhomon, Walter Rodney, Rawle Farley and Allan Young. Special mention is also made of *Themes in African Guyanese History* by Winston McGowan, James Rose, and David Granger, and while this fulsome reliance on well known sources acknowledges the academic credentials of *Scars*, it also helps to explain why the volume is presented with diffidence as only a first study, and the Kwayanas acknowledge themselves merely as compilers rather than authors.

The volume also has a polemical aim: "to launch a war against the myths invented by our historical and class enemies about the African" [p. vi]. One myth, at least, - that of the lazy and thriftless African - is smartly dispelled by analysing the effect of African achievement in setting up villages in the post-Emancipation period: "Without the village movement, both aspects of which [proprietary and collaborative] began in 1839, the country would have remained essentially uncivilised with an oppressive plantation culture. [p. 22] Foundations of civil society in Guyana were laid by African-Guyanese in the immediate post-Emancipation period. The villages were certainly the first democratic alternative to plantation culture, since Amerindian participation in coastal culture was limited.

But a tone of celebration or self-congratulation creeps into *Scars* along with its record of African achievement, for instance, when the authors praise freed Africans for giving the vote to women in their villages because it was: "like a many other aspects of the [African-derived] communal structure, far in advance of worldwide imperialist governments." [p. 23] This polemical aspect of *Scars* which may be influenced by the rousing rhetoric of the 1960s "Black is Beautiful" era of civil rights in the US, probably induces guilty awareness of a clash between the purely academic aspect of their volume, and their more polemical instinct for advocacy. Still, it would be a pity if this encourages the authors to defend their work, as they do in their "Afterword," against a more updated, scholarly work like Emilia Viotti da Costa's book on the 1763 uprising. For *Scars* falls between two stools, the polemical and scholarly; and the blend needs no apology, since it is matched by a hybrid style that successfully unites both the rousing, straight-talking fluency of the publicist, with the more studied brevity or factual solidity of the scholar.

DUTY TO MAIM AND KILL UNCHASTE WOMEN

Gaiutra Bahadur
Coolie Woman: The Odyssey of Indenture. pp.274.
London, Hurst & Co. (Publishers) Ltd. 2013.
ISBN 978-1-84904-277-2

Coolie Woman: the Odyssey of Indenture is the first book of Gaiutra Bahadur who was born in Guyana but studied at Yale and Columbia University before becoming a journalist. *Coolie Woman* tells the story of the author's great-grand mother - Sujaria - who was born in India, in 1873, and embarked as an indentured immigrant to Guyana (formerly British Guiana) in 1903. While the volume does attempt to reconstruct a biography of the author's great-grandmother, its exhaustive research and brilliant writing make for a denser narrative, partly a biography or family memoir, and partly an impressively detailed history of Indian indenture to the Caribbean and, in lesser degree, to Africa and Fiji. Through vigorous exploration of origins of Indian-Caribbean feminism, *Coolie Woman* also delivers an eloquent broadside against the principles and practice of British colonialism itself. The derivation of "coolie" from "kuli," the Tamil word for "hire," gives special resonance to the title "coolie woman" as a term of abuse.

It was the final emancipation of African slaves in 1838 that created an urgent need for fresh labour on Caribbean sugar plantations, and caused Indians and other smaller ethnic groups to be brought to the region as indentured workers.

Bahadur divides her book into three sections - "Embarking" "Exploring" and "Returning"- covering the whole indenture experience of Indians from their departure from India, indentureship in the Caribbean, return home, and the abuse of women continuously from start to finish.

From the beginning, a large majority of workers indentured to the Caribbean were men; but the ratio of much larger numbers of male over female workers created an imbalance with dire effects for the women, for example, promiscuity, family discord, rape and mutilation. Between 1859 and the end of the indenture system in 1917: "more than 167 women were killed by intimate or would-be intimate partners in Guiana." [p. 108] In a study done by the colonial office in 1871, it was also found that: "such murders occurred at a rate ninety times greater in Guiana than in India in the previous decade," [p. 109] statistics which frame: "indenture-era stereotypes of jealous husband and naughty wife, [and] Infidelity by promiscuous women, or fear of it in possessive men." [p. 194]

Although indentured men also killed themselves frequently, because of general hardship in a foreign land, indentured women were not only murdered, but became victims of attacks intended to disfigure rather than kill them: "Between 1886 and 1890, when twenty-five women were murdered in Guiana, thirty-five were wounded, usually with cutlasses. Noses, those representatives of women's honor, seemed to be a particular target." [p. 109] Bahadur tells the gruesome story of a man who, unable to reach his wife's face with a cutlass or knife, bit off the tip of her nose instead.

There may be many reasons for such grotesque cruelty, but even if the story about Lord Rama's expulsion and exile, in the Hindu sacred text the *Ramayana* supplies a general measure of solace to diaspora Indians, similarly exiled from home by indenture, Bahadur suggestively observes that the same text is: "preoccupied with women who break the codes of accepted social behavior... [and] Their punishment takes the breath away." [p. 106] The author speculates on: "what really caused Indian men to commit such chilling crimes against them [Indian women,]" [p. 123] and considers the possibility that, with the example of the *Ramayana* story of Rama and his consort Sita in their minds, Indian men saw it: "as their religious duty to maim or kill unchaste women." [p. 123.] In addition to standard historical texts, journals and documents, the use of sources such religious texts or local Guyanese songs, lamenting a woman's failure to give birth further illustrate the wide scope and vigour of the author's research.

If vigorous research is one reason for Bahadur's success in *Coolie Woman,* another is her strategy of fusing the personal story of her great-grandmother with the broad history of actual indentured women. Her information about Sujaria is frankly sketchy, merely the fact that she left India as a pregnant, unmarried woman, and settled in Cumberland village, Guyana, where she sold milk door to door, and at one stage became the wife of Shivrattan. Sujaria also has "cat's eyes," and is an "arresting beauty" with appearance "like a film star" and with skin that was "white like white people," giving rise to suspicion that she was Anglo-Indian. [p. 122] Bahadur's success is to fuse this meagre outline with abundant details, of numerous, actual indentured women, and create a convincing portrait of Sujaria as an authentic, fully fleshed, Indian indentured immigrant.

Bahadur's chief technique is to saturate her text with hundreds of questions, for example, on page 47, where she describes the scene at the depot for Indian immigrants in Calcutta before they board ship, a single paragraph contains ten consecutive questions relating Sujaria to Rukmini a nineteen year old hermaphrodite, Rashi an untouchable woman with a scarred nostril, and Tirnal a farmer from Mirzapur, travelling with five girls whom he could possibly be trafficking. By fusing Sujaria's plight with one that she shares with her fellow immigrants these questions clinch her indentured identity.

Similarly, although she herself did not return to India, [her tombstone exists in a cemetery in Guyana,] another paragraph on page 173 carries ten more questions strongly linking Sujaria with returning immigrants, and correctly situating her in the final stage of Embarking, Exploring and Returning. Bahadur also correctly situates the end of the indenture experience within a period of the early decades of the twentieth century when the struggle for independence was at its height in India, and Indian leaders rightly regarded abolition of indenture, which ended in 1917, as part of their own nationalist struggle.

"BIN BUNG MAN, BLIGE WUK EVRY DAY"

Dale Bisnauth
The Settlement of Indians in Guyana 1890-1930. pp.296.
Leeds, Peepal Tree Press, 2000.
ISBN 1-000715-163

The Settlement of Indians in Guyana 1890-1930 relates the story of Indian sugar plantation labourers leaving their plantations, at the end of their indenture period, to settle in new villages or other locations on the coastlands and river banks of Guyana. The author, Dr. Dale Bisnauth, a Presbyterian minister who served as Minister Education in the People's Progressive Party (PPP) government of President Cheddi Jagan, is also author of *A Short History of the Guyana Presbyterian Church* (1979) and *History of Religions in the Caribbean* (1989).

Indians first arrived in Guyana as immigrant workers in answer to a need for fresh labour after African slaves, who had worked on European-owned plantations for over two centuries, were finally freed in 1838. The new immigrants were usually indentured for a period of five years after which they could return to India or choose to remain in Guyana. But nearly three-quarters of the Indian immigrants remained after their indenture agreements expired and, by 1911, formed a majority of the Guyanese population which then consisted of two major ethnic groups -Africans and Indians – and small numbers of indigenous Amerindians and Europeans, together with equally small indentured groups of Chinese and Portuguese (Maderians). Much of Guyana's social and political problems stem from differing strategies used by European plantation owners to secure ethnic labour on terms that suited the rhythms and patterns of their plantation operations.

After African slaves were freed, indentured Indians were seen as undercutting the bargaining power of freed Africans by working for wages lower than the Africans were prepared to accept. For another, when Bisnauth's study begins, by the 1860s or '70s, time-expired Indians had already begun to move out of their plantations into new locations, between villages set up by freed Africans decades earlier, and sometimes into the villages themselves. Also, by the 1890s, Indians had accumulated savings from their meagre estate wages, and received land in lieu of a return passage to India that was part of their indenture contract. Free return passage was discontinued in 1891; but by then many Indians thrived as rice farmers: "The majority of rice cultivators were Indian immigrants whose indentureship had expired, and who lived off the estates in villages and settlements." [p. 155]

Although African-Guyanese had grown rice earlier, Indian-Guyanese created a new rice industry. Others raised livestock and cultivated ground provisions, and crops such as sweet potatoes, tomatoes, pumpkins and other vegetables. Some Indians even became shopkeepers and money-lenders. As it happened, during the 1890s, a boom in the colony's gold industry lured African-Guyanese from their coastland village homes to become prospectors in the forest; but after a decline in the gold industry, in the early 1900s, these prospectors found they could not pay the rates and taxes owing on their home properties, which were then bought at relatively low prices by Indian-Guyanese, only to cause or increase suspicion between Indian- and African-Guyanese.

By the turn of the twentieth century, prolonged depression in the sugar industry created such hardship on estates that many Indians sought dubious refuge in towns, most of all in Georgetown, where: "they [Indians] solicited jobs fetching people's baskets, packs or packages for a fee," [p. 176] and by night lodged in a "Coolie Hotel" where they passed the time, smoking and playing cards. Beggary was preferable to estate life because, as one poor wretch put it: "Me free man now, no bung - can walk wey me like, wuk wey me like. Manjah no abul ax um question. Bin bung man blige wuk evry day. Me own massa dis time." [p. 176] But, almost in contradiction to such poverty, by the early years of the new century, prosperous Indian businesses began to appear in Georgetown and feed further resentment or envy from African-Guyanese.

In addition to this insight into incipient African - Indian rivalry in Guyana, *Settlement* sheds light on Indian cultural indigenisation through indenture. Its back cover announces *Settlement* as: "a scholarly treatment of the role of ethnicity in a plural society and a cogent discussion of the processes of settlement and cultural change." Hindu caste feeling, for instance, gradually gave way to a creole sense of class in which respect for pandits, shopkeepers and sirdars was overtaken by the importance of pan-boilers, clerks, book keepers, sick nurses and dispensers on whom the society depended for its day-to-day survival.

As Bisnauth admits: "For most, at least during the period of this study, a new Indian-Guyanese identity, though latent, had yet to be grasped or acknowledged." [p. 83] Even if it was not clearly visible, this identity had taken root when the author observes that the building of mosques and temples meant that gods and practices carrying the inescapable imprint of the geography and culture of India were now transferred to Guyana, or that: "it was not unusual for Hindus to share in the celebrations of the Christian festivals of Christmas, Easter and harvest, and for Christians to participate in Hindu and Moslem celebrations." [p. 143]

Cricket also played a role in this amalgam of cultural mixing and transformation, as an East Indian Cricket Club appeared a full two years before a British Guiana East Indian Association. More importantly, the marked Indian indifference to politics during indenture began to change when J.A. Luckhoo, an Indian lawyer, was elected to political office, in Essequibo, in 1916. Also, in 1916, Indian-Guyanese played an active role in the debate on whether Sir Walter Egerton should be recalled from his post as Governor of British Guiana. By then, in Bisnauth's view, the Indian indentured community had acquired a Guyanese identity of its own, not because it had been: "assimilated into the larger creole society," but because: "it was largely shaped by local conditions."[p. 230]

ROOTS OF AN ETHNIC DILEMMA

Basdeo Mangru, Ed., C.F.Andrews
Impressions of British Guiana, 1930: An Emissary's Assessment. pp.122.
Chicago, Illinois, Adams Press, 2007.
ISBN 0-967009-32-4

Charles Freer Andrews (1871-1940) graduated in theology from Cambridge University, and entered the Anglican priesthood before going to India as a Christian missionary in 1904. Attracted by the movement for swaraj (home rule) in British colonial India, he became a strong supporter of Mahatma Gandhi whom he had first met in South Africa. In 1929, Andrews went to British Guiana to assess living conditions of Indians taken as indentured labourers to British-owned sugar plantations in the colony between 1838 and 1917. He was hosted locally by the British Guiana East Indian Association, and spent three months in Guyana before submitting a report to the British Governor Sir Gordon Guggisberg. Now, under the title *Impressions of British Guiana, 1930: an Emissary's Assessment*, this report has been edited and published by Guyanese historian Professor Basdeo Mangru.

By the 1920s, after indenture had ended and the supply of labourers from India had dried up, the gradual shift of Indian workers away from plantations created dire need for labour in Guyana. A delegation led by the Guyanese Attorney General J.J. Nunan, and Indian-Guyanese lawyer J.A. Luckhoo visited

India twice, in 1919 and 1923, in an effort to secure fresh workers under the so-called British Guiana Colonisation Scheme. But the Scheme failed following bitter controversy between those who supported and those who opposed further Indian immigration. Hence need for a reliable assessment of the conditions of Indians in B.G.

Andrews was ideally suited for the task. He spoke Hindi fluently; he knew India and Indian culture at first hand; and he had previously observed the living conditions of Indian workers in Malaya, Natal (South Africa), Fiji and Indonesia. Besides, as an Englishman with such qualifications, he could obtain ready access to everyone, from top government and plantation officials to members of the African-Guyanese middle class, and the lowliest Indian-Guyanese plantation workers. In addition, he brought a genuinely unbiased and humane concern seemingly to everyone and everything.

Take the issue of Guyanese schools, for instance, which were then managed by Christian denominations, but funded by the State. Andrews immediately spotted the injustice of a system in which only Christian instruction was given in schools supported by: "public money, a considerable portion of which is provided by non-Christian persons in the colony" [p. 77] Indian-Guyanese (Hindu and Muslim) children in these schools were inevitably given Christian instruction: "[Christian] hymns were taught to little Hindu children." [p. 70] And since there were few Indian-Guyanese teachers, Indian-Guyanese children: "are taught in a foreign language [English rather than Hindi] by [African-Guyanese] teachers who do not understand the East Indian nature." [p. 92] The solution, according to Andrews, was: "complete religious neutrality" [p. 77] similar to what obtains today.

Another educational problem was the practice of preparing Guyanese children for examinations set in England: "They [English examinations] have no touch with life here [in

Guyana] at all...The student loses sight of his own country and upbringing together." [p. 62] In this case, Andrews recommended examinations set by a West Indian Board, again similar to what exists today.

On Land Settlement Policy, Andrews thought the "ranges "or shared barracks housing plantation workers were unhealthy: "they looked very insanitary and filth was in evidence on every side." [p. 26] Such dwellings increased risk of disease, especially malaria, and could be improved by a generous policy of re-settling workers, for example, by offering them land in commutation of their return passage to India. Two acres were on offer, but Andrews thought it was not enough.

The colonial State also did not recognise the legality of marriages performed according to Hindu custom, and children of such marriages were considered illegitimate. One solution, advanced by Andrews, was simply for the State to regard such marriages as legal, as they would have been in India, since: "the very publicity of Hindu marriage is equivalent to a kind of registration." [p. 33] On the related issue of child marriage, Andrews held long discussions with Hindu pundits who agreed to raise the age of marriage to fourteen as a first step.

Other issues included control of malaria, the Indian contribution to rice cultivation, the use of Indian languages, absence of Indians in the police force, and the observation that rum-drinking: "was regarded as one of the worst forms of degradation within the [Indian] community." [p. 71] Both Andrews and another English missionary who had worked in India, R.J. Kidd, agreed that: "strong liquor drinking had been practically unknown in Indian villages...yet in Demerara [Guyana] it had become almost universal." [p. 89]

Some of Andrews's observations, for instance, those on Christian denominational schools, or on Guyanese school examinations set in England, illustrate their historical value in showing how things have changed since 1929. His proposals on race relations, alas, do not reflect similar change, and today appear both perceptive and poignant, if not prophetic, when he writes: "I wondered more than once whether some slight rise in psychological temperature might not produce a racial clash between East Indians and Africans of a very painful nature;" [p. 57] for this is exactly what happened in the 1960s.

Andrews thought ethnic animosity thrived on the "tragic" fact that: "Negroes and Coloured people...whose forefathers actually made British Guiana so fruitful ...are never likely to do more than patiently tolerate, in a friendly spirit, the East Indians who come into their country." [p. 57] As a neutral and sympathetic outsider, Andrews's opinions greatly illuminate the tangled roots of an ethnic dilemma that still threaten the survival of Guyana as a united country. Illumination of such vital issues, complete with the editor's footnotes, sub-headings, appendices, bibliography, Index and exhaustive Introduction, underline the value of Andrews' *Impressions* as a precious, cautionary commentary.

BRAWLING MADRASSIS: SOUTH INDIAN-GUYANESE

Moses Nagamootoo
Hendree's Cure: Madrassi Experience in a New World. pp.149.
Leeds, Peepal Tree Press, 2000.

Hendree's Cure: Madrassi Experience in a New World, the
first novel by Moses Nagamootoo, who served as Minister of
Information in the People's Progressive Party Government
of Guyana from 1996 to 2001, considers descendants of
Telugu- and Tamil-speaking indentured Indians who
boarded ship for Guyana at the South Indian port of
Madras, (Chennai) hence their being labelled "Madrassis."
By contrast, most indentured Indians left from the North
Indian port of Calcutta during the indenture period from
1838 to 1917.

In his "Foreword", Nagamootoo writes: "I have attempted
to recreate the lives, aspirations and oral traditions of the
early Tamils or Dravidians from South India and of their
off-springs who lived in my village." [p. 4] The village
is Whim, sandwiched between such African villages as
Lancaster, Liverpool and Manchester, and second only to
Port Mourant as a business centre on the Corentyne coast of
Guyana. Although, according to the author, the Madrassis
of Whim are a rambunctious lot, given to heavy drinking,
loud drumming, and Kali-mai puja worship involving
animal sacrifice, it is surprising to learn that during the
inter-ethnic political strife and violence in Guyana, in the

1960s, when many Indians and Africans were killed: "Not a single act of hostility took place between the two races [around Whim"]. [p. 143]

Nagamootoo has no time, in *Hendree's Cure,* for sophistication or etiquette. He uses a loosely episodic structure and a cataloguing, labelling or documentary technique that saturates us with myriad facts, figures and multiple names of characters, all of whom we could never remember because they are probably as many as those in Tolstoy's *War and Peace* which is at least ten times as long. There is not even a story as such, only a deceptively artless assemblage of sketches, portraits, episodes, anecdotes, incidents, memories, reflections or musings that feed into a rippling stream of oral narrative which seems, like Tennyson's brook, set to go on forever.

As the title of the novel suggests, there is an ostensible hero, Hendree, who has been taught by a "charcoal-black man-giant" (p. 53) drummer Changamma, and later presides as master drummer at village functions such as: "the ninth day christening of babies, seaside pujas, traditional weddings and dead-work." [rites accompanying a funeral] [p. 54] Hendree may gain some sympathy when he loses his wife Aydoo to a visiting Frenchman, but he is not deterred by such distractions, and sets about learning to "perform spiritual cures," [p. 124] not because he feels a spiritual calling or wishes to help people, but because: "In the healing business knowledge was power;" [p. 128] and by the time he heals or cures Joe-Joe whose right arm was mysteriously paralysed by guilt, he achieves a notoriety equal to that of Pundit Ganesh in V.S. Naipaul's novel *The Mystic Masseur.* Such are the trickster ethics of bare faced cunning and naked self-aggrandisement that ensure success and respect in rural, British Caribbean colonial, communities in the first half of the twentieth century.

What takes centre stage has less to do with Hendree than the village of Whim which, serves as the primary location and connecting link to the whole captivating parade of rustic gullibility and high jinks that pass for life in the village. Superstition is rife and: "Whim's own jumbie and churile stories were told at every wake." [p. 41] Cricket even is influenced, if not controlled by superstition when the pitch itself: "would come alive with the application of ingredients such as dried bird peppers, strands of horses' mane and dog's teeth" [p. 93.] For good or often bad measure, there are also plenty of spirits such as Moongazers, Dutch jumbies, or "backoos" not to mention mermaids or the "Water-mamma," all of which can be placated by magical arts, whether of Christian, Muslim, Hindu or Madrassi provenance.

We catch the improbable flavour of life in Whim from accounts, more likely tall tales, of extraordinary deeds that have entered village folklore, for instance, the brilliant exploits of the long distance runner Sonny Garbharran, or the extraordinary feats of the locally owned race horse "Bright Steel." But it is the local speech and narrative that contribute most to the spicy flavour of village life. When Hendree speaks out of turn, for instance, the reprimand from his guru Naga is swift and scorching: "You is a moon-pass coconut, a goodfunutting pin-stick floating like fraaf pon wave tap." [p. 58] Such is the feudal authority of this denunciation that it is accepted without demur. Nor should we expect less raucous or ribald speech when the author praises the charms of Naga's mistress Jessamie: "She was plump, fat like a pig on a slow fire and aroused appetite almost instantly." [p. 61] Raw language matches raw sexual desire.

Hendree's Cure is by no means the first work of fiction to chronicle Indian-Guyanese (village or sugar estate) customs and manners. A.R.F. Webber's *Those that be in Bondage* (1917) and Edgar Mittelholzer's *Corentyne Thunder* (1941) appeared much earlier, and were followed by novels and stories, for example, from Peter Kempadoo, Rooplall Monar, Janice Shinebourne, Sasenarine Persaud, Roy Heath, and Oonya Kempadoo although *Hendree's Cure* remains the most unsparing, affectionate portrait we yet have of brawling exuberance as the crowning glory of South Indian culture in Guyana.

As a politician Nagamootoo knows that his characters' blistering invective and histrionic, ready-for-a-fight bravado are, deep down, an expression of impatience with their colonial condition, and their longing for more meaningful resistance to a sense of powerlessness, inherited from decades of domination, exploitation and abuse. His "Foreword" simply states: "history needs to be recovered not only by scholarship, but also by acts of the imagination, especially when that 'history' has barely been chronicled in terms of conventional historical texts." That is exactly what *Hendree's Cure* does: it recovers aspects of Guyanese colonial history through a brilliant act of the imagination.

"A COOLIE LOOKING IN FROM OUTSIDE"

Jan Lowe Shinebourne
Chinese Women. pp.94.
London, Peepal Tree Press, 2010.
ISBN 13: 97818452231514

Jan Lowe Shinebourne's *Chinese Women* is her third novel which comes long after her first *Timepiece* (1986), and less long after *The Last Plantation* (2001) and a volume of stories *The Godmother and other Stories* (2004). With a Chinese father, and a mother who was half-Chinese and half-Indian, Shinebourne was born in Rosehall, a sugar estate in Berbice, British Guiana, where she grew up, before marrying an Englishman and moving to England where she has lived since 1970.

The narrator of *Chinese Women* Albert Aziz is an Indian Muslim who, like the author, is born in 1947. Albert grows up on a sugar estate in the county of Demerara, although his father works as field overseer in an unnamed sugar estate in Berbice, probably based on the author's memories of Rosehall. In any case, never before in her fiction, nor seldom elsewhere, is there another description of a Guyanese sugar estate more chilling than the one given by Albert: "The sugar estate gave me the feeling that very little divided beast and man. Both laboured, copulated, procreated and died exposed to the elements: in the mud, rain and canals, at the mercy of alligators, snakes, rats, vultures, mosquitoes and flies that sucked their blood and ate their flesh... You could see faeces floating in the canals and ditches where children played and people copulated. They even drank the same water they shat in" [p. 35]

This nightmarish vision was probably embedded in the author's consciousness from childhood without her being able to find the right words to fully express it. After a lifetime's thought and reflection lavished on three works of fiction, however, she finds simple but powerful words that finally exorcise inhibition, and proclaim the stark, unvarnished truth of British, colonial conditions on Guyanese sugar plantations.

In the 1950s, most Guyanese sugar estates were owned by the British company, Bookers, notorious for their apartheid practice of hiring only white administrative staff to supervise workers who were chiefly Indian. By the late 1950s, a liberal shift in company policy permitted Albert's father to be hired, and his family accommodated in the same housing quarters as white staff. By seeing how Whites live from the inside, Albert is able to give a fuller report on the scale of human exploitation on sugar estates: "the horrible daily spectacle of human misery." [p. 36] Even after his family lived alongside Whites for some time, he still detects: "the culture of surveillance where we had to pass through unwritten tests set by the overseers before we were allowed to live with them." [p. 72]

The inhumanity of British colonialism is only one aspect of the novel's more personal subject, Albert's life story, which appears in three parts, each outlined in one of three sections of *Chinese Women*. The first section discloses the calamity of Albert's accident at the age of ten, when he falls from a genip tree and breaks all the major joints in his body. Recovery comes after three years of therapy and specially devoted care by Dr. Webster, an Englishman. Albert leaves for Canada in 1974, and goes on to study engineering before becoming a millionaire by 2000, when he sells his: "first nuclear centrifuge design in the Middle East for a million US dollars." [p. 9]

Despite such success, Albert still squirms under the derogatory label he carries from Guyana where, as an Indian Muslim, he was defined as a *Fulaman,* or worse, as a *Fula coolie,* [p. 13] because of the low social status assigned to Indian-Guyanese sugar estate workers. Only at the end of the novel, after detaching himself from Guyana, Canada and the West to become an Arab Muslim does Albert discover self-respect and dignity: "As an Arab Muslim, which I am now, I would never be called a *Fulaman* again." [p. 91] This is partly why the novel ends with Albert deciding to leave his apartment in Calgary, Canada, to live in the Middle East to: "do the work of a Muslim, helping to build the nuclear programme that would lead to the destruction of Israel." [p. 93]

Another reason for Albert's decision is his "relationship" with the two Chinese women of the novel's title. The first, Anne Carrera, is an overseer's wife and neighbour during Albert's adolescence. Albert is totally fixated on her until he realises that she belongs to the dominant white group, although her husband may be Madeiran Portuguese rather than white, and she herself may be mixed and only half Chinese. Albert has an even greater obsession with Alice Wong, who was a Chinese fellow student in his school days, but from whom he is separated for more than forty years, until turning up in London where she lives, in 2006, and ardently courting her at the age of sixty. After showering her with extravagant offers of money and gifts, Albert is rejected and realises that: "Though I was a millionaire, I was still the coolie looking in from outside on the lives of white people." [p. 68] This is when he becomes convinced that his future lies with his Arab, Muslim brethren in the Middle East.

Perhaps Albert's decision to throw in his lot with Arabs agitating for justice in a post-9/11 world may at first seem far-fetched. Yet the surprising brevity of *Chinese Women,* only ninety-four pages long, and its potent language, already seen in its description of a sugar estate during colonial times, suggest confidence and an almost prophetic air that, in this era, pregnant with emergence of an Arab spring and signs of American decline, may well hint at apocalyptic change to come. True to her mixed, ethnic and cultural inheritance, Shinebourne grounds her novel firmly in history when she documents the humiliation visited on Guyana by European empires, British as well as Dutch, and the resilience of victims, not only Albert, an indentured Indian, who rises phoenix-like out of ashes, but indentured Chinese, described as: "the most tenacious of all the ethnic groups." [p. 51]

"THEY LONGED FOR IT [GUYANA]
I WAS ... IN FLIGHT FROM IT"

Rahul Bhattacharya
The Sly Company of People who Care. pp.278.
New York, Farrar, Straus and Giroux, 2011.
ISBN 978-0374-26585-4

The Sly Company of People who Care is the first novel of Rahul Bhattacharya, an Indian author who was born in 1979, lives in Delhi, and previously wrote a cricket book – *Pundits from Pakistan: On Tour with India, 2003-04*. Bhattacharya paid only two brief visits to Guyana in 2002 and 2006, and *Sly Company* does not tell a connected story as we might expect from a traditional novel. The narrative consists of what seems like a factual account of the author's travel through Guyana and neighbouring countries such as Brazil, Venezuela and Trinidad, along with commentary on Guyana's history, geography, politics, economics, sociology and culture, suggesting that *Sly Company* could, probably, be read as a travel book. But since fiction is flexible as a genre, there is no reason why Bhattacharya's characters, descriptions and dialogue may not also be seen as fiction. Certainly they benefit from fictional techniques.

Sly Company is divided into three parts, the first of which recounts hair-raising incidents on the narrator's trip to Kaieteur Falls using an overland route from Georgetown. The venture includes character sketches of porknockers with names like

"Nasty, Dacta Red, Roots, Labba, Baby and Foulis," which capture the rough and ready ways of living, and bare-knuckle escapades, that are part and parcel of survival in damp, hot house, tropical forest conditions where mortal danger may lurk at any turn. In one incident during "a session of semi-drunken cricket" [p. 48] a fire snake appears and is beaten with a stick and hoisted on a prong before its stomach is torn open with a knife and: "a frog fell out with a bloody splatter." [p. 48]

If this does not catch an atmosphere of living on the edge, consider an experiment of the narrator who keeps six yarrau fish in a bucket of water to observe their growth, only to see them cannibalise each other, until one supremo survives in water tinged with blood and floating pieces of fish. [p. 48] The narrator concludes: "In the bush everything could be wicked, everything left to chance." [p. 70]

Part Two offers an enlightening appraisal, from a sympathetic outsider's point of view, of the history of ethnic relations between Indians and African-Guyanese. As an Indian himself, the narrator's comments on Indian-Guyanese are notable: "Their [Indian-Guyanese] Indianness felt more intimate than mine. They longed for it; I had no such longing. I was wearied by it, and in fact in flight from it." [p. 100] Bhattacharya perceives reasons for troubled relations between Indians and Africans in Guyana: after Abolition, in an effort to keep freed Africans on the plantation at low wages, plantation owners destroyed African initiative in starting their own villages; but, out of similar economic motives, they later issued land grants to Indians and helped them to drain and irrigate their farms.

At worst the Africans saw the Indians as: "illiterate," barefooted, clannish heathens, misers who hoarded coins under their bed, who had strange customs and rituals and wore strange uncivilised costumes... At worst, the Indians saw the Africans as the condemned: ugly, black of skin, with wide noses and twisted coir for hair, mimics of the white masters, without a language, culture or religion of their own, frivolous, promiscuous, violent, lazy." [p. 109] Such information implies that, in addition to knowledge gained from observations on his visits to Guyana, the author of *Sly Company* also relies on research.

Part Three opens with the tension of police efforts to combat crime, and the relief of humorous anecdotes from Lance Banarsee (Uncle Lance.) We then get a salacious snapshot of the seamy side of nightlife on Sheriff Street in Georgetown (like Soho of London), followed by an even more salacious, often erotic romp of the narrator and his female companion Jan (Jankey Ramsaywack) through Venezuela and Trinidad. Bhattacharya displays a surprisingly sure grasp of Guyanese speech, for instance, in aphorisms like "Sorry fuh maga dog, maga dog turn around bite you," [p. 78] or "two man rat cyan live in one hole." [p. 127] He also flawlessly reports a woman's reason in court for burning another woman's forearm: "she ah lie like a dog, is she who jook me fust," [p. 87] and accurately reports a childlike Guyanese impulse for boastful bluster and baseless bravado, usually intended either to impress or frighten.

None of this explains the title of the book which derives from the author's discovery of a manuscript of Dutch colonisers who laid the foundation of Guyana as a nation. The first three words of a section of the pamphlet praising the "civilising mission" of the Dutch West India Company which led the colonising mission were "struck out" and "replaced by a single word SLY. " [p. 89] Then, in the margin, a sentence "they think like they care" was started and abandoned. Hence the author's ironic title for a Company which had enslaved, exploited and traumatised people for profit in ostensible pursuit of a civilising mission!

More ironic still is the epigraph to *Sly Company*: "All this was Dutch. Then, like so much else, it was English," a quotation taken from *Light Years*, a novel by American writer James Salter who, in casting a baneful eye on the predatory practice of bartering colonial peoples like merchandise, yokes together the rich and glamorous city of New York, which was originally owned by the Dutch, with a hapless colonial outpost like Guyana. Most ironic of all: in 1667, the Dutch exchanged New York (then named "New Netherland") for another hapless colonial outpost, Suriname - Guyana's neighbour!

INDENTURE FAMILY TRAGEDY

Ryhaan Shah
A Silent Life. pp.186.
Leeds, Peepal Tree Press, 2005.
ISBN 1 84523 0027

In the first three chapters of her first novel, *A Silent Life,* Guyanese Ryhaan Shah paints a sensitive portrait of close-knit solidarity and cosy warmth in an Indian-Guyanese family, chronicled by Aleyah Hassan her teen aged narrator. Like most Indian-Guyanese, Aleyah's family are descendants of indentured Indians who immigrated to Guyana between 1838 and 1917 to work as labourers on British-owned sugar estates. By the 1960s, when Aleyah begins her chronicle, she lives in a country town with her extended Muslim family that consists of her shopkeeper parents, younger brother and sister, and ageing maternal grandmother - Nani.

Pursuing a deep-seated passion for family history, Aleyah discovers that her grandfather Pa Nazeer displayed unusual talent as a dancer, while her maternal grandmother helped workers from nearby sugar estates to resist exploitation from their employers. We are told that: "They [estate workers] used to bring her [Nani] their troubles. They had trouble with their bosses, their wages, and the way they had to work. They worked worse than mules, they said." [p. 23] If this makes Aleyah's family look different or better off she cautions: "we weren't much better off than them [estate workers]" [p. 23]. The truth is that her family had a skeleton in their closet: talented Pa Nazeer had committed suicide, and the shame of this tragedy is never forgotten. An image of the rope with which Pa Nazeer hangs himself serves as a central motif that haunts us throughout the novel.

Aleyah is awarded a scholarship to study economics in England. After graduating with an M.A. degree, she joins World Aid, an organisation concerned with Third World development; and soon she is travelling to assignments all over the world as her career takes off and prospers. But her family's tragic past seems to jinx her success after she gets married to Dean Yacoob, son of a Muslim Indian-Guyanese family living in England. In sharp contrast to herself, Dean makes no headway in his job, and creates such problems that Aleyah is overcome by depression and has to be treated in hospital. In time, she and Dean separate, but she leaves their two sons in England with him, while she returns to Guyana.

The autobiographical structure of Aleyah's story also includes a chronicle of contemporary Guyana from the 1960s, when she is still studying, to the early 1990s when she returns to Guyana. While she is in England, for instance, in the 1970s and 80s, Aleyah receives regular letters from her family complaining about deteriorating conditions of everyday life in Guyana during the dictatorship of "the Kabaka," alias Forbes Burnham, who is never mentioned by name. The Kabaka's régime is riddled with racism and corruption generally, not to mention incompetence and specific hardships such as frequent blackouts, loss of electricity, erratic water supply, and shortage of essential foodstuff.

Eventually, Aleyah finds employment in the Ministry of Finance only to discover that, although democracy has been restored after decades of dictatorship, the new ruling party is no more effective than the Kabaka's in achieving change. Change is impossible because of deeply rooted social, ethnic and economic problems deriving from the past dictatorship and Guyana's colonial history before that. For example, when a small group of professionals discuss formation of a new political party that could change things, it appears to lose the battle before it even gets started: in a nation with historic ethnic, class, gender and other divisions, the group can muster only two Indian-Guyanese and one female among its ten members. The novel then comes to a seemingly abrupt end, with Nani revealing details about her family's indenture and the mystery of her role in her husband's death.

As a Guyanese addition to novels that imaginatively re-create personal narratives and circumstances of Indian indenture, not available in historical accounts, for example, Sharlow Mohammed's *The Promise*, Ramabai Espinet's *The Swinging Bridge* or Lakshmi Persaud's *Raise the Lanterns High*, *A Silent Life* presents a convincing description of the cruel ill-treatment of Nani's mother by her husband and mother-in-law in India until, out of sheer desperation, she is forced to abandon her twin sons and become indentured to British Guiana. Descriptions of the immigration depot in India, and of life on board ship to Guyana are thoroughly researched and Shah's reconstruction of the indenture experience is plausible and convincing.

But despite the author's successful reconstruction of indenture, Guyanese history, or the tragic fate of one family, Nani's revelation appears strangely muted at the end. In her climactic quarrel with Pa Nazeer when he threatens to kill himself, and when Nani reveals that it was she who gave him the rope to hang himself, her role in his death does not register the full force of the tragic blow intended. Partly because we already know about Pa Nazeer's tragedy throughout the novel, his death lacks a vital element of surprise from which not even Nani's potent revelation fully redeems it.

The relative ease of Aleyah's academic and professional success, in difficult circumstances, the suddenness of her depression, and stoic adjustment to her failing marriage also produce a similar effect which, together with the muted ending of *A Silent Life*, tend to diminish the aptness of the novel's stirring epigraphs from Martin Carter and Jorge Luis Borges, suggesting that both Nani and Aleyah bear the burden of a silent life or stoic resilience in the face of adversity, as seen, for instance, in Carter's : "we are the world's hope/ And so therefore I rise again I rise again." What is redeeming is the documentary skill of Shah's writing, for instance, her description of Georgetown as "Garbage City," [p. 162] her keen powers of observation, and ability to create convincing characters, and scenes or situations all of which enhance the promise of her first novel.

GOD'S UNIVERSAL VISION

Ryhaan Shah
Weaving Water. pp.254.
London, Cutting Edge Press, 2013.
ISBN 978-908122-38-4 (PB)

Weaving Water, the second novel of Guyanese Ryhaan Shah, could not be more different from her first *A Silent Life* (2005) the story of a Muslim, Indian-Guyanese narrator, and of her indentured immigrant family's mainly tragic experience in Guyana. *Weaving Water* also depicts tragic conditions of indenture in Guyana; but its Hindu characters are observed over a longer period than characters in *A Silent Life* - from 1917 to contemporary time, when Guyanese migrate in droves to foreign places in North America, and complain about corruption in their People's Progressive Party government. What also distinguishes *Weaving Water* from Shah's previous writing is her discovery of a unique narrative style of such fluency, grace and charm as to set it apart from much of Guyanese or West Indian literature.

Shah's style which mixes ordinary, everyday events with fantasy to form a genre, generally known as magic realism, was first popularised in the 1970s and 80s by Latin American writers notably the Colombian author Gabriel Marcia Marquez (1927-2014) whose novel *One Hundred Years of Solitude* (1967) remains a classic of the genre. But it is not clear whether Shah was directly influenced by Marquez or other Latin American authors. Her direct influences appear to come more from her subject - the metaphysics of a Hindu world view which she insinuates into *Weaving Water* with the inherited expertise of a born Hindu.

Two of the novel's chief characters, Rampat and Parvati, an indentured couple, travelling on the last ship with indentured Indians bound for Guyana in 1917, notice another young immigrant, Taijnie, giving birth to a baby girl aboard ship shortly before she dies and is buried at sea. Since Taijnie is travelling alone, her baby Neela is adopted by Rampat and Parvati, and later grows up with her adopted parents who have settled in the village of Coverton, in Berbice, Guyana.

Later still, as: "the baby born out of the belly of the sea," [p. 37] and one who is officially issued with a birth certificate giving her details as: "Father Unknown" and "Born at Sea" [p. 37], Neela gradually takes on supernatural associations and other-worldly expectations within a Guyanese Hindu, peasant community nourished by a thriving oral tradition: "about the journey out of India, about jumbies and [about] fairies and princesses." [p. 38] With equal surprise it is only a matter of time before Neela had: "already read the Bhagavad Gita" [sacred Hindu text] the whole of it, in Hindi, and knew all the stories of the deities." [p. 63] Nor are we surprised to learn that she also sang all the *bhajans* [religious songs] and *chalisas* [sacred chants] at the *mandir* [Hindu temple] until: "everyone said that the girl was a *devi* [goddess.]" [p. 63]

As a supernatural being, for example, mysteriously disappearing at night in the canal outside her home, Neela's exploits form a central thread in the novel's action; but Shah does not neglect more realistic social, political or ethnic issues. It is as if a magical blend of fantasy/reality involuntarily takes hold of her narrative, as it were, directing the author to create one enchanting scene after another, each surrounded by an almost dreamlike atmosphere, imbued with elements of fantasy, and accompanied by a constantly repeated, half musical refrain about Neela, for example: "In a village where little happened...gossip would fly, and stories would be made up. Neela herself had become part of that pattern, that weave. She was the reason why the milk went sour, the calf died or the baby was born dead...She was not only a fair maid and a water mama, but a sea spirit with unearthly powers." [p. 101]

Weaving Water depicts impoverished, Indian indentured labourers struggling for better working conditions. The novel also discusses relations between Indian immigrants from North India and those from the South, notably the so-called Madrassis, one of whom, Billa, has a close relationship of *jahaji bhai* [ship brother] to Rampat. Billa's physical prowess and general ebullience make him stand out, while his uneasy relationship with Sampson, an African-Guyanese giant, reflects the deep-seated nature of historic rivalry between African- and Indian-Guyanese.

The problem is that Africans who were brought as slaves to Guyana, worked on Guyanese plantations for two centuries before Indians took over their work which, they believe, gives them a stronger claim of legitimacy to Guyanese citizenship than the Indians who succeeded them. As Sampson's son Martin announces: "We [Africans] sweated and we bled for this earth, and you, [Indians] you came here just the other day and think you're better?" [p. 55] Not that Shah attempts to resolve the conflict, although Sampson's disappearance by supernatural means implies that no simple or ordinary solution is likely.

Never before, in Guyanese or West Indian literature, has the second novel of an author fulfilled the promise of their first like *Weaving Water,* not only because of Shah's expertise in magic realism, which enjoys inherent advantages of a subject (Hinduism) consisting of endless legendary exploits of gods, goddesses and sages, together with infinite resources of Hindu lore: "mysterious, ancient and deep;" [p. 45] but also because of her philosophical mastery of Hindu metaphysics.

The best comparison is with Shah's compatriot Sharon Maas, who also is not a born Hindu, but whose three novels *Of Marriageable Age* (2000), *Peacocks Dancing* (2001) and *The Speech of Angels* (2003) project a Hindu world view like that in *Weaving Water*: "it was the way of the gods that they moved in and out of your very lives to create, to destroy, to change and transform the world in order to fulfill the fate that was already written." [p. 153] As a Muslim author, Shah's triumph is to delve with such earnest and admiring sympathy into Hindu cultural heritage that, for the duration of her novel, at least, it invests her with God's own universal vision.

CHEDDI JAGAN: DISHONOURED PROPHET

Colin A. Palmer
Cheddi Jagan and the Politics of Power: British Guiana's Struggle for Independence. pp.363.
Chapel Hill, The University of North Carolina Press, 2010.

Colin Palmer's *Cheddi Jagan and the Politics of Power: British Guiana's Struggle for Independence* considers the political career of Dr. Jagan (1919-1997) chiefly between 1947 when he was first elected to the Legislative Council in Guyana to 1964, when Dr Jagan's People's Progressive Party (PPP) was defeated by an American-inspired change from the traditional first-past-the-post electoral system used in British electoral systems, to one of proportional representation where seats are awarded by the percentage of votes won, thus allowing opposition parties - the People's National Congress (PNC) led by Forbes Burnham, and United Force (UF) led by Peter D'Aguiar - to form a coalition that won elections in December, 1964.

Jamaican-born author Colin Palmer, Dodge Professor of History at Princeton University, is well known for his writing on slavery, African-American subjects, colonial Latin America and the Caribbean, for example, in his *Eric Williams and the Making of the Modern Caribbean* (2009).

Dr. Jagan's political career is unusually long, lasting from 1947 to his death in 1997, but although Professor Palmer's volume is not a full biography, it distils the essence of Dr.

Jagan's political contribution by focussing on crucial events in his early career, for example, the formation of the PPP in 1950, the party's historic victory in the first national elections based on adult suffrage in Guyana, in April, 1953, and suspicion of communism in several members of the PPP. This suspicion led to what the author describes as a coup d'état by the British Government under Sir Winston Churchill, who used force to dismiss Dr. Jagan's government and suspend the Constitution in October, 1953.

In eight chapters, a brief Conclusion and Epilogue, *Cheddi Jagan and the Politics of Power* also takes in equally important episodes such as the split of the PPP in 1955, the consequent spread of racial politics in Guyana, Dr. Jagan's victories in elections, in 1957 and 1961, and clandestine intervention of the US to engineer the critical defeat of the PPP in 1964. This meant that Dr. Jagan would remain as Leader of the Opposition from 1964 until 1992 when he finally served again as President of Guyana until 1997. By then, however, his performance as President must be regarded as too little too late, largely because of the severe blood letting of professional and skilled Guyanese who emigrated during the dictatorship of the PNC, from 1964 to 1992.

Nowadays, although he is dismissed as a political failure, for example, in Baytoram Ramharack's *Against the Grain* (2005), Clem Seecharan's *Sweetening Bitter Sugar* (2005), and Mohan Ragbeer's *The Indelible Stain* (2011), Dr. Jagan deserves credit for establishing the first mass-based, country-wide (not just Georgetown-based) party in 1950, and winning an historic election victory in 1953. The ensuing threat of communist subversion from his PPP that led to Suspension of the Constitution now seems as nothing more than a colossal mistake even if it inscribed the mark of Cain on Dr. Jagan, seemingly for life, while it not only left the reputation of his rival Forbes Burnham unblemished, but gave him a free hand to implement communist policies in Guyana, in the 1970s and 1980s.

Relying largely on archival sources such as records from British colonial governors and officials, as well as American politicians and diplomats, Professor Palmer flatly rejects the alleged communist threat of the PPP: "Her Majesty's Government's coup d'état [the Suspension] was based on a misreading of the political situation in the colony, and this invited a hasty overreaction." [p. 54] Certainly, Professor Palmer admits, Dr. Jagan and his fellow ministers were guilty of "vacuous Marxist rhetoric," but he concludes after Dr. Jagan's two administrations from 1957 to 1964: "The ideological pragmatism Jagan displayed in this instance characterized his behaviour until his defeat in 1964. He retained his Marxist rhetoric but he never governed as a Marxist, or even attempted to do so." [p. 153]

The tribulations inflicted on Dr. Jagan by the British over his alleged communism in the 1950s were nothing compared with the devilish American Cold War paranoia over communism unleashed on him and his party during the early 1960s, with active collaboration from Guyanese willing to sell their souls in order to destroy Dr. Jagan. Professor Palmer acknowledges, for instance, the: "diabolical policies of powerful outsiders [American mercenaries] acting in their own interest with the willing compliance of local [Guyanese] enablers."[p. 11]

Professor Palmer reminds us of Guyanese enablers whose motives in the American-inspired riot of February, 1962, were noted by the Wynn Parry Commission. Burnham, for instance, was described as being driven by a: "callous and remorseless attitude" [p. 219] and: "a desire... to establish a more important and more rewarding position for himself by bringing about Dr. Jagan's downfall,"[p. 227] while Peter D'Aguiar was concerned with: "representing his own interests and those of the colony's privileged groups." [p. 227] This false political unity, concocted out of wholly fabricated, transparent motives, brought the coalition between Burnham's PNC and D'Aguiar's UF to power, in 1964; but it was a mere ploy which quickly fell apart.

The crux of the matter is Dr. Jagan himself, his political beliefs and motives. Of one thing Professor Palmer is certain: "beneath all the rhetorical fulminations, vacillations, and incoherence, Cheddi Jagan's commitment to the welfare of British Guiana was never in doubt and shone through with admirable consistency and passion."[p. 158] Professor Palmer also quotes Governor Sir Ralph Grey, no admirer of Dr. Jagan, as saying: "Jagan is a nationalist, Marxist thinker, but not a Soviet-sympathizing, Soviet-dominated Communist doer." [p. 211] Seldom has a prophet been more dishonoured in his own country!

"A RING OF SPIES SURROUNDED...THE MINISTERS"

Jai Narine Singh
Guyana: Democracy Betrayed - A Political History
1948-1993. pp.224.
Kingston, Jamaica, Kingston Publishers Ltd. 1996.
ISBN 976 625 087-1

Jai Narine Singh's *Guyana: Democracy Betrayed – A Political History 1948-1993* succeeds his *Diplomacy or War: The Guyana-Venezuela Border Controversy,* (1982) and serves both as a somewhat sketchy political history of Guyana between 1948 and 1993, and as a confession of the author's erratic political career. Singh was born in 1908, and left Guyana in 1928 to study at the Imperial College of Tropical Agriculture in Trinidad and Tobago (Guyana's Northern neighbour.) In 1933, he moved to Venezuela (Guyana's Western neighbour) where he worked as a government agronomist. Six years later, Singh returned to Guyana and became a labour organiser and political activist attached, at one time or another, firstly to the British Guiana Labour Union that was started by Hubert Critchlow; then the British Guiana East Indian Association; and later the Manpower Citizens' Association. Finally, Singh studied law in England and was called to the bar in 1948.

In *Democracy Betrayed* a "Chronology of the Republic of Guyana to 1987" supplies a list or diary of years with significant events recorded for each year. The entry "1948" for instance, recalls the Enmore massacre when, during a strike of workers at Enmore sugar estate in 1948, five Indian-Guyanese workers were shot and killed by police. The tragedy spurred the struggle for independence and, unusually, is described in the third person, with the author, ever keen to assert a special place for himself in Guyana's history, claiming to play a leading role supporting victims of the massacre: "Singh leads funeral/ protest procession 16 miles to Georgetown: confrontation with authorities. As lawyer for victims' families, Singh eventually gains compensation for them, a vital first in Guyanese history." [p. xxv] This gives the impression that Singh's intervention on behalf of the Enmore victims was independent, singular or crucial, when the victims were also aided by other groups, for example, Dr. Cheddi Jagan, Mrs. Jagan and members of their Political Affairs Committee.

In the same way, Singh asserts his prominence in 1955 when the five-year-old People's Progressive Party (PPP) split into two Parties, one consisting mainly of African-Guyanese members, later re-named the Peoples National Congress (PNC) led by Forbes Burnham, while the other group retained the "PPP" name and consisted mainly of an Indian-Guyanese membership led by Dr. Jagan. Singh's 1955 entry states that: "Singh was the architect of the split, because Jagan was turning openly communist and receiving help from the USSR against the ideals of the coalition which had put independence and democracy first. Jagan walked out and formed his own communist faction of the PPP as opposed to Singh, Burnham and others."(xxvii)

More conventional accounts of the split tend to differ claiming, for example, that Burnham coveted leadership of the PPP at least from the Party's first victory in 1953, but that he bided his time until 1955, when he took the plunge because he saw that Dr. Jagan was increasingly discredited by the British. By this account, it was partly to dispel suspicion of ethnic partisanship in his new party that Burnham allied himself to Jai Narine Singh and Dr. J. P. Latchmansingh, two Indian members of the PPP, in leaving the PPP. Dr. Latchmansingh, a former PPP minister, and leader of the Guyana Industrial Workers' Union of sugar workers, is mentioned elsewhere but, surprisingly, does not appear in Singh's 1955 entry.

Perhaps the most interesting chapter in *Democracy Betrayed,* however - Chapter Seven – dramatises the situation of newly-elected PPP government ministers, in 1953, during the short period (133 days) before the British Governor, Sir Alfred Savage, deposed the new government and suspended the Constitution. Singh reveals that ministers are "invaded" [p. 47] by citizens from all parts of the country: "making requests and demands...for the most part, difficult to carry out, or practically impossible," [p. 47] so that: "many of the files dealing with important matters of government administration were left unattended."[p. 47] Not only that, civil servants deliberately mismanaged their instructions: "in order to embarrass the Government ministers," and "leading public servants betrayed the confidence of ministers."[p. 47] These public servants also: "took tales out of school to certain conservative persons who were opposed to the new order, persons such as the Hon. Sir Frank McDavid." [p. 47]

Singh's insight into the PPP's brief tenure in government as the ruling Party in Guyana reflects an insider's grasp of underlying dysfunction in practical, day-to-day administration of the nation's business which, more than sensational and loudly trumpeted claims of communist subversion, at least, partly, may have inspired the British decision to abort Guyana's first venture into broadly representative government, from April to October, 1953. Singh's portrait of radical administrative dysfunction has a ring of truth: it catches, for example, the toxic flavour of unsettling coexistence between British administrators, expatriates and their class of local admirers, totally flummoxed and frightened by the mass of ordinary Guyanese, suddenly aroused and intoxicated by a mere taste of what they thought was freedom.

Nor should we forget instances of strategic PPP misjudgement, for example, their foolish boycott of a social function at the Governor's house, and refusal of medals of the 1953 coronation of Queen Elizabeth which they rudely returned to the Governor, all of which needlessly inflamed hostility against them. In addition: "a ring of spies surrounded the actions and deliberations of the ministers [whose speech and action] was multiplied hundredfold and repeated in a distorted manner to the expatriates, their followers and the Governor." [p. 49] It all created a powder keg waiting to explode, and what it means is that, despite self-serving attempts to invest *Democracy Betrayed* with exaggerated claims of his self-importance, Singh's closely observed documentation, for example, of the riots and disturbances of the early 1960s, offers a reliable view of some aspects of Guyanese political history from an observer close to, but not at the centre of events.

"OFFICIALS AND PRIVATE CITIZENS INCITED MURDER, ARSON, BOMBINGS"

Stephen G. Rabe
U.S. Intervention in British Guiana.
Chapel Hill, The University of North Carolina Press, 2005.
ISBN 976-637-231-4 (pkp). First published by Ian Randle
Publishers Limited in Jamaica. 2005.

American intervention in British Guiana during the 1950s and 60s, has been known for a long time, but full details only came to light after declassification of official documents in the 1990s, and publication of studies either by independent scholars or individuals involved in the matter itself. As Stephen G. Rabe, Professor of history at the University of Dallas, Texas suggests in *US Intervention in British Guiana*, intervention was provoked by the Cold War which began in earnest shortly after the end of World War Two, when two super powers, the US and USSR, each playing sheriff in a Western film - dared the other to make a false move, as each touted its own favoured political ideology, American Capitalism on one hand, and Soviet Communism on the other. In this context, when the People's Progressive Party (PPP), led by Dr. Cheddi Jagan, won an historic political victory in Guyana, in 1953, the Government lasted only four months before they were thrown ignominiously out of office by British Governor Sir Alfred Savage who was backed by British troops.

American collusion in the débacle is discounted by Professor Rabe who suggests, instead, that the invasion was personally mounted by arch-imperialist, British Prime Minister Winston Churchill and his Colonial Secretary - Oliver Lyttleton - who suspected Dr. Jagan and his party of Communism. Whether this suspicion was justified or not, the Communist taint it stamped on Dr. Jagan stuck to him until after his death in 1997.

After 1953, following a four-year period of administration in Guyana by a Government of unelected appointees, fresh elections were held in 1957 although, by then, the original PPP had split into two factions, one led by the Indian-Guyanese Dr. Jagan, and the other by the African-Guyanese Forbes Burnham, former education minister in the short-lived 1953 PPP Government. The split was bad enough since it meant that Guyanese politics became a personal contest between an alleged Communist, Dr. Jagan, and an ostensible Social Democrat, Mr Burnham, whose party was re-named The People's National Congress (PNC). Worse still, the contest was seen as one between each leader's ethnic group, Indian-Guyanese represented by Dr. Jagan, and African-Guyanese by Mr. Burnham.

While racial confrontation still remains in Guyanese politics, Professor Rabe argues that it was not entirely the result of historical factors: it was also deliberately manipulated partly by outside (British and American) agencies which wanted to keep Dr. Jagan out of power, and partly by willing collusion from cynical and unscrupulous local leaders like Forbes Burnham who: "coveted power and acting on a global stage," [p. 53] and labour leaders like the disgruntled opportunist Richard Ishmael, who was incensed that his American academic qualifications failed to get him a teaching job at Queen's College, the leading Government Boys' school in Guyana at the time.

Although, after 1953, the policy of a ruling British Conservative Government was to: "destroy the PPP and convince Guyanese to join other political parties," [p. 48] Dr. Jagan's party not only won elections again in 1957, but created an impression, at least among perceptive observers, that he was neither Communist nor interested in advancing International Communism. All the British Governors who observed him at first hand in Guyana: "Governors Savage, Renison, Grey and Luyt consistently rejected U.S. claims that Jagan and the PPP secretly worked with Communists." [p. 177] Some colonial officials too, for example, Ian Macleod, at one time, the British Foreign Secretary, frankly admitted that if he had to make a choice "between Jagan and Burnham as head of my country, I would choose Jagan any day of the week." [p. 94]

But Fidel Castro's Cuban revolution in 1959 forced the Americans to dig their heels in so far as Guyana and the PPP were concerned. Castro's success with what the Americans deeply believed was an alien and hateful ideology, so close to their borders, inflamed their fear of Communism to unprecedented heights. So when Dr. Jagan and the PPP won elections yet again in 1961, and invoked the unspeakable possibility of Guyanese Independence under the PPP, American government paranoia reached breaking point, and induced the American Central Intelligence Agency (CIA) to join forces with American labour unions, AFL – CIO, in a deadly, clandestine operation to dis-empower Dr. Jagan and his party.

According to Professor Rabe: "U.S. officials and private citizens incited murder, arson, bombings and fear and loathing in British Guiana," [p. 75] and the result was that, following strikes engineered and supported by the CIA and the AFL-CIO in 1962 and 1963, and imposition of a new electoral system, proportional representation, in elections, in 1964, a new PNC government led by Forbes Burnham was finally installed.

Professor Rabe documents both the devious efforts by the US to bring Burnham to power in 1964, and the financial aid lavished on him afterwards, including support for his dishonest and fraudulent practices of rigging elections to retain power beginning in 1968; all this in spite of large scale theft and corruption during Burnham's first administration: "In 1967 Peter D'Aguiar discovered that approximately $58,000 had been illegally spent on a highway and that the director of audits could not account for another $11.7 million in government spending." [p. 152] Such frank exposure and meticulous documentation illustrate the historical value of Professor Rabe's book.

Equally important, *US Intervention in British Guiana* identifies an underlying contradiction in American foreign policy between passionate denunciation of Communist dictators by US officials, and consistent support of fascist dictators, throughout the twentieth century, especially in Latin America and the Caribbean. This contradiction may explain US intervention in Guyana, or their clandestine support of the Burnham and PNC dictatorship from 1964 to 1992.

"FAILURE ... TO LIVE IN THE REAL WORLD "

Daurius Figueira
The East Indian Problem in Trinidad and Tobago 1953-1962:
Terror and Race War in Guyana 1961-1964. pp.256.
Bloomington, IUniverse Inc. Indiana, 2009.
ISBN: 978-1-4401-5996-1

Daurius Figueira's *The East Indian Problem in Trinidad and Tobago* 1953-1962: *Terror and Race War in Guyan*a 1961-1964 is the third volume in a trilogy whose first two volumes examine declassified British and American files for revelations about two Trinidadian political figures Simbhoonath Capildeo, and trade union leader Tubal Uriah Butler. The third volume examines the files for revelations both about the political career of Dr. Cheddi Jagan of Guyana, and ethnic strife between Indian-Guyanese and African-Guyanese during the 1950s and 60s. In the words of the author, the files reveal: "covert and overt strategies [of Britain and the US] towards the creation of neo-colonial states, Trinidad and Tobago and Guyana, subservient and pliant to their [British and American] geo-political interests." [p. xi]

India's Independence in 1947 is seen as a catalyst of anti-colonial sentiment among Indian-Trinidadians, and a Report about anti-colonial speeches in an Indian Newsletter issued by the Indian Commissioner in Trinidad, in 1954, leads the British governor to comment on the: "harm this type of literature must do amongst semi-educated East Indians who compose one third of the population." [p. 5] In another Report, the governor claims that the underlying object of a visit of twenty-four Indian-Trinidadians to British Guiana, organised by the Indian-Trinidadian politician Bhadase Sagan Maraj, is: "to merge the [Indian] Associations of the two colonies into a single powerful unit and thus assist him [Maraj] in furthering his plans for East Indian domination not only in Trinidad, but on a regional basis." [p. 6] Whether true or not, such accusations make Indian-Trinidadians and Indian-Guyanese look threatening.

But the African-based People's National Movement (PNM) of Dr. Eric Williams wins elections in Trinidad and Tobago in 1956 and 1961, and Trinidad and Tobago becomes Independent in 1962, while the People's Progressive Party (PPP) of Dr. Cheddi Jagan which wins elections in British Guiana in 1953, is ousted by the British governor. Meanwhile, the PPP splits along ethnic (African/Indian) lines in 1955, and its Indian-based section, led by Dr, Jagan, wins fresh elections in 1957, and again in 1961; but Dr. Jagan and his party are suspected of communism and, as late as 1963, he is still requesting the British government to set a date for Guyanese Independence.

In a despatch written on 8th May, 1963, the British High Commissioner in Trinidad admits that Dr. Eric Williams: "has used the High Commission as the channel for receiving information about the developments in British Guiana." [p. 50] On 17thJuly, 1963, another despatch from the High Commissioner also observes: "Dr. Williams's concern about the spread of racialism and communism in the region from British Guiana; his loss of patience with Dr. Jagan; and his objections to a solution based on proportional representation because of possible repercussions in Trinidad." [p. 50]

The High Commissioner's despatch on 4th December 1963 refers to a speech of Dr. Williams as: "an impressive and formidable indictment of Dr. Jagan [one that is] understanding and helpful towards our [British] policies." [p. 50] Trinidad and Tobago is also the only black Commonwealth nation to join with Britain and other white Commonwealth nations who abstain from supporting a Ghanaian resolution in the General Assembly of the United Nations calling for Britain to set a date for Guyana's Independence.

Figueira, a Lecturer at the University of the West Indies in Trinidad, ties in this exposure of Dr. Williams's dubious political sympathies with Dr. Jagan's political exploits, at the time, to argue that they are both complicit in a "North Atlantic imperialistic agenda" [p. xi] managed by the US and UK. Although Dr. Jagan and Forbes Burnham, his African-Guyanese rival, both struggle for political power in British Guiana amidst chaos and mayhem in the early 1960s, Figueira lays blame for the ethnic rivalry, riots, destruction and death of those years squarely at Dr. Jagan's door: "This power of Burnham was never organic but the product of an abysmal failure of Cheddi Jagan to live in the real world. Jagan's denial fed Burnham's megalomania to epic proportions to the detriment of the people and the state of Guyana." [p. 167]

As Figueira sees it, the Americans want to keep Dr. Jagan out of power because of his communist beliefs. The British, on the other hand, do not believe that Dr, Jagan is a communist, and are prepared to devolve political power to him and his PPP, but: "the American agenda to remove the PPP from power trumps the British choice of the Indian- Guyanese as the race to carry the colony to Independence." [p. 221] Figueira argues that the Americans prevail over the British because of Dr. Jagan: "What Jagan failed to understand was that in 1963 the British colonial [power] was willing to give him racist hegemony in return for him walking away from his dogmatic Stalinist rhetoric and his embrace of Fidel Castro since 1959 at least until after Independence." [p. 231]

Figueira is optimistic in expecting the Americans, drunk with delusions of *realpolitik,* to simply accept a professed change of political outlook from Dr. Jagan. Figueira does notice that Dr. Jagan's own legislative measures and budgets during 1957 t0 1964: "were all within the boundaries of capitalist modernism." [p. 231] For despite his socialist rhetoric, Dr. Jagan's politics were never extreme in practice, as all governors of British Guiana, or visitors to the country from Britain's Colonial Office have attested.

If there was extremism, it was from the Americans whose fear of communism drove them to demand Dr. Jagan's head, like John the Baptist's, on a platter, while the British, weakened by World War Two, and wearied by Caribbean trappings of empire, reluctantly acquiesced to demands of superior American power. The American-sponsored removal of Dr. Jagan and replacement by Burnham is less due to Dr. Jagan's failure than to an inevitable transition of power from a Pax Britannica to a Pax Americana.

SIR JOCK AND "BOOKERS GUIANA"

Professor Clem Seecharan
Sweetening Bitter Sugar: Jock Campbell: The Booker Reformer in British Guiana, 1934-1966. pp.675.
Kingston, Ian Randle Publishers, 2005.

Despite its title, *Sweetening Bitter Sugar: Jock Campbell: The Booker Reformer in British Guiana, 1934-1966* is not a biographical study of Sir Jock Campbell (1912-1994), who was chairman of Booker Bros. McConnell and Co. Ltd, towards the end of the 1950s and early 60s. The author's aim is wider: "This is a book about Campbell and his times in British Guiana," [p. 15] the focus as much on Sir Jock as on the effect of his company's policies on Guyana. So although we learn much about Sir Jock's family, we also get slices of Guyanese history assiduously culled from original sources, including pamphlets, papers, articles, theses, books - published as well as unpublished - interviews with protagonists in the Campbell story, and personal observations by the author.

Professor Seecharan grew up on the Corentyne, the same part of Guyana as Dr. Cheddi Jagan (1918-1997), Indian-Guyanese leader of the People's Progressive Party (PPP), and main rival of the People's National Congress (PNC) led by the African-Guyanese Forbes Burnham (1923-1985). Dr. Jagan is a foil to Sir Jock in the unfolding drama of the latter's attempts to sweeten bitter sugar, that is to say, ameliorate the unsavoury consequences of British colonialism, in the form of African slavery and Indian indenture in Guyana.

As the descendant of a wealthy Scots-Irish family, Sir Jock was educated at Eton and Oxford (1930-1933) before visiting sugar plantations owned by his family firm, Curtis Campbell, in Guyana, in 1934. (Curtis Campbell merged with Booker in 1939). The visit was Sir Jock's road to Damascus: it opened his eyes to appalling conditions of his plantation workers, and his family's connection to slavery and exploitation: "I have always been conscious of the shame of my family having been slave owners." [p. 57]

Guilt is probably inspired by Fabian socialist ideas which Sir Jock imbibed at Oxford, and which may have inspired him to conceive of five responsibilities or principles of reform in his company: to shareholders, staff, labour, customers and the community. Yet "Jock was no revolutionary." [p. 98] On the contrary, Sir Jock acknowledges that the aim of business is to make a profit. But he is persuaded that benefits can accrue more widely if his five-fold responsibilities are achieved. *Sweetening Bitter Sugar* is an account of Sir Jock's attempt to implement these principles of capitalist reform in Guyana.

Dr. Jagan was Premier of Guyana in 1953, and 1957- 1964, and his main political support came from Indian-Guyanese workers on Bookers' sugar plantations. The issue of a new trade union, the Guiana Agricultural Workers' Union (GAWU), for these workers was crucial, in 1953, when the British suspended the Constitution and quashed a democratically elected government, led by Dr. Jagan who was suspected of communism. In the early 1960s, this issue was again crucial when Dr. Jagan's government was ousted by the British, in cahoots with the Americans, and a régime installed led by Forbes Burnham. Dr. Jagan's Marxist sympathies again served as an excuse to oust him, this time to placate US Cold War fears of communism.

Sir Jock comes out of all this as St. George, slaying the dragon of poverty and exploitation in "Booker's Guiana", despite obstruction from Dr. Jagan with his deep-seated sense of Indian-Guyanese victimisation by Bookers. The term "Bookers' Guiana" correctly describes the unholy stranglehold of Sir Jock's company on Guyana's economic neck, not only in sugar and rum, but shop-keeping, shipping, estate supplies, hardware, wholesale, retail, timber, saw milling, wharf owning, even a taxi service. But while Sir Jock emerges as enlightened, astute, noble, patient and tolerant, a reformer through and through, in health and housing, social welfare, wages and social amenities, Dr. Jagan: "could see only black and white, not the nuances which constitute reality; he lacked the flexibility of temperament... to move beyond the role of a crusader – he was not a statesman." [p. 150]

This phrasing alone suggests a style of chatty expansiveness, anecdotal zest, pungent phrase-making, oratorical fervour, and information of such encyclopaedic scope that it leaves little room for narrowness or partiality. This is why, for all Professor Seecharan's disappointment in Dr. Jagan, he still pays tribute to Dr. Jagan's historic political awakening of the Guyanese people in the 1940s and 50s, and undiminished passion for his cause. Nor is Sir Jock completely spotless: there may be doubt, for instance, about his behind-the-scenes role in the 1953 Suspension, and his non-support of the PPP-sponsored trade union, in spite of his claim to the contrary. In other words, although Professor Seecharan expresses forthright opinions of his own, the scope and eclecticism of his information allows readers to find evidence for contrary preferences as well.

For example, we get a more sympathetic impression of Dr. Jagan from Sir Jock himself than from the author: "I think he [Dr. Jagan] was a good man, and he was trying to do his best for the people of Guyana... he failed partly because of the

Cold War and because of the Russian communists." [p. 617] Sir Jock's opinion on Forbes Burnham is equally revealing: "Burnham was a criminal, an absolutely beastly man in every way." [p. 250] These are mere morsels of a rich feast of opinion, insight and information found in *Sweetening Bitter Sugar*.

Professor Seecharan may well be right that Dr. Jagan was not a statesman. But as Shakespeare's Hamlet might have said to his friend Horatio on the castle platform in Elsinore, Denmark: "there are more things in heaven and earth than statesmanship". It was not for his statesmanship that African-Buxtonians, inveterate Burnhamites to the last man, woman or child, forced an unscheduled stop on Dr. Jagan's funeral *cortège* as it passed through their village, in 1997: it was to render genuine respect and offer heartfelt farewell to someone they regarded, ethnically, as their bitterest rival, politically, as their chief stumbling block, yet for all, their fellow Guyanese countryman and hero.

PORTRAIT OF FLAWLESS PERFECTION

Baytoram Ramharack
Against the Grain: Balram Singh Rai and the Politics of Guyana.
pp.452.
Trinidad and Tobago, Chakra Publishing House, 2005.
ISBN 976-9504-91-2

Against The Grain: Balram Singh Rai and the Politics of Guyana is a political biography of Balram Singh Rai, an Indian-Guyanese lawyer who was born in 1921, and served in the government of the People's Progressive Party (PPP), under the leadership of Cheddi Jagan, from 1957 to 1962. Between 1959 and 1961, Rai was Minister of Community Development and Education, and in 1961, he became Minister Of Home Affairs, the first in the country's history. But Rai was expelled from the PPP in 1962, although he remained an Independent member of the Legislative Assembly until 1964, when he founded his own Justice Party and contested elections in the same year, without winning a single seat. He practised law until 1970, before leaving for the United Kingdom where he has lived ever since. *Against the Grain* also contains a Prologue (by Rampersaud Tiwari), and an Introduction (by Clem Seecharan), both of which offer brief, general observations on Rai's political career.

In 1953, while Guyana was still a British colony the PPP won a resounding victory in elections held, for the first time, under universal, adult suffrage, and a new, liberal Constitution. However, because of an alleged fear of communism among leading members of the party, the Constitution was suspended after about four months, and the PPP ousted from power by the British governor. In 1953, the PPP enjoyed enthusiastic support from the country's two largest ethnic groups, African- and Indian-Guyanese, but in 1955, it suffered a tragic split when the party's former Minister of Education, Forbes Burnham, broke ranks to form a rival party, later called the People's National Congress (PNC), consisting mainly of African-Guyanese members of the PPP. The result was that two ethnic parties eventually emerged – the PNC, consisting mainly of African-Guyanese, led by Burnham (African-Guyanese), and the PPP, consisting mainly of Indian-Guyanese, and led by Cheddi Jagan (Indian-Guyanese).

The PPP, under Dr. Jagan, won fresh elections in 1957 and 1961; but in elections held in 1964, following clandestine intervention from the CIA, and the American and British governments, a new system of proportional representation was introduced, enabling Burnham's PNC to win power. Thereafter, subsequent elections were rigged, ethnic or racial polarization increased, and an African-Guyanese dictatorship established precipitating massive emigration, a disastrous brain drain, and general, economic ruin. Astonishingly, Dr. Jagan remained as Opposition Leader from 1964 until 1992, when his party, now PPP/Civic, at last regained power in free and fair elections.

Rai's portrait in *Against the Grain* is one of almost flawless perfection: claims are made for his intelligence, integrity, morality, firmness, foresight, altruism, energy, generosity and modesty. His achievements as brilliant lawyer, Hindu leader and selfless politician are also admiringly emblazoned both in the text itself, and in more than one hundred pages of Appendices which reproduce his letters, speeches, addresses, or statements on religious, political, historical and cultural topics. Some of this information is undoubtedly useful, in so far as it helps to fill in the political history of post-colonial

Guyana, especially where a relatively minor figure like Rai is concerned; but Dr. Ramharack is indiscriminate; he includes too much; and his account is consequently more hagiographic than historical.

This is not to besmirch Rai's merits. As Education minister, during 1959 to 1961, in the face of widespread threats, and heated charges of communism and Godlessness, he successfully marshalled the PPP's case for abolishing the outdated and unjust system of "dual control" of schools controlled by both government and churches. Rai's forceful advocacy of reforms in recruitment to achieve ethnic balance in Guyanese security forces was also bold and far-sighted. But the abject failure of his Justice Party in 1964, and his political silence since 1965 deserve more comment.

Since Dr. Ramharack claims that Rai went against the grain of PPP communist ideology by not subscribing to the party's deluded and utopian mantra of "working class unity", and stresses instead: "the primacy of the racial/ethnic dilemma in Guyana" [p. 317], he implies that Rai was better positioned than the PPP to solve this dilemma. For him then to neglect Rai's subsequent political silence is either suspicious or careless.

The crux of Dr. Ramharack's argument is that Dr. Jagan and the PPP, through their inflexible and "vulgar Marxist-Leninist ideology" [p. 317], betrayed Indian-Guyanese interests, despite enjoying long and unswerving loyalty from Indian-Guyanese voters. Dr. Ramharack argues that, because of Dr. Jagan's ideological inflexibility, Indian-Guyanese were left in "a state of helplessness" [p. 315].

For anyone who might attribute Indian-Guyanese victimisation to Burnham or the PNC, Dr. Ramharack's answer betrays bitterness: "The PPP's umbilical cord was tied to the PNC's and the failures of the PNC were failures of the PPP." [p. 317]. This bitterness re-appears in the author's claim that Indian-Guyanese: "are themselves responsible for the injustices they experienced during the PNC dictatorship. Rai had done his best." [p. 306] This implies that Rai, potential saviour of Indian-Guyanese, was ungratefully spurned by the blindness both of PPP ideologues, and the Indian-Guyanese electorate.

Such bitter feelings of betrayal turn *Against the Grain* into a species of a historical revisionism. Although the volume weakly touts: "power sharing for all ethnic groups" [p. 324] it does not say how this elusive sharing is to be achieved. Instead commentaries by Keane Gibson – *The Cycle of Racial Oppression in Guyana*, (2003) and *Sacred Duty: Hinduism & Violence in Guyana* (2003) – suggest continuing ethnic ignorance of each major ethnic group by the other in Guyana. One danger is for *Against the Grain* to stir up Indo-centricity, in the same way that Keane Gibson's writing fans the flames of Afro-centricity. But racial conflagration is no answer. That is why, when we compare ethnic conflicts in places like Sri Lanka, Bosnia, Syria and other countries, the alleged deluded, Jaganite utopianism of "working class unity" becomes infinitely preferable to either Afro-centricity or Indo-centricity in Guyana.

FACTS, FIGURES, NAMES, DATES AND DIALOGUE

Mohan Ragbeer
The Indelible Red Stain: Destruction of a Tropical Paradise - A Cold War Story. pp.1390.
Self Published, 2011.

The Incredible Red Stain: The Destruction of a Tropical Paradise – a Cold War story by Dr. Mohan Ragbeer, a physician who practises Geriatrics and Family Medicine in Hamilton, Canada- consists of Book 1 - *A Journey into Darkness and Discovery* :*The Man from Port Mou*rant, which considers the career of Dr. Cheddi Jagan who was born in Port Mourant and became a politician; and Book 2 - *Return to Conflict, Intrigue, Anguish, Fire, Killings, and Exodus: The Firebrand from Central Kitty* which examines the political career of Forbes Burnham, who was born in the village of Kitty, and became the main political rival of Dr. Jagan.

"The Incredible Red Stain" refers to the apparently ineradicable influence of communist ideology on both Dr. Jagan, an Indian-Guyanese, and Mr. Burnham, an African-Guyanese, and the disastrous effect (stain) of their political policies on Guyana. According to Dr. Ragbeer, the red stain, in Dr. Jagan's case, led to the destruction of Guyana as a tropical paradise, while in Mr. Burnham's case, it led to fire, killings and the continuing flight of hundreds of thousands of his countrymen chiefly to North America, Britain and other parts of the West Indies.

After completing studies in dentistry, in the US, Dr. Jagan returned to Guyana in 1947, and along with his Jewish-American wife Janet Rosenberg and other Guyanese, including Mr. Burnham, formed the People's Progressive Party (PPP) which won elections in 1953 and became the first popularly elected government in Guyana. Since Dr. Jagan and the PPP were suspected of communism, the PPP government was dismissed by the British Prime Minister Sir Winston Churchill, and replaced by an interim Government of nominated members. In 1957 Dr. Jagan and the PPP again won elections, as they did yet again in 1961. By this time, however, the original, multi-racial PPP had split along ethnic lines, and was seen as a largely Indian party, while Mr. Burnham's newly-named party, the People's National Congress (PNC), was identified as African. With the introduction of voting by proportional representation in elections, in 1964, the PPP lost power to the PNC which, through support from the US Central Intelligence Agency (CIA) and continuously rigged elections, remained in power until 1992.

The general argument of *The Incredible Red Stain* is that Dr. Jagan's party, the PPP, espoused communist ideology during a period – the Cold War in the 1950s and 60s when two super-powers, the US which advocated free enterprise, and the USSR which advocated communism, controlled the world. At the time, it was evidently dangerous to introduce a communist régime in Guyana, a tiny country next door to the US, as was already illustrated by the experience of Fidel Castro who formed a communist Government in Cuba, in 1959, and subsequently lived in constant fear of a US-backed invasion. According to Dr. Ragbeer, vigorous attempts were made to turn Dr. Jagan from communism by far-sighted and well-intentioned Indian-Guyanese such as Dr. J.B. Singh a well known Indian-Guyanese cultural activist, and Tulla Hardeen, an enlightened Indian-Guyanese businessman and brother-in-law of the author who was rather less well known. However, Dr. Ragbeer concludes that these attempts were unavailing, and Dr. Jagan proceeded with alleged communist policies, which provoked the US to install Mr. Burnham and the PNC as the Government of Guyana, and inspire the fire, killings and exodus already mentioned.

The main lines of Dr. Ragbeer's argument are not new: they have gained increasing currency in recent years especially from Indian-Guyanese scholars such as Baytoram Ramharack in his *Against the Grain: B.S. Rai and the Politics of Guyana* (2005), and Clem Seecharan in *Sweetening Bitter Sugar: Sir Jock Campbell the Booker Reformer in British Guiana 1934-1966* (2005). Ramharack claims that B.S. Rai an Indian-Guyanese lawyer and former PPP minister might have been a more effective leader than Dr. Jagan because he was not communist, while Seecharan suggests that improvements for Guyanese sugar workers, initiated by Sir Jock Campbell, head of most sugar estates in Guyana, could have achieved change in Guyana if Dr. Jagan had cooperated instead of courting confrontation with the US. Both Ramharack and Seecharan agree with Dr, Ragbeer's negative conclusion that Dr. Jagan was impractical, naive:"quixotic, doctrinaire and indecisive." (Book 2 p. 446)

There is no doubt that *The Indelible Red Stain* is the author's *magnum opus*, "great" both in the sense of being a lifetime's achievement for the author, one that consumed his attention from 1997 to 2010, and "great" also in size as a two-volume work with one volume stretching to 700 pages, and the other to 690. In the end, though, *The Incredible Red Stain* will be judged less by its politics than by its structure and writing; for while the book's political argument is coherent, consistent (even repetitive, perhaps inevitably in such a lengthy text) it consists of at least four different strands narrated in the first person by the author.

The main strand is political; a second shows the narrator as a doctor on a forensic expedition to investigate a murder deep in the Guyana forest; a third narrative offers a superbly researched history of India, while a fourth presents an autobiographical account of events in the author's life. There are also useful maps and photographs which strengthen the documentary aspect of the work. The question, from a structural point of view, is whether these narratives cooperate to form a political, historical, sociological, autobiographical, documentary or perhaps an all-combined whole.

The Indelible Red Stain certainly contains elements of an encyclopaedic compendium or pot-pourri. Dr. Ragbeer's research is incredibly impressive, fortified both by its astonishing variety and bewildering detail of facts and figures, names, dates and verbatim dialogue. Above all, the author's fluent and graceful writing proves remarkably sustaining over long sections such as one on Indian history from pages 131 to 280 of Book 2.

LOW CUNNING: LOWER MOTIVE

Sir Shridath S. Ramphal
Glimpses of a Global Life. pp.624.
Toronto, Dundurn, and London, Hansib, 2014.

Over half of *Glimpses of a Global Life*, a memoir by Sir Shridath
Surendranath (Sonny) Ramphal, is devoted to his career as
Secretary General of the Commonwealth, the centre piece of
his so-called global life in international diplomacy, from 1975
to 1990. Since his birth in Guyana, in 1928, Sir Shridath follows
an ambitious plan established by his father J.I. Ramphal who
began as a school teacher, studied law, joined the civil service,
and became Labour Commissioner, the first local-born person
to hold the post in Guyana (then British Guiana).

Sir Shridath also qualified as a lawyer and served as Crown
Counsel in Guyana where, in 1953, after only four months in power,
the newly-elected People's Progressive Party (PPP) government of
Dr. Cheddi Jagan, was ousted by the British Governor. Later, Sir
Shridath took a keen interest in plans to establish the Federation of
the West Indies, and was shattered when the Federation, formed
in 1958, collapsed in 1962. With evident pique, he is convinced,
then and now: "that enlightened leadership from British Guiana
would have saved federalism." [p. 95]

Sir Shridath's public career begins, in earnest, in 1964, after
victory of the People's National Congress (PNC) led by Forbes
Burnham, in coalition with the capitalist United Force, (UF) led
by Portuguese businessman Peter D'Aguiar. Sir Shridath gloats

over Burnham's victory: "The mood in the country, and indeed in the Caribbean, was one of hope that 'BG's worst problems were ended and that the country could return to a constructive role within the region as an independent state." [p. 199] The implication of boundless relief suggests that what existed before, the (unmentioned, probably unmentionable) administration of Premier Jagan, had denied BG a constructive political role and, at last, had been removed. But the device that achieved Jagan's removal is not mentioned - proportional representation - a new electoral procedure. Proportional representation was devised by the US government of President Kennedy who leaned on their British allies, still the colonial rulers of Guyana, to impose it on the 1964 election because the Americans feared creation of another communist government, like Cuba, in the Caribbean, this time, under Cheddi Jagan.

For Sir Shridath, Dr. Cheddi Jagan, Premier from 1957 to 1964, is a stumbling block to Guyana's progress; but he does not mention Dr. Jagan's name because it is part of a calculated combination of evasion, ingratiation and manipulation, basic principles of a strategy to achieve fame and fortune for himself. The combination is seen at work earlier when he claims that lack of "enlightened leadership" prevented British Guiana from saving the Caribbean Federation, without acknowledging Dr. Jagan as British Guiana's elected government leader before 1964.

In addition, page 101 of *Glimpses* carries a *Daily Chronicle* cartoon with Ramphal standing close to Burnham, offering to help him carry heavy bags of burden as the newly-elected Premier, while Burnham replies "Thanks." Ramphal and Burnham are standing on a road clearly labelled "Road to Progress." Clever and cunning as Sir Shridath may be, his own words give away his enthusiastic but unstated preference for Burnham over Jagan. A seemingly uncontrollable orgy of self-quotation, sometimes pages long, then helps to blow

Glimpses up to over six hundred pages in length, and betray the author's hidden motive of relentless self-advancement through low cunning.

Sir Shridath's concerns over CARICOM and Caribbean integration are mere skirmishes compared to larger, international conflicts in the second half of the twentieth century, for example, the North/South economic challenge of growing disparity between rich and poor nations, and the possibility of nuclear holocaust, as a result of differences in political ideology between capitalist, Western nations led by the US, and the communist dogma of Eastern European nations in the Union of Soviet Socialist Republics (USSR) led by Russia.

This world stage is where Sir Shridath is seen at his best, organising conference after conference, enough to make himself look more like a prestidigitator than a diplomat. It is what US President Reagan perceives when he agrees that although the Cancun Conference, for instance, was constructive and positive: "too much time has been wasted on words and conferences. We need to turn our attention to practical issues." [pp. 318 -319] More practical goals are reached on African issues, for example, on action against Ian Smith's Unilateral Declaration of Independence in Southern Rhodesia, leading to emergence of the independent nation of Zimbabwe and, most importantly, on Commonwealth negotiations that promote an end to apartheid, and the imprisonment of Nelson Mandela in South Africa.

But all this is pursued in tandem with a curious neglect/disconnect with events in Guyana. In *Glimpses*, Sir Shridath detects a connection between his international successes from the advent of Burnham's rule in 1964 to his time as Commonwealth Secretary General: "I had, by 1974, come to the notice of the international community... A substantial element of the good opinion was a reflection of the standing of Guyana itself... I earned respect from Guyana's principled position... Guyana was recognised as being progressive but not extremist, non-Aligned in a principled way." [p. 210]

If anyone is surprised by these principles during a period of rigged elections, murders, (including the death of Walter Rodney, and 918 deaths in Jonestown), black outs, food shortages, massive emigration and much else, in Guyana, they surely will not be surprised by the last page of the last chapter of *Glimpses* which carries a strategically placed photo of the author and Nelson Mandela in close, fraternal embrace. For Sir Shridath who once lived temporarily in Marlborough House, and never ceased to glory in its royal connections, a photo of him in a bear-hug with the revered South African Mahatma (can anyone imagine Sir Shridath in jail for even one day?) is the final flourish of a master manipulator. It will delight his Burnhamite bedfellows no end, for all the wrong reasons.

RELENTLESS CLIMB TO THE TOP

Yesu Persaud
Reaching for the Stars: The Life of Yesu Persaud. Volume One.
The Caribbean Press, 2014.
ISBN 978 1-907493-74-4

Reaching for the Stars: The Life of Yesu Persaud Volume One
is a memoir by Dr. Yesu Persaud who was awarded two
Honorary Doctorates, one by the University of Warwick in
2008, and a second, this year, by the University of the West
Indies in Trinidad &Tobago. Dr. Persaud was born, in 1928,
on Diamond sugar estate, Guyana, where he lived and worked
until he left to study, in England, in 1955. He qualified as a
chartered accountant and returned home in 1966. While it
meticulously records events in the author's career up to 1976,
Reaching also throws light on social and economic conditions
in Guyana between the 1920s and 70s.

Most light is shed on the author's growing up in an
indentured Indian family of ten (two parents and eight
children) on Diamond sugar estate during the 1930s and
40s, before logies or former slave dwellings, long ranges of
wooden barracks divided into rooms by wooden walls, began
to be phased out. As Dr. Persaud suggests, his family was
lucky to have a logie with three rooms, when larger families:
"were huddled together in just two rooms." [p. 19] Even so,
in the 'lucky' case of Dr. Persaud's family, two of their rooms
served as bedrooms, while: "the third room was used for

everything else." [p. 19] It is hard to imagine how the third room served as kitchen, dining room, living room, not to mention as bathroom and other facilities, all on a floor of bare earth. Dr. Persaud claims that: "The question of hygienic and environmental considerations was both non-existent and immaterial.[p. 17] No wonder that the average life span of a Guyanese, sugar estate worker in the 1940s/50s, was not more than forty-seven years.

At the top of a feudal management structure was a (white) Administrative manager or attorney who represented the absentee estate landlord, and gave orders to a (white) Manager who, in turn, was above a (white) Deputy Manager, and was followed by a (white) Field Manager, in charge of distributing field work. Last of the white staff were the overseers who supervised so-called drivers, a handful of specially selected Indian/black workers, responsible for seeing that their fellow workers carried out prescribed tasks.

In this cruel and coercive working environment: "The [white] expatriate management, with few exceptions, treated the workers like dirt and their insults and invectives had to be borne no matter what." [p. 20] When white overseers first arrived in estate conditions, totally unfamiliar to them, they had to learn their job from local workers: "the learning process started under the tutelage of a Driver or Headman who, even when he was imparting his knowledge... had to be subservient and act with total humility." [p. 89]

Dr. Persaud's professional skill as an accountant comes through his superb gift for figures, names, titles and myriad details of whatever subject he discusses. Documentation of his home and primary school routine, for instance, is as rich in detail as the account of his early working and social life, his marriage, and work at Diamond estate until he realises: "As an Indian myself, I had reached the zenith of the estate pyramid with the position of Field Supervisor."[p. 88] The highest position to which an Indian could rise was Field Clerk, which was equivalent to an Overseer, reserved for whites only.

This meant that, as a Field Clerk, Dr. Persaud would be paid less than half the wage of an Overseer, and denied an Overseer's free housing. Such injustice drives him to the decision: "Higher education [in England] was the only answer," [p. 88] and, in 1955, with his wife and baby daughter left behind, to follow after he made suitable arrangements, he takes the plunge and moves to London.

In London, Dr.Persaud encounters problems of flat and job hunting, and colour prejudice typical in the experience of most West Indians, in England, in the late 1950s. Difficulties mount with his wife suffering from intermittent depression, and the arrival of another child to care for. But whether it is dealing with rapacious landlords, or coping with accounting studies at City of London College and Kennington College of Commerce, Dr. Persaud displays unbending resolution until he becomes a qualified chartered accountant in 1965, and returns to Guyana as Inspector of Taxes.

By the 1970s, however, when the Burnham dictatorship was tightening its grip, and nationalising foreign companies in Guyana. Dr. Persaud was offered the Holy Grail of Guyanese business as Executive Chairman of Demerara Liquors Ltd., Managing Director of the Demerara Sugar Co., as well as the job of overseeing :"the transition of Sandbach Parker[previously taken over by Jessel] to the Guyana National Trading corporation." [p. 196]

Dr. Persaud's documentation is magisterial. For instance, he itemises almost every stall and article for sale in Stabroek market [p. 159] and contrives anecdotes about expatriate estate staff such as George Greenfield (p. 55), and Jake McDonald (pp. 89-91) which are brilliantly informative; but his prime focus remains his self-portrait as a diligent, determined and resourceful, financial manager. It is a convincing portrait, although it also includes comments from an estate manager that Yesu, as a boy, is: "a very intelligent and smart young man [who] is going to go far in the world," [p. 88] and a confession suggesting that, five years before it occurred, neither Dr.Persaud nor Sir Jock Campbell, Chairman of Bookers - the largest sugar company in Guyana– realised that he (Dr.Persaud) would become: "the Group Financial Director of the Sandbach group in Guyana, and therefore even senior to Jock Campbell." [p. 158] If such self-congratulatory predictions may discompose less hardy sensibilities, they are probably essential to Dr. Persaud's ambitious, and relentless climb to the top.

"THE COLLECTIVE TRIBAL MEMORY IS LONG"

G.H.K. Lall
Sitting on a Racial Volcano, (Guyana Uncensored). pp.166.
2013.
ISBN: 0615787444 and ISBN-13: 9780615787442

Sitting on a Racial Volcano (Guyana Uncensored), G.H.K.Lall's survey of socio-political conditions in Guyana arouses memories of Bechu, an indentured Indian immigrant who, between 1896 and 1901, wrote a coruscating series of stylish letters to the press, critical of working conditions of indentured Indian immigrants in British Guiana, only to disappear abruptly, and leave a yet unsolved riddle about his true identity.

Like Bechu's letters, *Volcano* is both elegantly written, and full of fluently argued opinions bristling with style and excitement. Born Gabriel Lall in Essequibo, the author was briefly a civil servant during the early Burnham years, and migrated to the US where he worked in journalism for thirty years before returning home. Under the pseudonym "Hilary Kincaid" he wrote "*Birth of the Millennium – A Walk through Life's Pathways*, 2000, an electronically published volume of poetry, and *Soaring into Magnificence – Cancer – From Illness to Holiness, the Story of Ruth and her Life with Cancer*, Kindle Edition, 2011, an apparent memoir about a female relative's brave struggle with cancer. Lall has also written another volume *Guyana – A National Cesspool of Greed, Duplicity and Corruption (A Re-migrant's Story)*, 2012, whose subject mentioned as: "the dark underbelly that is Guyana today" sounds similar to *Volcano.*

The theme of *Volcano* is announced in the Preface: "The peoples of Guyana sit on top of a known, restless, threatening volcano. It is called RACE ... Race lies at the hub and heart of this society. Its spokes and arteries are easily recognized in the practice of politics, the existence of division, and the specter of fear."(pp. xii-xiii) In blunt terms, what the author argues is that deep-seated racial conflict, between Indian-Guyanese and African-Guyanese, who together account for more than seventy percent of the country's population, are set on a road to physical confrontation or civil war that can only be settled by partition: "The only way forward for this nation is SEPARATION. The only solution believed left that makes sense, and offers a viable way out of the malaise and morass is PARTITION." [p. 159] There are no ifs, ands or buts: by Lall's account, Guyana cannot be spared national self-dissolution and a possible blood bath to follow.

Lall's argument is that the current People's Progressive Party (PPP) government, especially under Bharrat Jagdeo and Donald Ramotar, have lost working class moorings inherited from original party leader, Dr. Cheddi Jagan, and has now adopted postures reminiscent of the twenty-eight-year People's National Congress (PNC) dictatorship which they replaced in 1992: "Then [under the PNC] Indians disappeared from public presence and significance; today the Black man is nowhere in sight much along the same lines... It [the PPP] ... is no less devastating [than the PNC] in terms of injury, indignity and injustice meted out to Black Guyanese. If anything it is more devastating." [p. 26] According to Lall, the current PPP: "must infiltrate, dilute, divide, and compromise any actual or potential opposition to its rule [including] trade unions, the media, the University, the army, the police force, anti-corruption institutions, PNC strongholds and the PNC itself (repeat, the PNC itself!)." [p. 29]

This tit for tat dilemma originates from each ethnic group's fear of the other: Indian-Guyanese, for instance, believe that: "the mainly Black opposition is waiting for its turn to steal and plunder at the public trough: and to drive Indians into oblivion with recriminatory zeal, if given a second chance. The collective tribal memory is long; it will not forget; it is unforgiving." [p. 53] Lall does not go back into history. The ethnically divided situation he describes did not openly exist in 1953 when a united PPP won national elections: it originated in a split of the PPP led by Forbes Burnham in 1955, with the result that: "Guyana is poised on an edge; one that is sharp and slippery, and extremely perilous." [p. 62] This dead end also comes from fateful changes, for instance, the apparent availability of a: "believed countless number of guns," [p. 56)] an: "enormous narcotics factor and the related abundance of dirty money," [p. 56] an army of available forces of: "loiterers ... and discontented and frustrated ex-security personnel. "[p. 56]

While it is impossible to verify all of Lall's "evidence" in *Volcano*, his litany of tragedies at Agricola, Linden, Lusignan and numerous other places in Guyana, together with phrases such as "approaching cataclysm" [p. 12], "day of reckoning" [p. 12] and "mortal foes locked in close embrace" [p. 164] drive home his claims of a deeply-rooted Guyanese malaise that is not only inveterately ethnic-based, but the agent of much continuing injustice, tragedy and grief in Guyana. He mentions similar post-colonial situations of ethnic-based unrest, killings and civil war in other places such as the Philippines, India, the Balkans, Sri Lanka and Russia. This alone, his recognition of the largely post-colonial origin of Guyana's troubles, suggests that Lall is no irresponsible, scare-mongering fomenter of incendiary feelings out of mischievous or publicity-seeking motives.

In 1960, Nigeria, a British colony, became an independent nation. In 1966, Chinua Achebe's novel *A Man of the People* portrayed his homeland as seething with ethnic, linguistic, religious and cultural divisions, implying that the country was on the brink of a military coup. Later the same year, Nigeria had a military coup, and other coups followed, along with civil war and brutal dictatorships. Today, nearly fifty years later, Nigeria functions or rather malfunctions; but still exists as a country. Whether it is apocryphal or not, when his fictional portrait of Nigeria was dismissed as being too pessimistic, Achebe observed that a truly pessimistic man would not write a book about his pessimism: he would simply shoot himself. That is why, far from *Volcano* being a prophecy of doom, it can, if read correctly, be heard as a herald of hope.

FACING UP TO ETHNIC RIVALRY IN GUYANA

Ruel Johnson
Ariadne and Other Stories.
Ruel Johnson, 2004.

Ariadne and Other Stories is a skimpy volume, barely ninety-two pages long, and self-published. About half of the nine stories are very short indeed: sometimes just over a page and a bit. But, as if to contradict its unprepossessing appearance, the volume was awarded the Guyana Prize for the Best First Book of fiction in 2002. What is more, the author, Ruel Johnson, was then the youngest writer ever to receive a Guyana Prize award.

Certain qualities of Johnson's writing may help to explain his success: originality, initiative, and a subtle mixture of confidence and defiance. The mere form of his stories is arresting and eye-catching. The title of the first story "Killing the Kitten" is weird enough to arouse suspicion, which deepens further when we realise that the slight, three-page narrative is simply a fragment: it scarcely qualifies as an anecdote, much less as a story with a beginning, middle or end.

The action in "Killing the Kitten" consists of two young lovers, Indian-Guyanese, Ravi and Bharti, discussing Ravi's discovery of an abandoned kitten which he throws into a trench. Ravi's cruelty is not isolated; it is matched by images of wind and ice that reflect the wider emotional coldness of human relations in the city of Georgetown, where this narrative and most of Johnson's stories are set. The fragmentary form creates the impression of a fairy story that appears innocent only on the surface, while much darker implications swirl underneath.

"Knock" is similar in form and content, and even shorter than "Killing the Kitten." It poses a dilemma faced by young Indian-Guyanese, Prakash, when he joins in a game of football with a group of Rasta African-Guyanese. As a visible outsider, Prakash is ignored by his fellow footballers, until he demonstrates skill as a player and is finally accepted. If "Knock" is clipped in form and condensed in substance, it is still twice as long as "Salvation" which examines the fate of an Amerindian warrior – Akawaio - who, out of pride, challenges a wounded jaguar with only an arrow as a weapon, and is killed.

Partly because of its extreme shortness in being merely a page and a half long, and partly because of its remote setting in a forest with wild animals, "Salvation" seems to fit the model of a fairy tale best of all. But in all three stories so far, and also in a fourth, "Legend," which is only slightly longer than the rest, the author presents fragmentary or seemingly casual and unimportant happenings that convey deeper meanings in the way that fairy stories or folk tales do.

The appearance of Indian-Guyanese as chief characters in two of the three stories so far illustrates the central importance of race relations in *Ariadne and Other Stories.* We are not surprised when, in "Legend," four friends from different Guyanese ethnic groups, are shown discussing the possibility of racial motives in the late President Burnham's decision to establish a statue of the African-Guyanese slave hero Cuffy in Georgetown, while he erects a monument to the Indian-Guyanese Enmore martyrs in the countryside. The aim of the story is less to suggest that Burnham was right or wrong, than to confirm the deeply rooted nature of ethnic animosity, rivalry and suspicion in Guyana.

"April", one of Johnson's longer stories, illustrates the originality and confidence of his thinking about race relations in Guyana. Not for him the spineless advocacy of a trite and artificial Guyanese nationality that will wash away ethnicity like sin. In "April" Johnson flaunts sexual explicitness like a banner of defiance against puritan inhibition, while he deploys Joycean, stream of consciousness prose to sing a glorious hymn of praise to the love making of an Indian-Guyanese man and his Afro-Guyanese lover in her black village. Johnson also acknowledges the real price of such bliss when, the next day, the path of the Indian intruder is blocked by six black men as he is about to leave their village. There is a suspenseful moment of uncertainty when violence seems imminent, but danger dissolves when the villagers suddenly decide to let the intruder through.

Stories like this give Johnson's writing a tone of tough-minded realism and unsentimental objectivity. Although there are other fictional works, mainly by Indian writers lamenting Burnham's depredation of post-colonial Guyana, there is no other fictional record that is quite as successful as Johnson's in facing up to ethnic rivalry and persistent threat of racial violence, in Guyana, in the 1980s and 90s.

Johnson's success is not merely the result of his skill in form and theme alone; it also derives from a Whitmanesque preoccupation with an individual style that reflects the natural zest and innovativeness of the culture to which he belongs. A story like "Baby", for instance, bristles with the Priapic, sexual energy and mischievous "joie de vivre" of the narrator's Uncle Maurice, Guyanese trickster and traveller extraordinaire. "Ariadne", meanwhile, the longest story in the volume, incorporates literary references and other technical devices in a love story of surprising tenderness. Most of all, Johnson fashions an individual type of language that describes local Guyanese football as: "the frenzied lingua franca of the poor, our own violent poetry in motion; our ballet and our tribal conflagration." [p. 37]

As for his use of Guyanese speech, Johnson does not miss a beat. Here is Ariadne complaining about a rumour that she will lose her virginity before the month is out: "That ass, Bruk-foot, tell him [a friend] that I going get 'bus' before the month done." [p. 26] ("Bus" equals sexual intercourse). With such command of local, Guyanese speech, and an oral form of story telling that does not shrink from frequently addressing the reader directly, Johnson imprints his own stamp of originality on his fiction, and throws down the gauntlet for writing still to come.

POWER SHARING IN GUYANA

Judaman Seecoomar
Democratic Advance and Conflict Resolution in Post-Colonial Guyana. pp.224.
Leeds, Peepal Tree Press Ltd. 2009.
ISBN 13: 9781845230272

When he died in London, in 2006, Judaman Seecoomar had not quite finished the manuscript of *Democratic Advance* and *Conflict Resolution in Post-Colonial Guyana*, the sequel to his first book *Contributions Toward the Resolution of Conflict in Guyana*, (2002) and it was left to his English publisher, Jeremy Poynting, to add finishing touches to the volume. In his "Editor's Note" Poynting writes: "What I have added is a paragraph here and there that makes the context of his [Seecoomar's] argument more concrete." If Poynting's intervention is mainly editorial or cosmetic, it removes any doubt that *Democratic Advance* is entirely Seecoomar's work.

Born in Guyana in 1932, Seecoomar moved to Britain in the 1960s; but he never forgot his homeland. He applied himself to lifelong study that not only gained him a Ph. D. degree, at the age of seventy, but allowed him to at least contribute to discussion of political problems that have dogged Guyana's development since Independence in 1966. While these problems stem directly from ethnic conflict between African- and Indian-Guyanese, they originate in the colonial policy of uprooting and exploiting populations from different continents, mainly Africa and Asia, through enforced labour on Caribbean plantations.

In his first book, Seecoomar analyses the historical background of colonial "divide and rule" policies that inflamed ethnic difference in Guyana, between descendants of African slaves and Indian indentured labourers, who were brought by the British to work on Guyanese plantations after slavery was abolished. In *Democratic Advance*, the author concentrates either on resolving ensuing ethnic conflict between African-Guyanese and Indian-Guyanese, or making concrete proposals for promoting advancement of practical, democratic structures in post-colonial Guyana.

Although Seecoomar draws on a variety of sources, he is most interested in the writing of the Dutch, Yale-trained, political scientist Arend Lijphart and his theory of consociationalism, a form of democratic government through power sharing designed, in particular, for societies divided by ethnicity, class, religion, ideology or other factors. Interest in power sharing for Guyana arises because the Westminster model of government, which the British left behind in Guyana and other former Caribbean colonies, has proved unworkable if not obstructive in post-colonial circumstances that are vastly different from those in Britain.

The case for power sharing is strengthened by its successful implementation, for example, in such European countries as the Netherlands, Belgium and Switzerland which also reflect divisions of language, ethnicity or religion. Hence the appeal of power sharing for Guyana or other post-colonial societies like Trinidad and Tobago, Fiji or Cyprus with populations writhing in differences of ethnicity, religion, class and language.

Power sharing is not an open and shut case. As Seecoomar puts it, in post-colonial Guyana, the need is for: "movement from colonial subjecthood to engaged citizenry" [p. 63] in order to achieve: "a truly functioning democracy" [p. 63], one in which the centralised patterns of the former colonial régime are replaced by local community structures, and grassroots participation that can promote equality. Yet the principle of proportionality which Seecoomar calls: "the linchpin of the power sharing discourse" [p. 80] and which should also produce equality, will not succeed in a country where one ethnic group has a majority. For all its eloquent advocacy then, by Lijphart, or by distinguished West Indians like Sir Arthur Lewis, power sharing is unlikely to work in Guyana where Indians have a clear majority over Africans.

Other factors limiting effective power sharing in Guyana are socio-economic differences between the two main ethnic groups, and: "the wider tendency in Caribbean politics for authoritarianism," [p. 105] two of the chief examples of which are Dr. Eric Williams of Trinidad and Tobago, and L.F.S. Burnham of Guyana who ruled continuously in their respective countries for two or three decades. It is for all these reasons that, along with power sharing, Seecoomar proposes a strategy of alternating government in Guyana: "The life of a parliament would be set at five years and each of the two main political parties would take charge of the government for one term." [p. 91]

There is much else in *Democratic Advance* either discussing the author's sources or elaborating on his proposals. In addition, almost one third of his book consists of appendices that include a lecture by the Guyanese scholar David Hinds "Race, Democracy and Power Sharing," a paper on Shared Governance by the Peoples National Congress/Reform, another by the People's Progressive Party/Civic Government on "Building Trust to Achieve Genuine Political Cooperation," and a Summary offering a draft "The National Development Strategy" that was presented by the late PPP leader Dr. Cheddi Jagan in 1997. His display of such details about local Guyanese politics, including different views from the two main rival

Guyanese political parties, illustrates Seecoomar's mastery of his sources.

His combination of Guyanese details in *Democratic Advance*, earnest probing of current theoretical sources, and his relentless effort to find solutions to Guyana's political problems also imply fierce patriotism. If we consider Seecoomar's long years of academic preparation despite ill health, his high-minded abstention from promoting partisan interests of his own (Indian) ethnic group, the mature, considered clarity of his writing, and his claim that: "study of Guyana is a metaphor for other multi-ethnic post-colonial states," [p. 20] we cannot miss an impartial, high-minded desire, grounded in love of country, to satisfy all Guyanese.

Whether or not this aim is achieved, and whether or not the rigorously argued power sharing proposals in *Democratic Advance* can succeed in extricating Guyana from further disappearing into a political quagmire, they surely cannot be ignored. As Seecoomar modestly writes, his proposals: "are not meant to be a blueprint. There is no blueprint. Rather they are a contribution to... serious debate." [p. 39]

ELECTORAL FRAUD AND IDEOLOGICAL SOMERSAULT

Chaitram Singh
Guyana: Politics in a Plantation Society. pp.155.
New York, Praeger Publishers. 1988.
ISBN 0-275-9289-2

Although Chaitram Singh's *Guyana: Politics in a Plantation Society* considers political developments in the former British colony during the pre-independence administration of Dr. Cheddi Jagan and his Peoples Progressive Party, (PPP) between 1957 and 1964, the volume mostly discusses developments during the régime of Forbes Burnham's People's National Congress (PNC) from December, 1964 to his death in 1985, together with events in early years of the Presidency of Desmond Hoyte, Burnham's PNC successor.

The author of *Guyana* is an Indian-Guyanese who studied at West point, the US Military Academy, where he gained a BS degree, and at the University of Florida where he earned an MA and Ph.D. Singh now teaches political science at Berry College, Georgia, in the US, and is also author of two novels *The flour Convoy* (2005) and *The February 23rd Coup* (2011).

An "Introduction" outlines basic details of colonial settlement in Guyana, first by the Dutch then, by the British who left a social structure deeply imprinted by habits, manners and practices that derive from the two most formative institutions of the colonial period – African slavery and Indian indenture. Consequences of slavery and indenture can be seen everywhere in twentieth century Guyana. After independence in 1966 we are told: "Blacks [Africans] dominate the civil service, the postal service, the army, the police force, the dockworkers," [p. 8] while Indians who form a majority of the population either supply the main labour force on sugar plantations, or work as independent farmers and businesspeople.

Toward the end of the colonial period, the first mass-based political party, the People's Progressive Party (PPP), was formed in 1950, and won the first general election in 1953, although this PPP government, led by Dr.Jagan, was forcibly dismissed by the British governor only four months later. Singh assesses this débacle: "The PPP ministers took office with an exaggerated view of what they could accomplish. They tended to be brash and their tactics confrontational." [p. 22] Two years later, the PPP split on ethnic lines when Forbes Burnham, an African-Guyanese who was minister of Education, left the PPP, and later formed his own party, the People's National Congress (PNC.)

The appearance of two parties, the PPP led by Dr. Jagan (Indian) and PNC by Forbes Burnham (African), soon produced bitter rivalry between Indian-Guyanese and African-Guyanese and, in due course, deadly ethnic conflict and social upheaval, especially after the intervention of the American CIA in the early 1960s. A new electoral system – proportional representation – was then imposed by the British, aided and abetted by the US; and in elections in December, 1964, the PNC, in coalition with a new party, Peter D'Aguiar's United Force (UF), won enough seats to form the government.

The corrupt nature of the new government quickly became clear when D'Aguiar, the Finance Minister: "became outraged by the scale in the corruption of the government as the PNC proceeded to reward its supporters. One of the most glaring cases surfaced in 1967 when the Director of audits could not produce proper vouchers for approximately G$20 million of government expenditures," [p. 40] after which D'Aguiar resigned his cabinet position. In elections in 1968 and 1973 the PNC also employed a range of fraudulent tactics from doctoring the electoral roll to tampering with counting of the votes which would ensure its hold on power for all future elections.

By the 1970s, after its guise of free enterprise and anti-communism had earned lavish rewards from its American sponsors for denying power to the PPP which the US regarded as communist, the PNC decided to change its political stripes: "The PNC has the distinction of having undergone the most ideological somersaults of any political party in Guyana... in 1955 Burnham sublimated the socialist beliefs he had hitherto professed...between 1961 and 1964, he [Burnham] collaborated actively with the capitalist-oriented United Force and accepted help from the CIA to create difficulties for the PPP government...After the 1968 election Burnham reassumed a socialist posture." [p. 45] Expedience or retention of power purely for the sake of itself, either through electoral fraud or ideological somersault, seems to have been a guiding principle of Burnham and the PNC.

In 1974, in pursuit of a new: "hegemonic role that socialist parties enjoy in Eastern bloc countries," [p. 72] the PNC announced a doctrine of party paramountcy through Burnham's so-called "Declaration of Sophia" which, according to Singh: "formally signified the end of liberal democracy in Guyana. It also implied that as 'the major national institution,' the PNC could not be replaced, at least not by constitutional means." [p. 72] Under such sub-headings as "The Guyana Defence Force," the "Guyana National Service," "The People's Militia," and "The House of Israel"- a "thug force" [p. 84] headed by a black American fugitive "Rabbi" Edward Washington, Chapter Four of *Guyana* unveils sobering details of how the doctrine of PNC party paramountcy functioned. Another sub-section of Chapter Four entitled "A Reign of Terror" recounts incidents of violence and terror inflicted on

Indian-Guyanese communities, and provides a clear outline of dictatorship.

Using Tables of Guyanese economic output from 1973 to 1983, Chapter Five drives home this outline of oppression and economic stagnation under Burnham and the PNC. To some extent, exposure of such ostensibly socialist failure and betrayal may be expected from a volume published by the Hoover Institute Press, whose mission statement includes tenets such as: "representative government, private enterprise, peace, personal freedom, and safeguards of the American system." (Internet) Yet it was the US, under President Kennedy, which imposed proportional representation to install the Burnham government in Guyana. Singh's *Guyana* suggests that the American political system itself or *realpolitik* - the practice of great powers imposing their will on weaker ones - is incapable of solving problems of political oppression or injustice outside their own immediate borders.

"ADVERSITIES OF BURNHAM'S GUYANA"

Conrad Taylor
Path to Freedom: My Story of Perseverance. pp.219.
TCF Business Group, US, 2011.
ISBN878-0-98498382-0-0-9.

Path to Freedom: My Story of Perseverance, the first book of
African-Guyanese Conrad Taylor, is a memoir of his early
life in Guyana up to 1969, when he and his school friend
Chaitram Singh won scholarships to study at West Point,
the prestigious American military academy in New York.
The two friends' four-year, West Point interlude, though
interesting, is brief, and *Path to Freedom* soon settles down to
one of the few, credible accounts that we so far have of social,
political and general living conditions in Guyana, during
1973 to 1977 after Taylor and Singh, against the advice of
friends and relatives living in Guyana, returned home from
their studies. Taylor's decision to return was ill-advised, as he
explains: "Naiveté and youthful idealism, however, clouded
my judgment." [p. 97]

When Taylor had left for West Point, the People's National
Congress Party (PNC), led by Forbes Burnham, had been in
power for only five years, which included a period in coalition
with the United Force (UF) led by capitalist entrepreneur Peter
D'aguiar. By 1973 Burnham had: "amended Guyana's constitution
to institute electoral changes that favored his future re-election
chances... [in a] virulent environment of fear and suspicion

that rewarded rumour mongering over competence...Innocent Guyanese were blacklisted without proof. Paranoia truly ruled... PNC party affiliation provided access to such things as business permits, social benefits, civil service positions, contracts and top Army posts. Matters of state became interchangeable with those of the PNC party." [p. 106]

Nor is all this accompanied either by the righteous anger of a political critic or the sage authority of a sociologist. As a West Point graduate, Taylor evidently has American political leanings; but what makes his memoir interesting is the candid, straight-talking, slightly hurt tone of an ambitious and patriotic young Guyanese who ventures abroad to acquire skills that may benefit his country, only to find his good intention blocked at every turn upon his return home.

From the beginning, the Guyana Government failed by following up with only six, of forty-eight student allowance payments, they had agreed to send Taylor and Singh at West Point. Neither were the two graduates awarded suitable rank or jobs upon their return to Guyana. In the end, after a frustrating, gruelling, and patiently documented struggle, they obtain unconditional release from the Guyana Defence Force, except that, in his typically arbitrary and cynical manner, President Burnham at one stage renegues on the verbal release he gives Taylor.

Taylor claims that, no matter what Burnham did, he remained in absolute control: in Guyana, ultimate power was his. One had to survive by appeasement, and Taylor had access to Burnham through his mother-in-law, Edmee Cummings, who was one of the dictator's most trusted and passionate PNC activists since their early days in Kitty. At a birthday party for Taylor's daughter, arranged by Mrs. Cummings, Burnham: "belied his reputation as a bully. There were no signs of authoritarianism in Burnham...He was not the power-hungry, egomaniacal politician of other days – [he was] –

caring – almost humble. He was the folksy, engaging man of the people that many Guyanese admired. He was the political moderate that moved the United States to orchestrate his win over Marxist-leaning Cheddi Jagan in the 1964 election." [p. 164] Yet: "Burnham was also paranoid about covert CIA action against his dictatorial Government. He had first hand knowledge about what had happened to the Jagan Government. He had collaborated with the U.S. in its demise. He feared a similar fate."[p. 108]

If there is room for comparison with other authoritarian Caribbean, political figures like "Papa-Doc" Duvalier of Haiti or Eric Gairy of Grenada, Taylor ignores it to enhance his description of Burnham's bullying actions and policies in Guyana. He reminds us, for example, of Burnham's introduction of the fateful doctrine of "paramountcy of the party" at the PNC's tenth anniversary celebration on December, 14, 1974, the so-called Sophia Declaration, which entailed that: "all branches of government – civil service, judiciary, and military – [became] agencies of the PNC." [p. 109] Loyalists were also cultivated to organise: "aggressive indoctrination programs to promote it [party paramountcy]." [p. 109] In pursuit of a general aim: "for Guyana to feed clothe, house itself," [p. 109] Burnham imposed "several utopian, anti-capitalist measures...banned all forms of imports into the country, including flour and rice," [p. 109] and as a result he: "catalyzed a sustained brain drain."[p. 109]

Despite its wider social/political implications, *Path to Freedom* remains a narrative of the author's personal experience. While Taylor quickly regrets his ill-advised return to Guyana in 1973, it was less quick to escape from what had become virtually a police state. Luckily, their daughter Candy was born in the US, which enabled Taylor and his wife to get American visas to travel to the US. Even so, more cat and mouse manoeuvres were needed to avoid detection until the very end when they left in January, 1977.

Taylor writes lyrically of his fate as a Guyanese during the 1960s and 70s. He claims to have had an idyllic, early, experience in the bauxite mining town of McKenzie (now named "Linden" after Linden Forbes Burnham) until the early 1960s when many Indian-Guyanese suffered from burnings, lootings, beatings and death during the Wismar massacre, only to be followed by a tit-for-tat response of thirty-eight African-Guyanese being killed by an explosion on a boat named "Sun Chapman." Having lived in the US during his West Point years and returned to Guyana from 1973 to 1977, when he saw no let up in ethnic rivalry in Guyana, Taylor ruefully reflects: "on how resolving the dashed hopes and thwarted dreams of my youth had strengthened my resilience; how the unexpected adversities of Burnham's Guyana had taught me perseverance; and how returning home might have been a beneficial coming-of-age experience, in the end." [p. 215]

SHADES OF MITTELHOLZER IN "JONESTOWN" TRAGEDY

Fred D'Aguiar
Children of Paradise. pp.363.
London, Granta Books, 2014.
ISBN 978-1- 84708-861-1

With six novels, seven volumes of poetry, and three plays under his belt so far, Fred D'Aguiar has become one of the most prolific authors in the Caribbean diaspora. Born in 1960, in London, England, where his Guyanese parents had settled, he was taken, in 1962, to live with his grandmother in Guyana, where he remained until 1972, before returning to London. After school, he trained as a psychiatric nurse, took a Bachelor's degree in African and Caribbean studies from the University of Kent, then abandoned doctoral studies to become a full time writer. Since 1994 he has lived in the US teaching at several Colleges before settling down at Virginia Tech.

Children of Paradise, D'Aguiar's sixth novel, imaginatively reconstructs "Jonestown," an allegedly Christian commune established by American evangelist and community organiser - Jim Jones - in the Guyanese jungle, in 1977. In November, 1978, following press reports of brutal ill-treatment and exploitation of commune members, a small, American committee, led by California's Congressman Leo Ryan arrived on a fact-finding mission that sparked such horrific violence that more than 900 people, including 304 children, mainly members or officials of the commune died, some murdered, and others seeming to voluntarily ingest a drink laced with cyanide. Jones himself was found dead with several gun shot wounds, believed to be self-inflicted.

Historical accounts of "Jonestown" exist in articles and volumes such as Shiva Naipaul's *Black and White* (1980); but *Children of Paradise* is a novel whose chief character is an unnamed, despotic ruler of a so-called religious community, in the jungle wilds of a South American country, also not named. Regular contact is maintained between the commune and anonymous government officials in "the capital" (actual Georgetown.) On the surface, at least, the ruler of the commune is addressed respectfully as the preacher or "Father," but the opposite gradually becomes clear: that he is a brutal dictator who demands and receives abject servility from terrorised and panic-stricken followers. Even if he may have succeeded in persuading some members of his commune that he is leading them to paradise, the preacher is the one most convinced by this delusion.

In a seminal incident where his pet gorilla "Adam" apparently kills Trina, daughter of Joyce, his former mistress and still trusted follower, the preacher miraculously resurrects Trina. Later, mysteriously, under his direction, Trina's hands: "can touch everything, even fire, and remain unscathed." [p. 37] This "resurrection" is then used to prove that the preacher is leading his followers to paradise: "He [the preacher] plucked each and everyone from their mad and aimless ways and brought them to the wilderness and placed them one step closer to paradise." [p. 37] But scepticism surrounds Trina's episode since she may have fainted rather than died, in which case her "resurrection" is fraudulent. Together with later events about Joyce and Trina's attempted escape, this increases suspicion that commune members are being deliberately duped by the preacher's deluded claims of leading his followers to paradise.

In addition to Joyce and Trina, the preacher has many faithful bodyguards, loyal prefects, and an entire cohort of officials including a doctor, pharmacist, chief accountant, chief electrician, project manager, and trusted assistants Nora, Dee and Pat. That the last three are young women who also serve as his concubines belie the preacher's claims of spirituality, and expose the delusion of his dream of (Guyana) as a country: "overflowing with minerals, precious metals, diamonds and timber" [p. 109] which, if he became president he could transform, along with the entire continent of South America: "linking all the nations and uniting them under one flag, the flag of worship of the Most High, for a heaven on earth, for the equal rights of all regardless of sex or standing in life." [p. 110]

This maniacal fantasy is flatly contradicted by the preacher's enforcement of his authority over members through such techniques as sleep deprivation, bullying, public beatings and humiliation at any sign of resistance to his orders. Jones's professed utopia is more like a gigantic chamber of horrors in which members are imprisoned, manipulated and exploited by a megalomaniac with an irresistible lust for power and control.

Inevitably, the preacher's bogus but compelling utopia eventually disintegrates, although D'Aguiar wisely resists a sensational dénouement similar to the mass suicide and carnage in the historical "Jonestown." Instead, he identifies specific elements of disintegration: one is the commune's violation of the Guyanese forest's pristine ecological purity, evident in the preacher's hostility to complaints by Amerindians about pollution of their river by chemicals and refuse from his commune; another is the escape of the preacher's pet gorilla Adam from confinement which may partly represent the emancipation of Africans from slavery. Adam's African link also takes in Captain Aubrey whose ship runs errands for the commune, but whose stories about the wily African spider Anansi conceal Aubrey's cherished desire to outwit the preacher and expose the deceit of his power-hungry rampage.

Imaginatively, D'Aguiar first came to grips with "Jonestown" in his book-length poem *Bill of Rights* in 1998. He confesses that the tragedy of "Jonestown" haunted him since 1978, and admits to influence from fiction by the revered Guyanese writer Wilson Harris, whose novel *Jonestown* (1998) elicits metaphysical comparisons with the mass suicide at "Jonestown," the holocaust of Jews in World War Two, and the genocide of Amerindians centuries earlier.

More interestingly, in terms of West Indian literature, speculation on religious hysteria in *Children of Paradise* may have roots in the Guyanese imagination of Edgar Mittelholzer's novel *Shadows Move Among Them* (1951) where a defrocked Anglican priest, Gregory Hawke, establishes a Christian commune among Amerindians, and runs into the same ironic conundrum encountered by Jim Jones and D'Aguiar's preacher: that practical implementation of their utopian vision was only possible through authoritarianism, suppression, and callous, cold blooded brutality.

ABORIGINAL SECURITY AND VISIONS AND
TERRORS OF THIS WORLD

Roy Heath
Orealla. pp.255.
London, Allison and Busby Limited, 1984.
ISBN 0-85031-528-X

Orealla is the seventh novel by Roy Heath (1926-2008) who
was born in Guyana and, in 1950, moved to England where
he remained for the rest of his life. Mostly set in Georgetown,
Heath's novels are so imbued with local sights, sounds, smells,
speech and unique features of the landscape that they offer
rare and penetrating insight into the history and culture
of twentieth century Guyana. Since he was born about the
same time as the action of *Orealla,* the novel remains a feat of
historical reconstruction even if Heath's portrait of Guyanese
social history is already well known from his other novels.

Although he is not the narrator, Benjamin, or Ben as he
is known in the novel, dominates the action of *Orealla* which
opens with his marriage to Tina and almost simultaneous
relationship with Mabel who becomes mother of his three
children. Strange how, in the midst of a Caribbean, colonial
environment regulated by values of race, colour and class,
in the first half of the twentieth century, someone like Ben
who is from the black working class becomes a part-time
journalist while holding a full-time job as driver of a horse and
carriage! Stranger still is Ben's brooding nature and his deep-

seated eagerness to settle scores. This gradually comes out after he is arrested trying to break into a home in a rich area of Georgetown. Instead of being sent to jail, Ben is assigned to work (and receive pay) as a live-in cabman for Thomas Schwartz: "a big man in the civil service responsible for the destruction of old currency notes." [p. 21]

Schwartz who is brown-skinned or "red" is called "Master" throughout the novel, and lives with his wife, known only as "mistress" in an opulent, Regent Street home that includes Edna the maid, and a syphilitic tenant named Fatpork. This sparse outline hints at a delicious irony in the author's view of the social prestige of the Schwartz family, or the unjust and racist colonial structure to which they belong. There is much gossip, for instance, about the family's shady origins, and rumour about their declining fortunes when Mr. Schwartz gave: "his wife's brother money to avoid an embezzlement charge and suspension from the Civil Service." [p. 24]

Orealla focuses on a dramatic contest between Ben and Schwartz who despises Ben for colour and classist reasons, and is infuriated by Ben's gratuitous impudence. It all comes to a head when Schwartz's wife goes away on one of her periodic trips to visit her sister in New York. Unexpectedly, while Ben is climbing a ladder to do repairs on the house, he sees Schwartz in bed with his wife's best friend. Ben successfully blackmails Schwartz by threatening to reveal his infidelity to his wife, and extracting a promise to increase his own pay and withdraw the rent charged for Ben's aboriginal friend Carl who also lives in the Schwartz residence. After Mrs. Schwartz dies and Ben can no longer blackmail Schwartz, the novel ends in a rather melodramatic dénouement with Ben shooting Schwartz and being sentenced to death.

But melodrama is merely a vehicle for profound reflections on the author's homeland. For instance, we cannot ignore the fact that, despite its title, the action of Heath's novel has almost no connection with Orealla, an aboriginal or indigenous village on the Guyana side of the (Corentyne) river that separates Guyana from Suriname. The chief connection is Ben's friend Carl, a Macusi, who is dismissed as a mere buck-man, and plays a tenuous role as a vagrant wandering around Georgetown which he: "hated with every fibre of his body." [p. 31] But although Carl hankers after Georgetown whenever he is in Orealla, Ben claims that Carl's Orealla offers: "the security of the womb... to which there was no return from the terrors and beauty of this world." [p. 247]

For all its pristine, idyllic closeness to nature, Orealla is no Eden. At best it is a lost or doomed Eden: "Orealla was doomed to be trodden into extinction by the horsemen of progress." [p. 246] While it is not asserted as doctrine, the notion of fate or destiny - of events taking their own course, independent of human needs or preferences - is explicitly mooted more than once in the novel whose final lines describe Orealla as a place: "where Carl and his clan were holding out against the advance of an alien way of life, with the dead hand of its justice sanctifying a crime of appalling enormity." [p. 255] What more can be expected of those living in a post- colonial society where, as victims of the historic crime of slavery/ indenture, they: "respected nothing except outward appearances and the fetish of skin-tone!" [p. 220]

In contrast, *Orealla* envisions a Guyanese culture consisting of an equal association of all ethnic groups, including aboriginals, sharing language that revels in idioms, images and expressions of speech that are either uniquely Guyanese or partly Caribbean, for example, "bishka" a card game, [p. 83]; "eye-turn" feeling dazed, [p. 106]; "bittle" food, [p. 155]; "gil" a penny, [p. 158]; "eye-pass" insult, [p. 180]; and phrases such as: "he got two woman an' want to huff my man from me," [p. 90] "the hum of voices sounded like a nest of marabuntas,"[p. 219] "she tumbled into adultery as a fly falls into a bowl of guava stew," [p. 220] and "you just lie there like comoodie when he swallow bush pig." [p. 224]

Shared language implies a common culture. This is not to mention threats and quarrels that are sheer music to the ears of Guyanese readers, and a description of Georgetown that is as evocative as anything Dickens ever wrote of London: "Georgetown itself with its inequalities, its prison, its avenues of jacaranda and flamboyant, its stretch of river and ocean, its fishing boats laid up in channels along stone jetties, its secret backyards, its sugar wharves... and administrative buildings conceived for permanence of an alien rule..." [pp. 246-7]

AFRICAN-GUYANESE SOUL

Roy A. K. Heath
Shadows Round the Moon. 254pp.
London, William Collins Sons & Co. Ltd., 1990, L12.95
ISBN: 0-00-215584-2.

Roy Heath (1926-2008) lived in England from 1950, but his memoir *Shadows Round the Moon* focuses mostly on his life in Guyana, (British Guiana) from his birth to 1950. Heath regales us with both the bristling tempo and rich colour of life in a typical British Caribbean colony, where the British formed the ruling class over a population mainly of Africans and Indians, with smaller groups of Europeans, Chinese, Portuguese, mixed blood coloureds and aboriginals. Social status is regulated by criteria of race, colour and class out of which the author emerges with a measure of privilege because of his educated, middle class, mixed, African/European stock, and residence in the city of Georgetown - administrative, commercial and cultural hub of the nation.

Roy's father died before he was two years old, and he was brought up by his mother mainly in different locations within Georgetown. On his maternal side, his relatives originated from the Caribbean island of St. Martin, while his father's family claimed connections in St. Kitts, Antigua and Barbados. Caribbean cosmopolitanism fortifies an impression both of culture and breeding: Roy's maternal grandfather Peter Moses de Weever was a pianist, his uncle Guy de Weever was author of an almost revered school text of Guyanese history and, like his mother before him, Roy himself became a school teacher and pianist. The circle of Roy's family revolved in a sophisticated aura of creole, colonial culture established by cultivated middle class families such as the Carews, Dolphins and Harpers, not to mention Guyana's finest poet, Martin Carter, who was Roy's friend.

A central theme of *Shadows* is the fate of this creole or coloured middle class, specifically in Guyana, if not in the wider Caribbean. By Heath's account, around the era of World War Two, his family and friends are living on borrowed time within a fragile edifice of education, sophistication, and gentility that is already beginning to collapse beneath their feet, because of the rapid deterioration of its economic foundation. Heath does not mince words: "The fundament of our class attachment – money – was conspicuously wanting" [p. 99]. Thus, when the head of a creole middle class family loses his civil service job and commits suicide, leaving house, piano and all behind, he fulfills a destiny of tragic decline for his mixed blood, middle class, programmed by colonial history: "There was nothing sadder than the remnants of affluence in homes marred by such tragedies." [p. 50]

The harsh truth was that although most professionals were creoles - black or coloured: "business was more lucrative than the professions" and "most business people were East Indians, Portuguese and Chinese." [p. 116] Creole decline goes hand in hand with the economic rise of Portuguese, Chinese and, most noticeably, Indians who were shedding their low status as indentured, rural, agricultural workers: "to buy their way into Georgetown creole society." [p. 214] This casts prophetic light on the sad, political direction of Guyana by acknowledging creole/black feelings of loss, dispossession, grievance or hostility that become fatefully entangled in newly emerging ethnic dispensations by the 1950s, only to erupt into deadly, political tensions by the 1960s.

Paradoxically, in the midst of such sorrow, *Shadows* contrives an heart-warming evocation of Georgetown in the 1930s and 40s when exaggerated respect for elders was still the norm, and belated principles of Victorian discipline were enforced by severe habits of strict, puritanical abstinence, or brutal, physical chastisement that improbably functioned alongside loud and outlandish gestures, for instance, during Christmas festivities when masquerade bands gaily roamed in city streets, and colourful eccentrics daily passed themselves off as self-educated philosophers, prophets or pundits, dispensing arcane, unwanted wisdom in public or, with only slightly less discrimination, in barber, tailor, and rum shops.

Shadows abounds either in such characters or scenes, incidents and anecdotes that display similar eccentricity. Heath writes, for example: "the history of drama in Guyana cannot ignore the public quarrel... above all its spontaneity" [p. 46]; he also illustrates the coarse language and hilarious invective used in these quarrels, mostly by women, and admits that such quarrels were compelling, public entertainment. In this colourful pageant of Guyanese culture, as the volume's title implies, memories and reminiscences of the past become like dreams or shadows: "under the lamplight and the drifting moon." [p. 202]

To top this rich and glorious pageantry of local colour, Heath's style is also cut from uniquely Guyanese cloth, for instance, residents of Georgetown are called "Georgetonians"- his own coinage - and local images or phrases add authentic seasoning to his narrative, while a woman's laughter: "possessed the quality of bright moonlight, eerie and disturbing, and her dreams were full of snakes and ants," [p. 54] and his short-lived pleasure in becoming a civil servant is compared to: "a woman's make-up in a persistent downpour". [p. 221]

As an eye-witness record of notable events such as the Great Fire of Georgetown in February 1945, the impact of US troops in Guyana during World War Two, and the economic effects caused by the departure of these troops, *Shadows* at least passes muster as a reliable work of social history; but when one adds the self portrait of the author and his family, his wider reflections on social history, psychology and anthropology, the originality of his locally enriched style, and his superb evocation of Georgetown in the 1930s and 40s, the stock of *Shadows* rises well beyond the range of most Caribbean memoirs.

Heath's writing does for Georgetown what the fiction of Dostoevsky and Dickens does for St. Petersburg and London respectively: it immortalises the city. Despite examples of ethnic or social difference, deep-seated feelings of cultural mimicry, colonial dependence, and pitiful lack of political awareness, Heath's portrait of his native city in *Shadows* invokes achingly elegiac, paradoxical feelings of bittersweet nostalgia for a bygone era of bemused, colonial innocence, now forever vanished, not only from Georgetown, but from Guyana, and the wider Caribbean.

A DESERT OF DEBT AND DESPAIR

Roy Heath
The Ministry of Hope. pp.320.
London, Marion Boyars, 1997, L16.95.
ISBN 0-7145-3015-8

Kwaku Cholomondoley, hero of *The Ministry of Hope* - Roy Heath's ninth novel- continues picaresque adventures started in the author's sixth novel *Kwaku or the Man who Could not Keep his Mouth Shut* (1982). Kwaku's adventures which earlier appear in the 1970s, or soon after the start of the Burnham régime in 1964, now unfold during the 1980s and early 90s in *Ministry*, when, after twenty-eight years of dictatorship, Burnham's party - the People's National Congress (PNC) - had reduced Guyana, in the words of a minor character, to: "a desert of debt and despair." [p. 205]. The difference between the two novels is between humour and irony: while brilliant jokes, good humour and drollery produce no more than a light-hearted, rollicking romp in *Kwaku,* they conjure up much darker, more sombre images in *Ministry,* where black humour and comedy are sometimes pickled with irony of raw savagery.

In the earlier novel, Kwaku starts out as a lowly shoemaker who gains affluence as a faith healer, only to sink back into penury and lose friends, family and everything. At the beginning of *Ministry,* where our somewhat chastened hero is bent on recovery, he leaves Berbice for Georgetown, armed with an introduction to the Permanent Secretary in the Ministry of

Hope. The reader does not miss contradictory values, twisted motives and sinister dealings when Kwaku learns that the Ministry's real name is one that ironically means "without hope" [p. 45], just as the Permanent Secretary, whose correct name is never given, is called the Right Hand Man, although he sits on the left hand side of the Minister during meetings.

Kwaku is given a flat, and a job as messenger at the Ministry of Hope; but when he confides in his benefactor, the Right Hand Man, about his plan to start a business selling antique chamber pots, the Right Hand Man opens up a lucrative chamber pot business of his own. Undeterred, Kwaku relies on his trickster wits to cope with the treachery, suspicion, fear, blackmail, bribery and coercion that surround him, and soon leaves the Ministry to set up a thriving business in his old vocation as a faith healer.

Ministry makes no bones about rank corruption in the fading years of the PNC dictatorship: "The atmosphere created by the dominance of a single political party caused blackmailers and informers to thrive and made cripples of honourable men, who were not above selling a compliant mistress's services to earn promotion in an underpaid administration." [pp. 102-103] Equally damning details are given by one of Kwaku's cronies: "A local bank that lends money to party people and doesn't bother to demand repayment; Government vehicles unaccounted for; the Government auditor producing no report for years; Treasury accounts years behind... people who practise corruption, lies and thuggery." [p. 264]

Yet *Ministry* is no mere diatribe against political corruption: the novel also presents a colourful array of characters whose lives intersect and nearly collide with dramatic, sometimes deadly effect. Clifford Correia, for instance, head of the Currency Exchange Centre in Georgetown, and collaborator of the Right Hand Man in shady, financial dealings across the Rupununi border with Brazil, embezzles one thousand

US dollars, and is forced to stay in the Rupununi with his aboriginal mistress and family, while his wife Amy continues in Georgetown as secretary to the Right Hand Man. But after Amy becomes her boss's live-in mistress, Correia returns to Georgetown and blackmails the Right Hand Man, now Minister, into supporting his candidacy in approaching elections. Intrigue, treachery and blackmail mix with politics to produce a thrilling climax in which Correia is mysteriously murdered, and the Minister given forty-eight hours to leave the country or face prosecution for murder.

Nothing confirms Heath's skill as a novelist more than this ability to link these hair-raising, largely political twists and turns with Kwaku's more humorous, domestic squabbles, and amusing social connections to eccentric cronies such as Suarez and Bertie, and the oddly named Surinam, a painter who is eventually confined to the asylum in Berbice. So many contrasting characters and varied activities within the political structure of the novel make for a racy narrative, diverting enough to suppress any sombre tone rising out of all the amorality and anarchy.

Heath's skill shines even brighter in comparison with other novels that consider the PNC dictatorship in Guyana, for example, Nirmala Sewcharan's *Tomorrow is Another Day* (1994) and Lakshmi Persaud's *For the Love of my Name* (2000) which may expose collective perils of political oppression, but do not capture the impact of oppression on individual Guyanese with nearly as much conviction. Delicacy of irony, Chaucerian rather than Swiftian, enables Heath, through subtlety and indirection, to uncover gross, public mischief, intermixed with peccadilloes of private life, and expose the tragedy of unlimited political power on rulers and ruled in post-colonial Guyana. Heath scarcely mentions Indian-Guyanese who, historically, are regarded as chief victims of PNC corruption in post-colonial Guyana; but sheer genius enables him to unveil corruption through an ironic portrait of African-Guyanese both as chief supporters of the PNC, and equal victims of the régime.

If the Australian Patrick White is remembered as a reliable chronicler of the fictional, Sydney suburb of Sarsaparilla, and R.K.Narayan as the author who put Malgudi, fictional name of the Indian city of Mysore, on the literary map of the world, Roy Heath deserves similar honour for his minutely pencilled, brilliantly etched portrait of the buildings, streets, trenches, politics and manners of Georgetown, and the very feel, smell, sight and sound of the people who live in it. Instead of politics itself, it is rather the subtle impact of politics on everyday lives of ordinary Georgetonians in *Ministry* that clinches Heath's reputation as Guyana's finest novelist.

FIDELES UBIQUE UTILES

N.E.Cameron
A History of the Queen's College of British Guiana (Guyana).
pp.143.
Toronto, Vantage Systems, Second Edition, 2009.
ISBN 978-0-9696531-1-1-0

The first edition of *A History of the Queen's College of British Guiana*, written by Norman E. Cameron (1903-1983), appeared in 1951, and was printed in Georgetown, British Guiana by F.A. Persick Ltd. Cameron, who won the Guiana Scholarship in 1921, gained an M.A. degree from Cambridge University where he specialised in mathematics. He first taught at his own school – The Guyanese Academy – from 1926 to 1934, before becoming Senior Master at Queen's College (QC) from 1934 to 1958, and Deputy Principal from 1958 to 1962. He later also served as Professor Emeritus of mathematics at the University of Guyana.

In his *History*, Cameron maps out the historical development of QC with chronological precision, relying on crisp, short chapters often with many sub-headings, and a multitude of facts, figures, lists and sometimes lengthy quotations that make for a graphic presentation with a distinctly documentary appeal. His style is somewhat staid and steady, even earthbound, but eloquent enough for its chief purpose: unearthing important steps in QC's development, and highlighting the personalities or achievements of those connected with the school.

As we learn from Cameron's *History*, on 11th July, 1844, (Anglican) Bishop William Piercy Austin held an Inaugural Meeting to discuss his idea of a new school that would keep: "the children of the more wealthy [English residents] in the colony [British Guiana] for a longer period" [p. 2] in order to encourage patriotism for Guyana in them before they left for further education in Britain. On 5th August, 1844, Queen's College Grammar School, as it was first known, opened its doors to fifteen students under two tutors in the old Colony House, near what was then the Victoria Law courts. It was a fee-paying church (Anglican) school with a curriculum consisting of Greek, Latin, Mathematics, History, Geography, Writing and Arithmetic.

By 1875 when its enrolment had reached thirty-five, QC took a major step in shedding its church affiliation and becoming a Government institution. There were still two Departments, "Modern" and "Classical," but a wider number of subjects: Reading, Writing including Dictation, English Grammar, Arithmetic, Algebra, Euclid, English History, Geography, Latin, Classics and French. Exley Percival (1848 – 1893), the first Principal after QC became a Government institution, is still the second longest-serving in that position: from 1877 to 1893. As a mark of his formative influence, not only was a school "House" named for him, but QC boys: "provided an inscribed granite slab for his tomb in Le Repentir Cemetery." [p. 37]

With typical diligence, Cameron records details (with accompanying photographs) of QC's main premises from 1854 to 1918, and later at Brickdam from 1918 to 1951, and Thomas Lands from 1951. Nor does he forget the growth of the school in numbers and influence; academic awards and scholarships won by QC students, for instance, the Gilchrist Scholarship that lasted from 1871 to 1888; the better known Guyana Scholarship which started in 1882; and myriad extra-curricular activities stretching from drama and the choir, to the

Cadet Corps, formed in 1889, the scout troop, and numerous sports from athletics to soccer, cricket, hockey and much else.

In addition, the 2009 edition includes an Appendix with "Reminscences – My Recollections of QC (1945-1980)" by Clarence Trotz, a QC student from 1945, Master from 1957, and Principal from 1975 to 1980. Trotz updates Cameron's *History* beginning with the retirement of Captain Howard Nobbs as Principal in 1952 (Nobbs's term began in 1931) and his replacement by V. J. Sanger-Davies who initiated changes such as the admission of students from other schools to study science that was unavailable in their former schools. By 1962, however, when Sanger-Davies retired, he was replaced as Principal by a Guyanese, Doodnauth Hetram, ending the one hundred-and-eighteen-year-old practice of foreign-appointed Principals, in the same way that Frank Worrell's appointment in 1960 ended the time-honoured practice of appointing only Whites as West Indian cricket captains.

This colonial practice had served QC well, after all, and it was perhaps fitting that, as the leading secondary school in the nation, QC should reflect a Caribbean-wide transformation from colonial tutelage to national self-esteem, later to be confirmed by Independence itself, in Guyana, in 1966. Hetram served as principal from 1963 to 1969, and was succeeded by Clement Yhap (1969-1971), Morrison Lowe (1971-1974) and Trotz during whose tenure, in an equally radical transformation, female students were admitted to the school for the first time in one hundred and thirty years.

In addition to Norman Cameron, who deserves to be forever honoured for his selfless labour of love in recording the historic role of QC in Guyanese education, we must also thank contributors to the 2009 edition: Dr. Joycelynne Loncke for her "Professor Norman E. Cameron: Biographical Notes;" Clarence Trotz for his judicious update that ensures continuity for Cameron's pioneering work; Patrick Chan for his informative "Reflections of an Alumnus (1954 -1961);" C.I.C. Wishart for his review "The Queen's College of Guyana Association (UK)"; and *The Illustrated London News* (1963) for an article "Queen's College, The Buildings and Activities at this Multi-Racial School," reprinted by paid permission along with photographs. But none of this, along with a list of Guyana Scholars (1882-1990) in the Appendix, would have been possible without the inspired initiative of members of the Queen's College Alumni Association (Toronto) who orchestrated the entire 2009 updated edition of Cameron's volume, including photographs.

Unless I am greatly mistaken, the first edition of this volume was launched at QC, in 1951, when I believe I heard Captain Nobbs begin with the opening line of his Foreword: "Mr. Cameron, the indefatigable worker that he is ..." [p. ix] "Indefatigable" was a new word for me; nor was it the only thing that I learned in my seven years at QC. That is why, for me at least, the word vindicates our school motto of boundless loyalty and service - FIDELES UBIQUE UTILES – so eloquently proclaimed in the writing of Norman Cameron.

RIGHTEOUS INDIGNATION AND FLAMING PASSION

Mona Williams
Bishops: My Turbulent Colonial Youth. pp.162.
Wellington, New Zealand, Mallinson, Rendel, 1995.
ISBN 908783-05-0

Bishops: My Turbulent Colonial Youth, describes Mona
Williams's strenuous effort to gain entrance into Bishops High
School, and her studies there from 1955 until she enters the
Sixth Form five years later. Bishops was then the only girls'
Government secondary school with trained, foreign teachers
and special teaching facilities in the colony of British Guiana;
and Mona, her sister Claire and brother Keith were entirely
dependent on their mother, a school teacher, whose family
situation was typical of Guyana in the 1950s when: "You had
to look to your wits, your brawn and your family to survive."
[p. 76] Since her mother cannot afford fees to Bishops, Mona's
best option is a scholarship for which she must lodge with the
family of Mr. McGowan, head master of a school on the island
of Wakenaam, where she is coached and often beaten; but
Mona scores 93.7% in an intensely competitive, make-or-break
scholarship exam, and eventually wins a coveted scholarship
to: "the Promised Land of Bishops' education."[p. 51]

For a country girl like Mona, however, just gaining entrance
to the Promised Land of Bishops' education is not enough; for
Bishops is in Georgetown, the colony's capital city and seat of
Government, headed by a British Governor, whereas Mona's

mother lives in McKenzie (now Linden) a bauxite mining town, sixty miles up the Demerara river, and accessible only by river. This means that Mona, Claire and Keith must share rented Georgetown lodgings that can be cramped, insanitary or not always able to supply adequate meals. Frequent need to change lodgings also creates an unstable, nomadic existence for Mona and her siblings.

In such conditions, as a black student living on the margin of survival in colonial Guyana, Mona finds what she expects upon her entrance in Bishops: "All de big shot people's children go there. Like de people round de Governor. De big business people, de sugar estate managers and de rich white people, [and] their children." [p. 41] What boggles Mona's mind though is to hear a white student from Britain say: "We don't have to sit an exam [to enter Bishops] if we're white." [p. 60] After her life-and-death struggle to enter Bishops, this example of the racist structure of British colonial Caribbean society in Bishops, absolutely floors Mona, inflaming her already mixed feeling of: "awe and excitement" [p. 43] about her new school.

Racism infects both Bishops' selection of students, as well as the school's curriculum. When she asks her English mistress, for instance, if her class can study a West Indian novel in addition to the standard fare of Shakespeare and Dickens, she is told: "the Caribbean is yet to produce writing worthy of the name literature." [p. 89] Similarly, her history mistress does not believe that Guyanese history is worth studying: "B.G. is too young to have a history to speak of." [p. 91] According to Mona: "The culture of the school made me feel ashamed and stupid to ask for our own music, our food, our novels, poetry and plays, our art or our dances although I knew I should never feel this way." (pp.90-91) Such élitist attitudes at Bishops produces self-hatred among students, as Mona writes: "I knew of older Bishops girls who clearly, by the things they said, despised themselves for being black." [p. 95]

By her account, the turbulence in Mona's colonial youth is caused mainly by the racial ethics of her school and her single-parent family's poor conditions (her father is absent throughout, having gone to England since Mona was three.) But she is not alone. In time, Mona finds like-minded nationalistic individuals such as Helen Taitt, a ballet dancer who runs a dance school, and offers her a part-time job as a ballet instructor. Such is her ambition and drive to succeed that Mona also finds another part-time job, although, once again, she is dogged by racism when she admits: "Portuguese, Chinese and pale others as sales staff, yes; but a jet black sales girl? Come, come!" [p. 107] This proves that racism is rife not only in Bishops, or education, but in business and Guyanese society as a whole. Still, by 1960, apart from establishing her credentials in the performative arts at Bishops, winning first prize in poetry recitation and third prize in singing, Mona passes her Ordinary Level exam and has her scholarship extended to enter the Sixth Form at Bishops.

For all its unsparing documentation of hardship and injustice, both physical and psychological, the narrative of *Bishops* also adroitly manages to be lively, spirited and entertaining, adorned with Guyanese proverbs like: "to a starving picknee one milk-breast is better than a flat chest." [p. 101] or with profligate word coinages and original expressions like "joy-crazy' [p. 39] and: "belly-rumbling-hungry-day," [p. 69] or yet again with descriptions of local culture, food, music, speech idioms and humour, or anecdotes and dialogue that proudly proclaim *Bishops* as the handiwork of an inspired and well practised Guyanese story-teller.

Still, there is a touch of anachronism in feelings of nationalism that come from a Guyanese teenager, almost a decade before Guyana's Independence in 1966. It seems that, writing in 1996 about events that occurred forty years earlier, the author adapts her time sequence for greater dramatic effect. For one thing, Dr. Cheddi Jagan was not leader of the Opposition in Guyana in the 1950s. For another, the author's nationalistic feelings from pre-Independence 1950s Guyana are conflated with the rhetoric of the 1960s' Civil Rights Movement in the US where Mona later went to university. Other idiosyncrasies include spellings such as "lightening" for "lightning," [p. 102] "Hindu" for "Hindi," [p. 127] and the misspelt names of West Indian cricketers such as Ramadhin [p. 65], Kanhai and Worrell. [p. 147] But such minor flaws do not deny *Bishops* a place as one of the most outspoken of Guyanese memoirs or autobiographies with its own refreshing blend of youthful vigour, righteous indignation and flaming passion.

POWER OF THE WITHERING GLANCE

Philippa Perry
B. G. Bhagee: Memories of a Colonial Childhood. pp.243.
Self-Published, 2011.
ISBN-13: 1461192910, ISBN-10: 1461192196

Philippa Perry's *B.G.Bhagee: Memories of a Colonial Childhood*
consists of thirty-eight sketches, each about four to six
pages long, recalling episodes in the life of the author
(née Carrington) who was born in 1945 and grew up in
Georgetown, Guyana. Some episodes consider Philippa's
experience as a student, while altogether they form a portrait
of her (mainly black) Georgetown community as a whole.
Another title of her book - "B.G. Days"- appears on alternate
pages of *B.G.Bhagee,* emphasising an idea of the book as a
portrait of "Days," that is, daily routine or ordinary life in
colonial Guyana, during the 1950s and 60s.

"Lot 10", the first of four sections, takes its name from
the author's address: Lot 10, First Street, in Georgetown,
Guyana's capital city. "Lot 10" consists of twelve sketches
describing Philippa's family and neighbourhood: she is
one of seven children and her family own a property that
contains their own home as well as other buildings in
which: "an assortment of tenants and poor relations jostled
each other to survive." [p. 11] Philippa's portrait of her yard
tells all: "Nothing was hidden, you could see people at their
open doors and windows... all around you the chattering,

arguing, singing, laughing and warring, with the radio on its single station blaring forth accompaniment." [p. 11] Nor are animals excluded from this milling medley of madness: "When the humans paused for breath, there were sounds of animals: the squawking of chickens that every family prized, and the yelping of dogs that belonged to no one in particular."[p. 11]

Despite what seems like pandemonium, though, life in the yard seems strangely peaceful: no physical violence is reported; even if dark motives lurk in: "the seething resentment that my mother harboured, set amongst her husband's relatives, never free from their watchful eyes. The grudges that other tenants held simmered below the surface...because we were the grandchildren of the owners and did not have to pay rent." [p. 12] Under the surface life is fraught with suspicion, rivalry, and hidden danger, magnificently evoked when: "they [neighbours] waited for us to stumble and fall. Goodwill was scarce; they waited for tragedy to strike." [p. 12] Such malice! So succinctly expressed!

Nor, as Philippa notices, are her immediate family members exempt. Her Aunt Cil's hopes of marriage, for instance, are thwarted by Aunt Irene who intercepts and confiscates letters sent by Aunt Cil's Guyanese boyfriend in the US, all because she [Irene] wants to keep Aunt Cil at home as her baby-sitter. Similar incidents move Philippa to claim: "Our family history had its share of cruel stepmothers, children starved and beaten, wicked wiles to keep lovers apart, and poisonings and suicides with household fluids." [p. 71] It sounds like a tropical version of a history of the Borgias transferred from medieval Italy to Guyana, and it illustrates courage in an author resolved to spill the family beans at her own peril. An "Author's Note wisely advises: "all the events [in *B. G. Bhagee*] happened, they are true...Some names were changed to protect me from the wrath of my relatives." [p. 3]

Section Two of *B. G. Bhagee* considers the author's experience first at primary school – St. Ambrose Anglican which claims special status as: "the élite of primary school(s)." [p. 90] It was founded in 1855 and Miss Friday who was trained in England: "was the first local woman to become its headmistress." [p. 99] Philippa proves to be a star student at St. Ambrose, and not only wins a scholarship to Bishops, the leading girls' Government secondary school, but tops the exam list with the highest marks of all students in the colony.

Section Two also covers Philippa's time at Bishops from 1956 to 1963. Since she regards Bishops' teachers as: "the academic élite who radiated confidence and demanded excellence," [p. 118] Phillippa has unswerving faith in their ability to prepare her for the slings and arrows of the real world: "By their [her teachers'] example we learned to appreciate the subtlety of insult and the power of the withering glance, a new world opened for us and Bishops armed us with weapons to survive in it." [p. 118] But before she can take her Advanced Level exam she is awarded a scholarship to Connecticut College in the US. In those Cold War days, the author's scholarship was inspired by ideological rivalry between the US and the USSR, which prompted an initiative by the US government to counterbalance the award of similar scholarships being offered by East Germany and the USSR to members of Guyana's allegedly communist Opposition party - the Peoples Progressive Party.

The last two sections of *B.G.Bhagee* "Kith and Kin" and "Afterwards" enlarge scope of the volume's social context with fourteen additional sketches about relatives, friends and political issues after Guyana becomes a republic in 1970 and: "turned the country into a nation of beggars , everybody waiting for handouts, old clothes, food from overseas." [p. 223] These wider issues shift the volume more toward the genre of a memoir rather than autobiography or fiction. But literary categories overlap, and what we finally get is a richly detailed, endearing and enchanting picture of Philippa's community, sternly unsparing and truthful, yet warmly consoling in its mature tolerance of human failings.

Hers is an almost completely African-Guyanese community based in Georgetown, Philippa's great-grandfather being of African-Barbadian descent, and her father first working in Georgetown as a carpenter, cabinet maker, and later as a security guard. This produces a typically Georgetonian point of view that gives Philippa away when she visits Essequibo and condescendingly observes: "Essequibo seemed at the end of civilization." [p. 138] As corroborated by other examples of Guyanese writing from authors like Godfrey Chin and Mona Williams, as well as Sharon Maas and Roy Heath, the socio-economic dominance and prestige of Georgetown is indisputable in colonial Guyana.

MITTELHOLZER'S FLUENCY AND MAAS'S INDOPHILIA

Sharon Maas
Of Marriageable Age. pp.530.
London, Harper Collins, 2000, (First Published1999).

Guyanese-born Sharon Maas has so far produced three novels –
Of Marriageable Age, Peacocks Dancing, (2001), and *The Speech
of Angels* (2003) – all of which are set, at least partly, in India.
African, Amerindian, Dutch and British in ancestry, Maas
acknowledges that her first novel was inspired by Pratima,
her childhood friend and daughter of the Indian-Guyanese
historian Dwarka Nath. No doubt it was this association that
led to Maas's first visit to India in 1973 when she spent two
years in an ashram.

Of the three main characters in *Of Marriageable Age*, Paul or
Nataraj (Nat) is first seen as a child in a Christian orphanage in
Madras (Chennai) in 1947, Sarojini (Saroj) is born like the author
herself, in 1951, and grows up in Georgetown, Guyana, in the
1950s and 60s, while Savitri, the daughter of an Indian cook, first
appears in South India, in 1921, and participates in somewhat
improbable relationships with Nat and Saroj. At first we are told
that Nat is of mixed English and Indian blood, and adopted by
an English doctor living not far from Madras. Later, inspired by
his father's selfless medical work among Indian villagers, Nat goes
to England to study medicine; but after exciting and distracting
social and sexual adventures in swinging, 1960s London, he
returns home empty-handed without a medical degree.

As Nat's career reflects India in a troubling, transitional stage of development, immediately after Independence in 1947, the chapters on Saroj offer an equally disturbing portrait of British Guiana, in a dire political struggle for Independence during the 1950s and early 1960s. Saroj is the daughter of Deodat Roy (Baba) a prominent Indian-Guyanese lawyer, and strong supporter of Dr. Jagan's People's Progressive Party. But believing that Dr. Jagan's party has betrayed Indian-Guyanese, as a racial group, Baba forms his own All-India Party for Cultural Progress which is, no doubt, a fictional portrait of the actual Hindu dominated Justice Party that was founded by Balram Singh Rai. Baba does not mask his racist Indo-centric views: "Some races are born with a higher spirit, born to lead, others are born low, capable of menial tasks." [p. 146] On the other side, by also recording that: "Indians feared to go out onto the street. They were attacked, robbed, mutilated, killed, raped by Africans," [p. 147] Maas successfully captures the trauma of racial rivalry between Indian- and African-Guyanese that was exploited politically to create general mayhem in Guyana in the early 1960s.

With equal success, the author captures the inner domestic turbulence in Saroj's family. Saroj's mother (Ma) is quietly diplomatic and devious, while her father is brutally authoritarian, once beating her mercilessly for associating with their African-Guyanese neighbour. Together with Baba's attempts to arrange a suitable Hindu marriage for her when she is "of marriageable age"- fourteen - this beating arouses a fierce spirit of rebellion in Saroj. The phrase "of marriageable age" has strong resonance in a narrative with several tough, resilient female characters like Lucy Quentin, mother of Saroj's close friend Trixie, who is an outspoken feminist and strong opponent of arranged marriage.

Meanwhile, in South India, in the 1920s, Savitri's parents work for an English family, the Lindsays, and as a child Savitri falls in love with the Lindsays' son David; but the relationship is opposed on all sides, and David eventually goes to England where he becomes a doctor and marries an English woman. During World War Two, David leaves his wife in England and returns to become reunited with Savitri in Singapore where she becomes pregnant. When Singapore is overrun by the Japanese, Savitri escapes and learns that David has been killed in the fighting, although this turns out to be false.

This improbable relationship between David and Savitri is typical of many surprising if not bizarre twists and turns in a novel with action that sprawls over continents and lasts for decades. Not only does the child of Savitri and David turn out to be Nat, but Savitri marries a fellow Indian by whom she has three children all of whom, as well as her husband, conveniently die off. Following such adversity, Savitri answers an advertisement for a brahmin wife placed in an Indian paper by Saroj's father Baba, and goes to Guyana where she becomes Ma - Saroj's mother.

There are numerous other unlikely, coincidental or random happenings. When Saroj and Trixie go to England to study, for instance, Saroj is casually spotted by Nat at a railway station and a romance ensues. Trixie gets married to Saroj's brother Ganesh, and Baba who has also come to England, gets a heart attack, and begins to change his extremist views about race. In the end, intractably tangled complications between Nat and Saroj are resolved so that they can marry and settle in India.

It seems somewhat contrived for everything to fall so neatly into place at the end. Yet the novel is popular and has been translated into several languages. Nor can we deny that Maas's characters are interesting and their relationships intriguing, if too coincidental. Her writing also is fluent and her descriptions fresh, original, almost photographic in accuracy, for example, her portraits of Georgetown and London in the 1960s, and

Madras in the 1920s and 30s. Whatever else it may not have, Maas's first novel has superb documentary value.

What is more, reliance, even excessive reliance, on coincidence may not be the liability it seems, for it is apparently influenced by tenets of "advaita" Hinduism that recognize no caste distinctions, only: "the vast mysterious interconnectedness of all humans." So what we regard as coincidence becomes merely failure to understand divine intelligence. As the author writes: "There is intelligence that links or guides us in ways beyond our understanding." Not very different from Hamlet's: "There's a divinity that shapes our ends/ Rough-hew them how we will."(*Hamlet*, Act V, Sc.,2, ll. 10-11)

HARRIS, HEATH, HINDUISM AND THE GUYANA FOREST

Sharon Maas
Peacocks Dancing. pp.485.
London, HarperCollins, 2001.
ISBN 0-00-711847-3

While *Peacocks Dancing* is not a sequel to Sharon Maas's
first novel *Of Marriageable Age* (1999), it is haunted by
similar ghosts from Guyana's post-colonial history, and
India's ancient civilisation with its branches of rarefied,
Hindu philosophy. *Peacocks Dancing* consists of six Parts,
sixty-four chapters, an Epilogue, and regular entries by the
narrator Rita Maraj into a diary that brings welcome order to
gusts of sprawling action. Rita, daughter of Indian-Guyanese
Ronnie Maraj and a coloured or mixed blood mother, dies
before the story begins. Through scenes of her early life in
Guyana and later travels in India, Rita extracts much colour
and variety out of Guyana's colonial history, and ethnically
mixed population drawn partly from India, through the
indenture system.

Part One of the novel which introduces Rita, her father and
stepmother Marilyn Prabudial is a masterpiece of Caribbean
fiction that displays as much insight into West Indian history
and society as V.S.Naipaul's classic "Trinidad" section of his *The
Middle Passage.* Nowhere else, at least not in Guyanese fiction,
do we find a more complete portrait of Guyana's capital city,
Georgetown, its streets, buildings, layout, vegetation, people and

manners and - considering Georgetown's historic importance - of the social and economic life of Guyana as a whole.

On pages twenty-one and twenty-two entire Georgetown families, all neighbours, are identified by their race, colour or religion. Simple skin colour identifies Rita's school friends, for example, Polly Wong is "blanched-almond-cream," Donna De Souza is "olive-toned," Christine Knight is "honey-skinned," and families such as the Roys, Farouks and Isaacs are "various shades of gold- brown," while Rita is merely dismissed as "the darkest." Not only that, names such as Wong (Chinese) De Souza (Portuguese) Farouk (Indian/Muslim) Maraj (Indian/ Hindu) add an element of ethnic classification that further defines the mixed, polyglot nature of the Georgetown middle class of which the author's own (Westmaas) family is a well known example.

The author's sensitive psychological study of her characters raises the excellence of Part One to the level of Mark Twain's frontier society where youthful innocence and fearless energy combine forces to oppose stifling convention. Rita, for instance, betrays contradictory feelings, at once acutely caring and protective of animals, yet fiercely hostile toward Marilyn, who retaliates with cunning calculation that would defy the wiles of the most wicked stepmothers in fairy tales; and it precipitates a titanic struggle between two formidable antagonists that reduces Ronnie to a rubble of insouciance and complaisance, dotish rather than doting to his daughter, and mere putty in the hands of his wife. After Marilyn's pregnancy miscarries, flames of conflict in the Maraj household rise higher and higher, especially in Part Three, when Marilyn loses two other pregnancies and finally gives birth to a girl - Isabelle.

Relations between Rita and her step sister now take centre stage in the novel, and in the second half of *Peacocks Dancing*, teenage Isabelle fails to realise her dreams as a beauty queen in Guyana, and sets off with Rita on a somewhat whimsical quest to India, seeking a possible inheritance from the Rani of Mahapradesh, whose grandson Kamal, her proper heir, studies engineering in the US and returns to India with a white American bride who dies from food poisoning after giving birth to a daughter - Asha. Kamal - Asha's father - chooses to live as a monk in an ashram in North India although, when he discovers that Asha has been sold into prostitution in Madras, he drops everything to search frantically for her.

Isabelle is cordially received by the Rani who enjoins marriage between her and Kamal which would, at least, create the possibility of a male heir to her. Soon afterwards, though, Rita separates from Isabelle and joins in the search for Asha as well, uncovering the dark side of Madras with pimps and enforcers, dirt, squalor, exploitation, child prostitution and disease including AIDS. When she is eventually discovered by Rita, Asha is a mere skeleton, incapable of speech and held in a virtual prison. But when Rita takes Asha home in a taxi, Isabelle dashes out to meet them and is knocked down.

This is one of several accidental or sudden deaths in the novel (Ronnie Maraj's entire family were killed in a road accident.) It takes a superbly skilled story teller to marshall a narrative of so many sudden twists and turns toward a smooth end when Rita transfers the HIV positive Asha to live with Rani, and in her final diary entry, acknowledges the return of Kamal that makes: "an audience of two"[p. 485] and creates: "the flawless union of minds and hearts." [p. 485]

There is more to *Peacocks Dancing* than the sensational narrative suggested by the novel's front cover advertisement of: "an exotic story of richness, ruin and roots." From early on Rita imbibes wisdom from her maternal grandmother who leads her to discover spiritual enlightenment in the Guyanese forest. This further leads Rita into: "the quest for myself; for my place in life." [pp. 344-345] What she seeks is the ineffable in Hindu philosophy: "knowledge undefined yet true and whole, unproved because unprovable, arising as a flame of insight, with her [Rita], being, vast and free of thought, as its medium." [p. 345]

Knowledge, truth and beauty go together: hence symbolic reference to peacocks in Maas's novel emphasizing the notion that: "only beauty must exist in the world." [p. 79] Comparisons are possible with philosophical fiction by Maas's fellow Guyanese Wilson Harris who indulges in philosophical meditations prompted by the Guyanese forest in his novels, for example, *Palace of the Peacock,* or another Guyanese, Roy Heath, who also explores Hindu philosophy in his novel *The Shadow Bride.* Strange that colonial fragmentation inspires sublime creativity in Guyanese artists and such contention or strife in politicians!

DESTINY IN HINDU METAPHYSICS

Sharon Maas
The Speech of Angels. pp.374.
London, Harper Collins, 2003.
ISBN 0-00-712-386-8

As the last of three novels - the first two being *Of Marriageable Age* (1999) and *Peacocks Dancing* (2001) - *The Speech of Angels* carries give-away signs of Sharon Maas's preferences in the substance and style of her fiction, for example, her abiding fascination with India, Hinduism and a Hindu notion of Fate or Destiny, her roving eye both for details of living conditions and sweeping, panoramic descriptions of India, and her flawless fluency of style. Although it originates in India, Bombay [Mumbai] in particular, the action of *Speech* spreads out to Germany and England, and while there is no mention of specific historical events or dates, the presence of regular airline flights and other features of modern life suggests a near-contemporary period of action when the usage of "Mumbai" for "Bombay" had not yet fully caught on.

The title of the novel is taken from Thomas Carlyle's remark: "Music is well said to be the speech of angels," which is the last of three epigraphs that appear immediately before the Prologue to the novel. The four parts of the novel that then follow are each prefaced by a further music epigraph, for instance, Victor Hugo's comment: "Music expresses that which cannot be put into words and that which cannot remain silent," and J.S. Bach's statement: "The goal and final purpose of all music should be, for none other than the glory and praise of God." Already, from the ethereal quality of these comments, we sense the abstract nature of the author's concern with Fate or Destiny as "the most intricate web of causality" [p. 290] that links all living things together into one grand global scheme.

This does not mean that the action in *Speech* is itself abstract or unconvincing, merely that music is the novel's thematic centre piece, and the consuming interest of its chief character, Jyothi, an Indian girl rescued from the teeming slums of Bombay by a German couple, Jack and Monika Keller, who come to India to adopt a child. (Jack is an American who lives in Germany.) Still, although events in the novel are not unconvincing, they tend to satisfy mechanical demands of the author's plot a little too conveniently, as in the death of Jyothi's mother in a road accident and the later discovery of her father's death clearing the way for Jyothi to be formally adopted by Jack and Monika.

Monika returns to Germany ahead of Jack to set up their new family living arrangements while Jack and Jyothi, who is only six years old, follow shortly afterwards. On their flight over to Germany, Jack meets a young English woman Rachel Fitzgerald who stops off in London while he is in transit, but not before he has kissed her. It is the type of chance encounter in Maas's fiction from which we may expect great and unexpected significance later on.

Jyothi thrives, if not at school, in her new home, where Jack coaches her as a violin player. Soon, pushed and prodded more by Monika than Jack, she reveals herself as a gifted musician who, after some time, gains a reputation for successful performances at music recitals and concerts. But while Jack is supposed to be visiting his parents in the US, Monika discovers letters confirming his regular, secret correspondence with

Rachel. Whether this discovery destabilises her or not, Monika suddenly dies in an accident soon afterward, clearing the way for Jyothi to move to England to live with her new parents - Jack and Rachel.

The connection with Rachel becomes more complicated when, as a teenager, Jyothi meets Dean the son of Rachel's brother Will and his Indian wife Soona. About this time too Jyothi feels that her music has lost its soul. Her artistic inspiration is in crisis as well, as she struggles with her feelings for Dean. Then, while Dean, Jyothi and her parents visit India, Jyothi goes to the hill station of Rishikesh and, in a remote area that encourages meditation or reflection, follows a stranger - Rabin - to listen to sitar music played by Swami Satynanda. Jyothi is transfixed by the pure spirituality of the Swami's music and, following discussion with Rabin, realises that, for true excellence, her music must not only be technically perfect, but selfless, spiritually pure like the Swami's. Probably, at the same moment of this crucial insight, we are told that Dean has a climbing accident reminiscent of one in which his father had died. Dean survives, but both events can be attributed to "capricious Fate" [p. 286] or "Fate's invisible games." [p. 286]

By now, in her mid-twenties, as Jyothi struggles to resolve crises both in her musical career and love for Dean, her story meanders somewhat through her struggles until she is convinced of Dean's insincerity and finally rejects him. But her music crisis is more intractable. Following Swami Satynanda's example, she is tempted to abandon the violin for the sitar; but Jack dissuades her from doing so. For the sake of purity, in order to play the violin with the spirituality of the Swami, she must first recover her true Indian identity and change back from "Jade," the Western name she adopted as a celebrated musician, to her Indian name "Jyothi." As it happens, in a universe governed by Fate, it turns out that Rabin knew Jyothi as a child, and is now willing to teach her as she plays the sitar to gain the spiritual wholeness necessary for attaining true excellence with the violin. Only when we consider the author's overarching theme of music as her attempt to reach God by tracing the wonderful workings of Fate, can we better understand Mass's reference to: "the hand that moved the strings that caused the fantastic interplay of individuals – lives twisting and turning, touching and moving on." [p. 59]

BEWITCHING NOSTALGIA

Michael Gilkes
"The Last of the Red Men"
(Unpublished)

"The Last of the Red Men," by Guyanese-born Michael Gilkes, won both the Trinidad and Tobago National Association Cacique Award for best drama production in 2006, and the Guyana prize for drama in the same year. Gilkes began as a pharmacist before becoming an academic, and author of such acclaimed critical works as *Wilson Harris and the Caribbean Novel* (1975) and *The West Indian Novel* (1991). He combined an academic career with playwriting, and his play "A Pleasant Career," based on the life of Guyanese novelist Edgar Mittelholzer, won the Guyana prize for drama in 1992. Gilkes is also an actor, film producer and poet whose first volume of poems *Joanstown* won the Guyana prize for poetry in 2002.

"The Last of the Red Men" consists of two acts with the playwright as the only actor throughout. In Act 1, Scene 2, for instance, he appears as an old man in his 80s, slumped in a wheel chair in his senior citizens' home or almshouse, as this institution is known in Guyana. In Act 2, Scene 1, he appears as a presumably vigorous young man, dressed in short-sleeved sports shirt, slacks and sun-glasses, and riding a bicycle. The complete contrast in roles illustrates the versatility of Gilkes's virtuoso performance.

The chief character in the play is Roger Algernon Fitzwilliam Redman, the pompous formality of whose name alone gives away his cultural background in Guyana, a former British Caribbean colony, and part of the so-called New World where the indigenous people – First Nations - were regarded as "red" men by European colonizers, no doubt because of their reddish brown skin colour. More specifically, the protagonist's name "Redman" reveals his origin in an ethnic group of mixed blood people, descended mainly from (white) European plantation owners and (black) African slaves. Members of this group were also saddled with the disparaging designation of "red, and even more disparagingly, were regarded as "no nation" by fellow Guyanese; for in British Caribbean colonial society they occupied a neutral or middle position between the ruling, white upper class, and a largely black (African) or indentured (Indian) working class. But it is the stirling contribution of this group, as stalwart artists, professionals, teachers and administrators in Guyanese society, that forms the main theme of the play.

While race and colour coincide with class in Caribbean history, "The Last of the Red Men" stresses class more than race in a spirited effort to defy the racist and inhuman nomenclature and value system bequeathed by colonialism and African slavery to the region. In one of his compulsive rants, Redman defines "red" as "not rich, not poor, not white, not mulatto, not coloured"; and he illustrates his definition by mentioning teachers, artists, novelists, poets and civic leaders – actual people who will be readily recognized by a Guyanese audience, for example, Frantz Fanon, C.L.R. James, H.A.M. Beckles, Rudolph Dunbar, Edgar Mittelholzer, Guy Sharples, A.J. Seymour, George Lamming and Derek Walcott.

Many of these people are black rather than "red," yet Redman defiantly claims, "For us, they are all red men." His claim, in other words, is based on the historic debt owed to the

Guyanese or Caribbean middle class for their distinguished social services and general "standards of reliability, of integrity, of excellence," especially during the colonial period. But he also recognizes their declining influence after Independence in the 1960s. This decline explains why the play is described, in Redman's consistently waggish words, as a "post-mortem on the cadaver of the middle class." It also explains a prevailing elegiac tone, symbolized visually by the protagonist's physical frailty, and more explicitly by a somewhat adventitious mock trial in the final scene, when the middle class is accused of pride and snobbery, and "tried" for "suicidal homicide."

If all this sounds distant, abstract or too academic, it is misleading; for it is all transmitted through scenes of vibrant, dramatic action, bursting with realistic, rib-tickling zest and vitality, partly because they carry a mischievous blend of ridicule, invective and sarcasm, deliciously spiced with a bawdy Caribbean flavour. For instance, we relish Redman's pungent speech when he pours scorn on politicians as "ill-informed, illiterate, ill-mannered opportunists scuttling like cockroaches through sewers." In similar language Redman rails against everyone and everything when, like Shakespeare's King Lear, he evokes a spirit of cynical scepticism that makes the natural order of things in the world seem unnatural.

Nothing could be more perverse or unnatural than Caribbean colonialism and slavery. It is why Redman can dismiss ordinary Guyanese people for "catching their royal poverty-stricken asses," as if they deserve to do so, or why he fulminates against the "whole blasted almshouse of the Caribbean" as if the entire region also deserves victimization. Nor does he spare himself, admitting with equally deserving self-deprecation, that he may be considered "an eccentric old fart," living in a euphemistically named almshouse "The Palms" which is nothing but "a geriatric zoo."

Whether we agree with them or not Redman's fast and furious fulminations deftly weave a magisterial critique of Caribbean history and sociology into a rich tapestry of brilliant local colour splendidly displayed within a frame of bewitching nostalgia.

As far as technique is concerned, the sharply ironic contrast between Redman's outward physical frailty, and the fiery vehemence of his wicked wit and mockery is only one of several dramatic devices exhibiting Gilkes's superb stagecraft and artistic control.

There are, for instance, several off-stage voices and changes of scene that create variety, and help to blunt the possibility of monotony or boredom that are endemic risks in a solo performance. Redman addresses an imaginary reporter, and plays a tape recorder of his recollections which, with typical bathroom humour, he publicly announces that he will turn off whenever he wishes to use the toilet. The result is an original piece of Caribbean theatre that improbably captures the swashbuckling verve of V.S. Naipaul's demotic language in *Miguel Street,* and the perfervid intensity of Derek Walcott's Caribbean soul-searching in *A Dream on Monkey Mountain.*

STOIC ACKNOWLEDGMENT OF UNRELIEVED ADVERSITY

Eric Walrond
Tropic Death. pp.192.
Toronto, Collier-Macmillan Ltd. 1972.
(First published in 1926.)

Tropic Death, a collection of ten stories by Eric Walrond (1898-1966), appeared in 1926 as the first and only full length work of an author who was born in Guyana, but moved with his (Guyanese) father and (Barbadian) mother to Barbados where he first attended school. Walrond continued school in the Canal Zone, Panama, where he later worked as a journalist. In 1918, he moved to New York, studied at City College and Columbia University, and was deeply influenced by Marcus Garvey's Universal Negro Improvement Association. Preoccupied with the "plight of the Negro," he established himself as a prolific writer on racial issues for a wide variety of magazines in the 1920s, and with *Tropic Death* being published to great acclaim, he was recognised as a member of the Harlem Renaissance.

"Tropic Death," title of Walrond's collection and its final story, implies that life for his characters, chiefly black or brown workers in tropical Caribbean, colonial territories, in the early decades of the last century, consisted mostly of unremitting toil to keep body and soul together. Toxic, colonial issues of class and colour were also complicit in ensuring that Walrond's characters lived on the edge of poverty, sickness and starvation, never far away from death. "Drought," the first story, paints a bleak picture of Sissie running: "a house on a dry-rot herring bone, a pint of stale, yellowless corn meal, a few spuds," and "thumping the children around for eating scraps, of eating food cooked by hands other than hers." [p. 26] Such was the hunger that one child, Beryl, dies from eating marl – dust from crushed stone.

In "Panama Gold" fire spreads from a canefield to burn down Poyah's shop while he is still inside, and in "The Yellow One" where a mestizo Cuban helps a mixed blood woman - La Madurita - during their voyage by boat from Honduras to Jamaica, a fight erupts between a Negro and another light-skinned Cuban, causing La Madurita to be crushed to death. The author's clinical, almost dismissive comment is: "In the scuffle the woman [La Madurita] collapsed, fell under the feet of the milling crew." [p. 66]

In "Wharf Rats" too the chief characters, a St. Lucian family in Panama, face overwhelming odds. Possibility of a blooming love affair promises to relieve tension over the struggle for survival, but when a son of the family - Philip - later dives into the sea for coins thrown by tourists from a ship, he is devoured by a shark. Again, Waldron's terse comment on the tragedy betrays his stoic acknowledgment of the unrelieved adversity that is, evidently, all that his characters can expect out of life: "it [the shark] bore down upon him with the speed of a hurricane. Within adequate reach it turned, showed its gleaming belly, seizing its prey."[p. 84] Nothing could be more under-stated or matter-of-fact!

Similar satirical wit gives a sharp edge to "The Palm Porch" where Miss Buckner runs a brothel. Miss Buckner's sombre combination of false respectability and evil cynicism prevail when one of her clients, a drunken English vice-consul, who proves embarrassing, is later found dead (no doubt following orders from Miss Buckner) and quickly removed from her premises. This fictional world of unrelieved doom and gloom also appears in "Subjection" where Ballet objects to cruelty inflicted on a fellow worker by their supervisor, a white, American marine at the Panama Canal site. Other workers who know what is good for themselves keep quiet and, as expected, Ballet is later shot, execution style, by the marine. In typically laconic fashion, all that we learn from the Canal Record is that: "the Department ... kept the number of casualties in the recent native labor uprising down to one." [p. 112]

Walrond's tough-minded portrayal of the bleak fate of Africans in the Caribbean and the US, at the turn of the twentieth century, fifty years before the Civil Rights movement, and a full century before the election of a black American president, is nothing but the unvarnished truth as seen, perhaps most starkly, in the title story when Sarah Bright and her son arrive in Panama from Barbados looking for her husband, only to find him in the depths of deprivation facing a slow, horrible death from leprosy.

Hints of obeah are prominent in three stories. In "The Black Pin" two feuding black female neighbours discover how obeah can be re-directed to achieve revenge/justice. In the grotesque ending of "The White Snake" the only story set in Guyana, a woman's baby becomes: "the fresh dead body of a bloaty milk-fed snake the sheen of a moon in May," [p. 143] while in "The Vampire Bat" following his arrogant dismissal of obeah as blind superstition, a white West Indian soldier, Bellon Prout, freshly returned home from service in the Boer war, is killed by a vampire bat.

The resounding literary success of *Tropic Death* is due mainly to brilliantly precise writing. Walrond uses simple words with exact meanings, and intersperses songs, rhymes, hymns, legends and folktales which, along with phonetic, creole speech, make for a lively narrative that reflects the richness of Caribbean, oral traditions. One example of his expertise is his original creolising of the convention of the heroic or epic simile from classical poetry in "The Black Pin" where he evokes the full extent of Zink Diggs's devastation of her neighbour's property: "No rock engine, smoothing a mountain road, no scythe let loose on a field of ripened wheat, no herd of black cane cutters exposed to a crop, no saw, buzzing and zimming, could have outdone Zink Diggs's slaying and thrashing and beheading every bit of growing green." [p. 124] All this, directly in front of the victim, Diggs's hapless neighbour April, who can only stand by, open-mouthed and helpless, disbelieving and defeated. That a writer of Walrond's calibre was silent for the entire second half of his life remains one of the saddest tragedies of Guyanese and West Indian literature!

NIHILIST, OPTIMIST OR REALIST?

Pauline Melville
Eating Air. pp.476.
London, Telegram, 2010.
ISBN: 978-1-84659-081-8 (First published in 2009)

Pauline Melville who was born in Guyana and now lives in England is author of *The Shape-shifter,* a collection of stories that won the Commonwealth Writers Prize for best first book in 1990, a second volume of stories *The Migration of Ghosts* (1998) and two novels - *The Ventriloquist's Tale* which won the Whitbread prize for best first novel in 1997, and *Eating Air.* If Guyana serves as a partial location for many of Melville's stories and first novel, the action of *Eating Air* unfolds mainly in London, England, with some scenes in Italy and countries that neighbour Guyana like Brazil and Suriname.

In *Eating Air,* what may have looked like an instinct for compulsive movement and border crossing, in the author's earlier fiction, changes into an urgent desire for political revolution. We encounter revolutionaries if not revolution throughout the novel. Note, for instance, a quotation from Jean Genet which serves as epigraph to Part One: "I am drawn to peoples in revolt," and the epigraph to Part Two which is from Flaubert: "Of all history I understand nothing but revolt." [p. 128]

We also meet characters like Victor Skynnard, Mark Scobie and Hector Rossi, ageing Marxist revolutionaries, who failed to usher in a communist utopia by abolishing international capitalism in the 1960s and 70s and now, in an age of suicide bombers, collaborate with contemporary terrorists, eager to redress the continuing injustice of Western domination over the rest of the world. As Hector's younger collaborator Shahid tells him: "Islam is not just a religion. It's a political ideology similar to yours. Look. Communism didn't work. Capitalism doesn't work. The only solution left is Islam." [p. 86] Hector's mention of libertarian or "democratic communism" invokes Shahid's mere scorn: "That's so last century. That's so over." [p. 88]

In the 1960s and 70s when left-wing groups like the Baader-Meinhoff gang in Germany and the Brigate Rosse (Red Brigade) from Italy attracted international headlines, Mark and Hector were members of the Italian group, and Hector served time in an Italian jail for his role in the murder of Signor Agnelli from the Fiat car firm. But in *Eating Air* the machinations of these revolutionaries and their younger collaborators to kidnap banker Stephen Butterfield, and attack his HCB bank in Holland, form only one strand of the novel's plot. Their efforts prove fruitless; Hector is gored to death by a wild boar, their kidnap plan foiled, and the novel ends with a rather bizarre, suicide bombing type accident when an aeroplane ploughs into a built up urban area with horrific consequences.

During their adventures, though, the failed terrorists and their intended victims from the world of finance, for example, Stephen Butterfield, Eddie Sursok a Syrian-Palestinian banker, and Johannes (Johnny) Caspers, a Jewish-Surinamese, cross paths with an even more motley group of protagonists including a Surinamese, Elissa (Ella) de Vries, a dancer at the Royal Ballet in London, her idiosyncratic husband Danny McLeod, Hetty Moran an American female adventurer, the Situationist architect Michael Feynite, and a transvestite pilot Felix (son of Johnny Caspers) who flies the aeroplane in the apparent accident mentioned earlier. This suggests a distinctly ludic, serio-comic approach to ostensibly serious subjects like art, injustice, politics, revolution or terrorism - "striking a blow for a billion oppressed people," [p. 437] or opposing "corrupt democracies" engaged in "wars, mass killings, torture." [p. 438]

Not surprisingly, opening epigraphs to *Eating Air* and its title announce Melville's ludic approach. In her first epigraph, Shakespeare's Hamlet simulates deliberately playful or demented behaviour in replying to his stepfather Claudius: "I eat the air, promise cramm'd," and in the second, a poem by Sylvia Plath, the persona, speaks with evident exaggeration of eating "men like air." Not only that, the narrator of *Eating Air* Baron S, yet another Surinamese, plays music in the evenings at: "Mambo Racine's, a casino, dance hall and brothel" [p. 9] in London, and claims, in a tone strongly tinged with dark humour, that: "My style is that of a graveyard dandy." [p. 9] Baron S also prefers fiction that: "celebrates the marvels of reality," [p. 13] and later candidly confesses: "I'm a novelist. It's not my job to provide moral support. It's my job to set the moral compass spinning." [p. 449] "Art" he pontificates elsewhere "is what those of us do who are too frightened to be terrorists." [p. 470] It may explain why a novel that purports to consider principled resistance to worldwide injustice seems given largely to idle speculation.

Yet, as quotations above may suggest, despite its antic display of what seems merely mental jousting, *Eating Air* serves up both solid erudition and writing that bubbles with wit and wisdom, for example, "Having a great enemy is almost as good as having a great friend," [p. 68] or "Everything we feared from communism is being brought about by capitalism" [p. 70] and: "It is not doubt that makes a man mad. It's certainty." [p. 73] In addition, Melville acknowledges influence from distinguished antecedents, and admits her novel is a: "loose reworking of themes from *The Bacchae*."[p. 477]

In his play Euripides hints that our failure to distinguish boundaries between values associated with the god Dionysius – emotion, instinctiveness, revelry - and those represented by reason, self-control and reality, often leads to tragic suffering. This is most vividly captured in a tortured romantic relationship between Ella and Donny, a Dionysian figure *par excellence.* Donny is described as: "a connoisseur of pure rebellion." [p. 278] He comes and goes as he pleases, and obeys no law or rules. When asked what he believes he replies: "Nothing. Children. The innocence of children. Humanity." [p. 227] He claims he is neither an individualist nor nihilist, but an optimist. Donny's romance with Ella also reflects influence from Shakespeare's poem "Venus and Adonis." More importantly, it illustrates Tolstoy's: "Once admit that life can be guided by reason and all possibility of life is annihilated," [p. 337] Melville's epigraph to Part Three, which brilliantly encapsulates her entire novel.

NEW AGE NOVEL: SURVIVAL OF THE BODY

Tessa McWatt
This Body. pp.325.
Harper Collins Publishers Ltd. 2004.
ISBN 0-00-200565-4

This Body is the third novel of Tessa McWatt who was born in Guyana, in 1959, and brought to Canada by her family when she was three years old. She was educated in Toronto and later worked, both in Toronto and Montreal, before moving to England where she is now Senior Lecturer at the University of East London. Her background probably explains her concern in *This Body* with subjects such as migration, homelessness and identity.

This Body is divided into three parts. Victoria, the chief character, is a middle-aged Guyanese woman who, like the author, lived in Toronto before moving to London, England, where she cares for Derek, the son of her sister Gwen, following Gwen's death in a car accident in Guyana. Derek who is eight years old, at the start of novel, is a budding teenager at the end, and clandestinely reads from a stack of letters which his aunt received both from his mother and from Kola, his aunt's former lover in Toronto. If Victoria's interest in these letters is to re-live her past as a sort of salve or protection against the worst anxieties of immigrant alienation and ageing in her sixties, Derek's motive is to track down his father whom he has never seen: all he is told is that his father was last known to be in Miami.

Much of Part One of the novel concentrates on details of Victoria's early life and her work as a cook. *This Body* provides actual recipes, some half a page in length, and extensive, often mouth- watering discussions on the merits of certain ingredients, and preferences in methods of preparing food. It rounds out a portrait of Victoria as a spirited and independent, if somewhat unstable individual who also runs a catering business jointly with her English lover Lenny Brown.

Victoria's day-to-day interaction with Derek is the mainspring of matters, and it takes on elements of suspense and romance when Derek connects his search for his father with his reading about King Arthur and his knights of the Round Table. For example, he fancifully imagines his father: "like a knight [who] had fought for the rights of poor people in Guyana, and provoked the government to the point of endangering his own life." [p. 127] In addition, Derek learns from Victoria of "kanaima," an Amerindian spirit of revenge which he enthusiastically enlists, along with its distinctly Guyanese flavour, into the search for his father.

In the Second and Third parts of the novel, complications develop as Derek makes friends at school with a girl, Kendra, an association that strengthens the relationship between Victoria and Kendra's father Alexander Hodge. Eventually, the association becomes close enough for Victoria, Alexander, Derek and Kendra to go off to France for a holiday by car and, yet later, for Victoria and Alexander to become lovers. Victoria's need for this affair, no doubt another balm to her ageing and footloose, immigrant status, confirms the deep-rootedness of her anxieties, and it is not surprising that when she takes Derek on a trip to Guyana, in another grasp for stability through psychic re-connection with her cultural roots, the venture falls flat when she suddenly cuts the trip short and injures her ankle in Barbados.

All this becomes more interesting because of the author's tightly packed narrative style employing energetically researched details that help to authenticate people, places and events, for instance, Victoria's recipes already mentioned. There are also similar details about characters we seldom or never meet, for instance, Kola whose biography is fully sketched in, along with his feuds, intrigues and wanderings from Kenya to Canada, back to Kenya, then to London where he is murdered in murky circumstances. Purely as a technician, at least, McWatt is highly skilled.

This Body is also packed with items of pervasive sexual interest, not only Victoria's many affairs, but reminders that her father so indulged himself sexually with random partners that Victoria believes she may have many relatives whom she does not even know in Guyana. Victoria also observes a man masturbating in a train, Derek sees Victoria having sex with Lenny in a hotel room, and Derek and his school friends discuss sex and artificial insemination casually and jokingly, suggesting that *This Body* may be something of a new age novel where relationships are transient and, as Victoria claims almost at the end: "Everything is an accident." [p. 301]

Certainly much of Victoria's life seems accidental. On their trip to Guyana, her sudden decision to return seems impulsive when she tells Derek with a seemingly compulsive feeling of weariness: "I want to go home, child." [p. 300] As the author reports: "Derek is confused by the word. How many places can home be?" [p. 300] Although the author writes with enviable conviction about life in Guyana, Canada and England, none of these places is home to either Victoria or Derek. But, at last, Victoria ends Derek's romantic pursuit of his elusive paternity by revealing that he cannot know his father because he was conceived by artificial insemination. Hence the bleakness of the final lines of the novel as Derek reflects that: "being born means I have this body, and that dying means, simply, that I leave this body, and there's more." [p. 325]

These lines echo the final words in V.S Naipaul's story "One out of Many," in his book *In a Free State*, (1971) where the narrator Santosh, a traditional Hindu from India, is disoriented by new-fangled American manners, in the same way that the lives of Victoria and Derek are disfigured by their legacy of family displacement, during colonial upheavals of population. Although the title of McWatt's novel is taken from a poem "Anodyne" by the African-American writer Yusef Komunyakaa, her concern is also post-colonial: anyone shorn of their history, culture and customs, is programmed merely to satisfy basic needs of hunger, shelter and sexual gratification, just to sustain their body.

"RACE HATE WILL MAKE THIS COUNTRY CHOKE IN ITS OWN BLOOD"

Brenda Chester DoHarris
A Coloured Girl in the Ring: A Guyanese Woman Remembers.
Lanham, Maryland, Tantaria Press, 1997.
ISBN 0-9659444-0-9

Although the first half of the title of Brenda DoHarris's novel, *A Coloured Girl in the Ring,* is taken from an innocent and playful nursery rhyme, her novel contrives a profoundly insightful study of life in Guyana, from 1958 to 1964, when the narrator was at secondary school; and whether one regards it as autobiographical fiction or fictionalised autobiography, *A Coloured Girl in the Ring* offers a memorable evocation of familiar sights, sounds and scents in colonial Guyana, and of Guyanese history, geography, sociology, politics, and commonest events, all densely crowded around a story about family, friends and neighbours, and most of all about the narrator herself.

Using a method of itemising, cataloguing or listing that goes back to one of the earliest of English novels, Daniel Defoe's *Robinson Crusoe,* DoHarris assiduously researches, collects and records names, places and events that we instinctively remember from Guyana in the 1950s: not only common items of food like coague, sugar cake and rice pap, dumplings, fufu or black pudding, but furniture like the Berbice chair, Morris chair, chiffonier, the Phillips radio with Sarah Vaughan singing

"My Tormented Heart", calypsonians singing "All Day All Night Miss Mary Ann", and Lighthouse cigarettes, Nugget shoe polish and Reckitt's Crown blue. In a magisterial description of Stabroek market, nearly a page long, and matched only by passages in novels such as Jan Carew's *Black Midas,*(1958) and Sharon Maas's *Peacocks Dancing.* (2001) DoHarris itemises everything from dray carts and Bookers' taxis to mangoes, mittai, cassava pone and genips, stinkin' toe, pointer brooms and trusted medications like Dodd's Kidney Pills, Sloan's Liniment, and DeWitt's pills. (pp.187-188)

This catalogue alone would likely not achieve the conviction that it does, were it not for the volume's language and dialogue of demotic Guyanese speech. When DoHarris conjures up phrases like "Afta rall" for "after all", or sentences like "Wake up yuh lazy behine an' bring dung de posy" [p. 99], heightened by idiomatic expressions like "yuh cork duck" [p. 91] or "time longer than twine" [p. 130] she hits the bull's eye of accent, rhythm and intonation in authentic Guyanese speech that makes 1950s Guyana materialise, like film, before our eyes.

If this vision appears idyllic or nostalgic, it is not the whole truth: the central theme in DoHarris's novel is that she – the coloured or brown girl – is entrapped in a ring of deprivation and exploitation in colonial Guyana, and that her best option is: "to escape the ring, to go abroad and seek education beyond the mudflat" [p. 137]; for the larger truth is that all Guyanese, including the narrator's parents, friends and neighbours are encircled in the same ring that is geared to their self-destruction. What follows then is a struggle against self-destruction, as we see when the narrator's father overcomes dire poverty to become a government dispenser, and her mother escapes from her own father's beatings to become a nurse. However, when her father is transferred to a new post in the Guyanese forest, he becomes forever separated from his family, leaving the narrator to rely only on her mother to achieve her ambition of studying abroad.

Of the narrator's neighbours, Mr. Braithwaite is a drunkard who kicks his family out; Misses Ada, Ida and Edna hold body and soul together by making and selling black pudding; Gatha is jilted and left with child by policeman Eustace; Eustace meanwhile loves Shirley, a striptease dancer who is first mauled by her lover's wife, and later murdered by Eustace; while Eustace, later still, commits suicide by throwing himself in front of a moving train.

Similarly raw, brutal and pitiful events overtake the few Indian-Guyanese who live in the narrator's village: Balgobin the milkman, Bahadur the grocer, and Ragunandan a cake shop owner. Like the narrator, Ragunandan's daughter Drupattie wins a scholarship to secondary school, but when she falls in love with Steven Osbourne - an African-Guyanese boy – her family's racist objections force her into an arranged Indian marriage that abruptly ends her academic career. Steven is later beaten by Indian-Guyanese, and Drupattie's uncle is stabbed, presumably by African-Guyanese, such actions being symptoms of ethnic rivalry that leads to politically-inspired riots, killings of members of both ethnic groups, and widespread destruction in Guyana, in 1962. In the end, the village madwoman - Banga Mary – offers perhaps the most prophetic analysis of such self-destruction: "One day race hate will mek dis country choke in its own blood" (197).

Because of its self-destructiveness, *A Coloured Girl* turns out less of a nostalgic idyll than a mixed, bitter-sweet chronicle, unsparingly realistic, poignant, and heightened by a feminist perspective that rightly celebrates the sustaining role of women in colonised societies. As she is about to leave for study abroad, the narrator is given two gold bangles by her father's aged and poverty-stricken mother who counsels her: "You are a woman now, an' yuh mus' kerry some'ting of me wid you… to let you remember de women yuh come dung from." [p. 101]

This is one of several instances where the narrator breaks the strict, chronological sequence of her narrative – another is when she later meets Steven Osbourne in New York - to extract profound pathos from characters, women as well as men, who display unyielding willpower if not to escape, at least, to struggle defiantly against the confining constraints of their colonial ring. DoHarris strikes gold with such pathos which, if we connect it to her father's reading of Shakespeare's sonnets in the Guyanese Interior, and to Edgar Mittelholzer's characters listening to European, classical music in the same forest, in *Shadows Move Among Them* (1951), proves it is a vein of pure, unadulterated, Guyanese gold.

"GOD DOAN COME BUT E' DOES SEN"

Brenda Chester DoHarris
Calabash Parkway. pp.158.
Bowie, Maryland, Tantaria Press, 2005.
ISBN 0-9770728-0-0

Calabash Parkway is the sequel to Brenda Chester DoHarris's first novel *A Coloured Girl in the Ring: A Guyanese Girl Remembers* (1997) which revels in heart-throbbing nostalgia for Guyana in the 1950s and 60s, a period of painful transition when Guyana moved, or staggered from its centuries-old status as a British colony to the longed-for glory of a newly independent nation. But while her personal or family history is front and centre in *Coloured Girl*, the author chooses to step back from the main action in *Calabash Parkway* in which she appears largely as observer, listener and narrator. Instead, two other characters from *Coloured Girl*, 'Gatha and Evadne, fellow residents of the author's home village of Kitty, are moved to centre stage of the second novel where the warm nostalgia of the 1950s and 60s is replaced, ironically, not with the glory of Independence, but with inglorious economic hardships and political horrors that induce tens of thousands of Guyanese to emigrate from their homeland.

DoHarris's second novel unites both the naturalness of a lowly fruit (the calabash) representing the Caribbean with the artificial affluence of a highway (Parkway) representing the US, as a way of focusing on Guyanese immigrants living mainly in

New York, during the 1970s and 80s. The novel's appeal stems mainly from a central tension between the desperate efforts of the main characters to escape from scandalous conditions in post-colonial Guyana, and their equally desperate struggles to cash in on the elusive affluence of the American promised land.

The Prologue of *Calabash Parkway* introduces 'Gatha who, in *Coloured Girl*, was notable merely as the jilted lover of Eustace, a policeman who later kills another of his lovers before committing suicide. In *Calabash Parkway*, however, 'Gatha is transformed into a more mature woman who, after reaching New York, mainly through luck, strikes out on a career of stunning resourcefulness and perseverance, working night and day, sending money home to her family in Guyana, prevailing over one setback after another , for example, losing her savings to burglars and having her visa application to the US being rejected, yet, finally, after ingeniously thwarting immigration authorities to re-enter the US via Canada, and re-join her American lover Jack Feelings, suddenly succumbing to a heart attack in Jack's arms. No doubt, her tragic death turns her success into a Pyrrhic victory; but her career is an absorbing saga of immigrant persistence, resilience and sheer guts. It also wonderfully dramatises the global inequality between North and South by depicting this rather abstract dichotomy, in concretely human terms, of people being forced to struggle for survival in alien and daunting circumstances not of their own making.

If 'Gatha dominates the action of *Calabash Parkway* from the Prologue to its final chapter, Evadne is not far behind. And just as luck first brings 'Gatha to New York as the paid companion of Eunice who is dying of cancer, so does a chance meeting bring Evadne to New York as the wife of a Guyanese-American Compton Thornhill. Nor are Evadne's struggles in New York any less compelling than 'Gatha's. Indeed, in some ways, they may be more so; for Evadne's relationship with

Compton becomes complicated when his former lover Jennifer gives birth to his daughter, Joy; and Evadne and Compton buy a house from Jennifer's sister producing complications with Jennifer shooting and killing Compton. So, although Evadne does not die like 'Gatha, she is disoriented enough to need recovery and regain her "psychic wholeness" [p. 131].

Perhaps the most striking feature of all is the documentary fidelity with which DoHarris evokes Guyanese culture and society, predominantly its African variety, both at home and abroad. Nothing proclaims the Guyanese identity of her narrative more than the idiomatic creole expressions or colloquialisms which, in addition to the speech of her characters, crowd almost every other page of *Calabash Parkway*, for example, "hungry daag a nyam kyalabash" [p. 1] or "God doan come, but 'e does sen'" [p. 16] These expressions both confirm Guyanese cultural authenticity, and provide philosophical commentary like the Chorus in Greek classical drama. Nor should the humour of these expressions be forgotten, especially when they combine with quotations from what the author calls the "spitpress" or rumour mill to stamp the narrative with its unmistakable Guyanese identity.

Since both novels have many of the same characters and concerns, it is natural for readers to compare *Calabash Parkway* with *Coloured Girl*. The main difference is that the substantial American setting in the *Calabash* causes the author to switch back and forth, in time and place, between New York and Guyana. But although switching is smooth, on the whole, it encourages reliance on coincidence, for example, chance meetings and sudden deaths, which can detract from full conviction. The relatively more coherent structure of *Coloured Girl* is probably what explains its greater dramatic power. Not that high drama is missing from *Calabash Parkway*. Two examples are 'Gatha's compassionate acceptance of Joy, daughter of her rival Jennifer, at Compton's funeral; and the reunion of Drupattie's daughter Samantha Seelochan with her father Steven Osbourne.

Calabash Parkway also abounds in examples of children separated from their parents and being brought up by the love and caring of others. It reflects the drama of flexible family structures that are vital in resisting the multiple fractures and dislocations caused by colonial and post-colonial trauma, and emigration in Guyana. No doubt, this type of social solidarity is influenced by the attitudes and rhetoric of US black civil rights and feminist movements of the 1960s as we see, for example, in a letter from Jack Feelings [p. 123]. It is rhetoric that asserts a peculiar black or African-American claim to "soul", and although "soul" is neither uniquely African nor black, it certainly flourishes both in the author and her characters in *Calabash Parkway*.

IMPROVED RACE RELATIONS IN ANGLOPHONE CARIBBEAN

Clive Sankardayal
The Brown Curtains. pp.288.
New York, Jako Books, 2007.

Although Clive Sankardayal's *The Brown Curtains* is neither explicitly political, nor exclusively Guyanese, it is strange how accurately the author's début novel captures the flavour of Guyanese politics, during the 1960s, when dictatorship and decline inflicted a sense of national collapse severe enough to drive tens of thousands of Guyanese to seek refuge in foreign lands. Fictional portraits of these immigrants appear in fiction by, among others, authors such as Fred D'Aguiar, David Dabydeen, Cyril Dabydeen, Sasenarine Persaud, and Brenda DoHarris, for example, in Britain, Canada and the US. But, after 1960, Guyanese settled in Caribbean islands too, albeit in smaller numbers than in Britain or North America, and *The Brown Curtains* adds one more item to fictional studies of Guyanese immigrants, this time, in other West Indian territories.

Up to the time that the novel's narrator, Guyanese school teacher, Ronald Singh, migrates to St. Lucia with friends - Rajendra Girdharry (Raj), Bramnarine Tiwari (Bram), and Narendra Chatterpaul (Nar), life in his West Coast Demerara village of Zeelugt, according to Ronald, was not bad until: "politically instigated race riots, pitting Indian against

Africans, forever changed Zeelugt." [p. 18] Worse still, riots: "spread over the land rapidly and destroyed the social fabric of society." [p. 18] It amounted to ethnic cleansing in which one ethnic group: "was forced to exchange dwellings and settle in a community of their own race in order to ensure safety for their families." [pp. 18-19] Migration was also driven by widespread bribery and corruption in government and: "kick down the door robbery." [p. 31] There is no doubt that Guyanese fleeing such conditions preferred the metropolitan centres already mentioned, but as we see from *The Brown Curtains*, West Indian islands like St. Lucia (and Barbados) sometimes served as stepping stones for Guyanese immigrants intent on reaching the more glittering Shangri-la of cities like New York or Toronto.

Ron and his friends settle smoothly in Mon Repos, St.Lucia, getting jobs and living together in a rented house with brown curtains. They buy groceries from Regis, a local entrepreneur, who uses his premises to stage films and other forms of entertainment, including cockfighting. If the four friends inevitably miss their families and frequently reminisce about their homeland, they nevertheless relish the absence from fear and tension that they left behind. Their main St. Lucian contact, with shop-keeper Regis, is more business-like than casual or social. Of the four Guyanese friends, only Raj, the youngest, really mixes socially, for instance, by developing a close relationship with a St. Lucian girl named Felicity.

During the school holidays, Ron, Bram and Nar return home to Guyana for a visit, and not until then does the novel really pick up steam. First, there is the predictable excitement and banter of Ron's joyful reunion with his wife Geetangali (Geet) and their children in Guyana, then their attendance at an Easter fête with loud music, kite flying and festive celebrations such as climbing the greasy pole: "Women and children sat carelessly and rocked to the blare of Indian music...Man, box, bird, diamond shaped and star pointed kites claimed the air and darted to and fro crazily." [p. 176]

It makes for a relaxing and enjoyable Guyanese home reunion, but it also brings news of Raj's relationship with Felicity which hits the Indian village of Zeelugt with the force of a tsunami. Ron, for example, is confronted from every quarter by dark hints, and suspicious, fearful mutterings of threatened violation: "I hear Girdo son [Raj] living with a black girl? True?" [p. 185] Nor does Raj's father Girdharry leave any doubt about his fellow villagers' unease when he candidly admits: "If Raj marry a black girl he go put me to shame." [p. 190]

To prevent this impending calamity, Girdharry arranges a marriage for Raj with the daughter of Ramroop, a rich Indian shop-keeper. He also pleads with Raj: "If was an Indian no matter she not Hindu, we woulda come around, but a black girl! My God, Lord Krishna! Why you punish me so, Raj? Is obeah they obeah you?" [p. 264] But all entreaties are in vain, since Raj goes ahead and marries Felicity, anyway. Yet this victory of true love over ethnic prejudice is more apparent than real, for the novel ends with a discussion of Raj's marriage between Ron and Mr. Girdharry in which the narrator feels a burning pain: "as if a centipede had just sunk its poisonous mandibles into my [his] flesh." [p. 288] The image captures the pain of Zeelugt villagers who believe that inter-racial marriage violates ancestral beliefs, especially when these prejudiced beliefs are compounded by "politically instigated race riots" and ethnic cleansing during the 1960s.

At the same time, Raj's marriage is advanced as a sign that traditional divisions of race, class, colour, and religion are beginning to loosen their grip on the Caribbean. The novel is awash in raw, coarse and bawdy humour of dialogue that crosses boundaries of race, class and colour, as seen, for instance, in the Guyanese Easter fête already mentioned, and in the Gros Islet street jam that later follows in St. Lucia. Cricket games in the novel also include players from different ethnic groups.

Not for nothing did the novel win the St. Lucia National Arts Award for Prose in 2005, a signal honour for a Guyanese author whose characters, despite differences of race, religion and diet, settle with such ease in St. Lucian society. Nor is it any wonder that *Brown Curtains* is announced on its back cover as: "one of the few West Indian novels to explore intra-Caribbean migration and cultural differences among CARICOM countries." It is ground-breaking and judicious exploration that holds out hope of improved race relations in the Anglophone Caribbean despite the hurt feelings or pain it may cause traditionalists.

"HUMBLED IN [GUYANA'S] MIGHTY CATHEDRAL OF FOREST"

Charlotte Williams
Sugar and Slate. pp.192.
Kingston, Jamaica, Ian Randle Publishers, 2002.
ISBN 976-637-065-6.

Sugar and Slate is a memoir by Charlotte Williams whose father, Denis Williams (1923-1998), enjoys an iconic reputation as painter, writer, anthropologist and art theorist among his Guyanese countrymen. In 1946 Denis won a British Council scholarship that took him to England where he studied art, established his reputation as a painter, and married a Welsh woman, Katie Alice, with whom he had six daughters. In 1957 Denis moved to Africa (Sudan, Nigeria, Uganda and Ghana) where his young family lived with him for a time before they moved back to Wales. Later, Denis returned to Guyana, and *Sugar and Slate* describes his daughter's journey exploring her identity as a person of mixed race who is also Welsh. The title of Charlotte's memoir refers both to her father's origin in a sugar-producing British Caribbean colony, and her mother's birthplace in the Welsh town of Bethesda, famous for slate quarries.

    Sugar and Slate is divided into three sections: "Africa" introduces Charlotte's family history including her parents' initial meeting in London, during the late 1940s, her childhood in Africa, in the 1950s, and her adult life in Beiteel a seaside town in Wales in the 1960s and 70s; "Guyana" gives Charlotte's impressions of Guyana following reunion there with her father in the 1980s; and "Wales" reflects both on her identity and her father's funeral in Guyana in 1998. Despite a discursive narrative with much going back and forth between episodes, a consecutive sense of chronology springs almost spontaneously out of the author's stubbornly unrelenting search for her true identity.

Ideas of freedom and independence for former colonies, like those in Africa and the Caribbean, germinate spontaneously at the end of World War Two, and explain why visitors to Denis and Katie Alice in London, at the time, included Michael Manley, Jan Carew, Wilson Harris and Forbes Burnham: "They were the Caribbean writers and artists and future leaders with visions and big thoughts. They were planning a different world." [p. 10]

When Charlotte's parents moved to the Welsh town of Beiteel there were no Blacks, although Blacks were not unknown in Wales, in port towns like Cardiff and Swansea. In 1892, for instance, a Training Institute had been set up in the small town of Colwyn Bay to train Africans as Christian missionaries who were expected to return to Africa and preach the gospel; but racial prejudice reared its head when some Africans remained and intermarried. In all-white Beiteel Charlotte felt alienated: "any associated reference to blackness haunted me. The word Africa alone did it to me for years." [p. 43] Although she was regarded as white in Africa, in Beiteel she was black: "I knew I stood for something but I had no idea what... black stood for nothing, nothing at all." [p. 47]

Denis had returned to Guyana in 1968, and had divorced not only Katie Alice, but his second wife Toni who was part-English and part-Scandinavian. By the time he met Charlotte again, in Guyana, in the 1980s, he had married a third wife, Jenny, this time a Guyanese. From her arrival in Guyana, Charlotte was appalled by irresponsible work habits of the airport staff, and later by the harsh combination of poverty, breakdown, dereliction and distress, for example a lorry accident had pulled down power lines and half the city would be without electricity for days; sections of the Demerara bridge broke loose and floated away; a child who is knocked down by a minibus bleeds to death - no ambulance; and Charlotte picks up an elderly woman who had collapsed on the pavement after waiting all day in vain to see a doctor at the Public Hospital in Georgetown: "The Burnham era had left a deep scar on the country's economy – low wages, food shortages and high crime." [p. 112]

Charlotte's observations are highly original, and her descriptions nothing less than brilliant in *Sugar and Slate*. When she visits Guyana's tropical interior, she is: "humbled in the mighty cathedral of forest" [p. 140] which, at night, becomes: "a sparkling vision of lights, flashing fountains of scintillating shapeless patterns across your eyes, like seeing stars from a blow to the head." [p. 145] Her summing up of the whole Caribbean as: "a congregation of the dislocated and the dispossessed!" [p. 149] is both perceptive and poetic.

Her father emerges almost as central to the story as herself. Denis, after all, had written a novel *Other Leopards* (1963) in which the hero, Lionel Froad, is a blend of two competing characters – Lionel, his educated European side, and Lobo his emotional African side. This psychic conflict dogged Denis all his life, and in one of his frequent rants against colonialism he rhetorically asks: "How can you speak, act, create anything if your every thought has been shaped for you by the European... [and] your language has been relegated to the status of babble?" [p. 53] He had also written books on art, and explored the pre-history of Guyana, while refusing funding for his research from Western sources or collaboration with Western academics. His daughter wisely comments: "He [Denis] had rejected the West but not the Western... he was rebuffing Lionel in his search for Lobo." [p. 115]

Charlotte longed for Guyana as ardently as Denis had pursued Africa, but her head finally prevails over her heart when she realises: "I had been chasing an idea of Guyanese-ness that would never be mine." [p. 184] The truth is she was neither Guyanese nor Welsh, and she had to change: "her perception of what it was to be Welsh or what it was to be Guyanese, or both." [p. 184] Charlotte concludes: "to be mixed race is not to be half of anything; mixed but not mixed up," [p. 191] and, in the end, she takes her father's advice: "You [Charlotte] have a symmetry with Wales you won't find here [in Guyana] ... Go back and find your own Wales... Go home." [p. 162] Charlotte does.

TALES OF GUYANESE DIASPORA IN TORONTO

Barney Singh
Tales in the Guyanese Vernacular.
Internet, Kindle Publication, 2012.
ISBN-13:978-1480186644.

Tales in the Guyanese Vernacular collects twenty-one stories by Basil Aybarran Singh aka Barney Singh (1927-2013), a Guyanese who studied Engineering in England and Holland in the 1950s, before returning home. In 1963, he migrated to Toronto, Canada where he lived until his death in 2012. In his "Acknowledgment," to *Tales,* Singh pays tribute to: "many persons who invited me to tell my stories at their functions and parties and to those who kept saying 'Write it down,'" suggesting that, along with his wife and five children, Singh enjoyed a rich, social life that included story telling in what he describes as: "my first language," a creole version of English that is known in Guyana as "creolese."

Apart from their colourful vocabulary and subject matter, Singh's stories touch an immediate chord of recognition, among Guyanese or West Indians, through their casual informality and random, oral structure, combined with a deeply rooted instinct for wit, laughter or comedy. As we gather from what the author has already said, his basic aim in *Tales* seems to be good natured fun and frolic among Guyanese countrymen and friends, peppered with banter, raillery, jokes, witticisms, farce, teasing, clowning and sheer foolery. Even if some stories contain characters, complications and situations of climax followed by resolution, more often than not what we get are mere snippets of action, anecdotes, brief incidents or bare sketches that justify themselves purely by their comic potential.

"Miss Ellany," for example, a deliberate play on the word "miscellany," consists of seven unconnected anecdotes introduced by a brief *apologia* from the author explaining that, despite their unstructured appearance, his stories contain: "a prolific supply of treasures" for which "miscellaneous" becomes: "an unsatisfactory word as it implies the flotsam and jetsam of life and unimportant details that may be ignored." On the contrary, each anecdote: "brings a smile or jogs your memory." For instance, "Life after death" will appeal especially to cricket fans by describing two friends in heaven recalling their unbridled delight in past cricket contests.

"Prophet Wills" offers the tragi-comic portrait of a well known Guyanese eccentric, noted for dressing in excessively formal, but badly soiled clothes, and given to didactic speech or exaggerated and misplaced erudition, for example, in declaiming: "Oh Supreme Omnipotent, a ferocious canine has hold of the lower extremity of my anatomy," when all he means is "Oh God, a bad dog bit my foot." "Basra", meanwhile, recalls pleasant memories and nostalgic glimpses of history evoked by the paddle wheel steamer "Basra" on a Guyanese river; and "At de Mall" meditates on the wonder and incongruity of two Guyanese women using creolese to discuss goods on display in the stores of a mall in Toronto. "No Signature" is another story that consists similarly of unconnected but amusing incidents or anecdotes.

Many stories consider immigrant struggles to find employment or adjust to life in Canada. In "Putuss," for instance, the hero despairs of finding employment until a fellow Guyanese advises him to anglicise his name from "Putuss" to "Percy" and adapt his strategy. In another story, Ramotar is so confused by Toronto that after buying a ticket, he runs behind the bus instead of boarding it. He does this regularly to save the fare until his wife wryly advises him to try running after a taxi instead since he would "save" more from the higher taxi fare.

In yet another story, when, through hard work, Rookmin achieves money and prestige in Canada, she becomes conceited or "brigah," adopting a Canadian accent and what she thinks are superior manners that encourage her to disdain commonplace things, and snub familiar people while on a trip home to Guyana. But on a visit to Bourda market, she suddenly screams: "Oh rass, man! De crab bite me fingah. Oh God! Somebady help me loose off dis tentaleh from me fingah." If Rookmin's come-uppance produces raw humour, her predicament rises to the level of a folktale when it ends with the sage aphorism: "Pyass all yuh want pun yuh mattie man but not pun crab. Crab is no respecter of persons."

In his "Addendum" Singh reprints two stories from Michael McTurk's *Essays and Fables in the Vernacular of the Creoles of British Guiana* (1899) which employs creolese at a stage of its evolution when it was most strongly influenced by the speech of Africans or former slaves. Singh updates both stories with versions of his own reflecting influence from later indentured immigrant groups like Indians, Chinese and Madeirans. Comparisons between Singh's stories and creole narratives by other West Indian writers are also interesting, for example, between Ramotar and the Jamaican lady Tanty who fears the double decker London bus would capsize in Samuel Selvon's novel *The Lonely Londoners*.

As the author explains, his writing in "Tales" originates in spoken performances, but their inherent orality does not automatically trivialise Singh's stories or transform them into exotic displays of the diasporic experience of Guyanese or West Indian immigrants, simply to relieve longings of nostalgia or homesickness. As Singh hints, immigrants, West Indian or otherwise, are not the simple flotsam or jetsam of life: their struggles in adjusting to a new culture should be seen as authentic "treasures" rather than adventitious or unimportant details. Singh's stories are an expression of cultural survival staking a claim of authenticity for Caribbean people, side by side with other ethnic groups, in a new, complex, dynamic and ever-evolving multicultural environment in Canada. This, at any rate, is Singh's hope since his "Acknowledgment" also mentions that, having been captured in print, his stories: "will stay 'alive' and accessible to many generations of Guyanese."

POST-COLONIALISM IN INDIAN-GUYANESE-CANADIAN WRITING

Cyril Dabydeen
Drums of my Flesh. pp.234.
Toronto, TSAR, 2005.
ISBN 1-894770-25-0

Drums of my Flesh is the seventeenth book and third novel of Cyril Dabydeen who is also author of eight collections of poems and five volumes of stories, and two anthologies of poems and one of fiction. Dabydeen was born in Guyana in 1945 and, in addition to his remarkable productivity since arriving in Canada, in 1970, is something of a literary pioneer. Apart from the Barbadian Austin Clarke and late Trinidadian Sonny Ladoo, Dabydeen is the only other well known West Indian writer who had begun his career in Canada by the early 1970s. *Drums* won the Guyana Prize for Best Book of Fiction in 2007 and was nominated for the IMPAC Dublin Literary Award also in 2007.

Drums consists of a Prologue and Epilogue as well as forty-four chapters divided into seven sections. While the Indian-Guyanese narrator of the novel Boyo is a Canadian immigrant speaking throughout the novel to his half-white, Canadian-born daughter Catriona, in a park in Ottawa, the autobiographical incidents he recollects take place during the 1950s and 60s, chiefly in two heavily Indian or Hindu populated districts in his homeland: the sugar estate of Canje, and the village of Brighton, both in the county of Berbice. Information about his Guyanese past is meant to help his daughter cope better as someone of mixed blood and culture in Canada.

The plot follows the narrator's family history in rural Guyana where Boyo's alcoholic father Gabe regularly abuses his mother Dee, causing her to flee with her children - Boyo, brothers Dev and Anand – from their home in Brighton, on the Corentyne coast to their grandmother's (Dee's mother's) home in Canje. Grandma's home becomes a refuge with Dee constantly glued to her sewing machine, earning money for an independent life. Boyo and his brothers, meanwhile, make periodic visits back to Brighton where they catch crabs, observe life on a farm, and mingle with both their father and his mother whom they know as Ma.

They also encounter Fatima, their father's mistress who is described as his "consort," someone who: "appeared and disappeared at will... Something instinctual being renewed or relived each time they were at it." [p. 137] In Brighton, most of all, Dee's sons meet Gabe's cherished friend and counsellor - Jaffe, an old and half-blind Muslim man who believes he is descended from Alexander the Great, and is fondly regarded by Gabe as a prophetic figure, legendary world traveller and: "an eternal witness to all the world's beliefs." [p. 81]

As far as family history goes, the narrator's mother remarries and two more children Stan and Sarah are born; but trouble erupts both between Dee and her second husband, and between Gabe and Fatima who finally leaves, setting Gabe free to re-marry. Dabydeen's portrait of lives disfigured by poverty and violence is matched in fiction by other Guyanese writers, for instance, Lauchmonen (pseudonym for Peter Kempadoo) and Rooplall Monar. Like *Drums,* the action of Lauchmonen's novel *Guiana Boy* takes place on the Corentyne coast, and although it acknowledges similar physical hardship and struggle, also suggests an idyllic picture of boyhood adventures in a tropical milieu. Monar's stories are enacted in districts in the county of Demerara where they wholly confirm similarly loose family relationships and bare, rough and ready survival so typical of rural Guyana during British colonial times, up to the 1950s and 60s.

But Boyo's narrative of his Guyanese childhood is not presented in the consecutive, linear fashion implied by this brief synopsis. For all its potentially dramatic scenes of family conflict and travail, for example: "My father in a drunken stupor, rolling in a ditch. Somewhere," [p. 158] the novel's action seems deliberately staged, and staid, inviting little reaction to themselves as events linked in consecutive, purposeful order. Instead, chapters appear as virtually independent poems evoking general thoughts, feelings, themes and motifs. The narrator truthfully claims: "a fanciful tale I'm weaving of an insubstantial but real world." [p. 163] Thus, far from establishing imaginative order over the insubstantial flux and disorder of ordinary life, as dictated by older theories of art, Dabydeen consciously revels in postcolonial or postmodern celebration of disorder and flux in a Guyanese context.

As we know, Dabydeen is no novice in fiction: *Drums* emerges at the height of his literary powers. In an interview in 1991, he uses the example of a pendulum to explain how his imagination swings from Ottawa to Guyana or the Caribbean. As an immigrant writer in Canada, Dabydeen deploys action consisting of a bare outline of events, before they are quickly overlaid by an almost involuntary interaction between "images and echoes" that flood the author's mind from the Caribbean. This is why the author admits to splicing time and space, tropical and temperate worlds in *Drums*. His success is to ensure that these spliced "images and echoes" fit into a metaphysical structure linked or related to the novel's action.

Dabydeen displays versatile skills as a writer of fiction and poetry, making it difficult to decide if he is more successful in one genre than another. His greater productivity in poems and short stories suggests that he finds these (shorter) forms more congenial than the novel. Still, *Drums* regales us with a profusion of allusions and references to universal subjects and topics in history, geography, philosophy and the world's religions, myths and legends all geared to foster Catriona's global Canadian outlook. Whether strictly linked or not, the poetic richness of these allusions and references is an achievement by itself.

INDIAN-GUYANESE-CANADIAN: WHERE IS HOME?

Cyril Dabydeen
My Multi-Ethnic Friends and Other Stories. pp.204.
Guernica EditionsInc.Toronto, 2013.
ISBN 978-1-55071-705-1

The work of Cyril Dabydeen, an Indian-Guyanese who has lived in Canada since 1970, seems rather neglected for someone credited with four novels, eight volumes of poems, four anthologies and eight collections of stories of which *My Multi-Ethnic Friends and Other Stories* is the most recent example. Neglect seems all the more likely when we consider the enthusiastic reception given to the work of two other authors who are Dabydeen's closest Caribbean-Canadian-contemporaries, Austin Clarke of Barbados, and Dionne Brand of Trinidad and Tobago.

Clarke's first novel *Survivors of the Crossing* appeared in 1964, and his *The Polished Hoe* won the most glittering Canadian literary prize, the Giller, in 2002; he is also honoured as virtually the creator of black Canadian literature. After her first book of poems *Foreday Morning* in 1978, Dionne Brand took the Governor General's Award for poetry in 1990 and 1997 when her *Land to Light On* also claimed the Trillium Book Award. By contrast, Dabydeen's first Canadian work *Distances*, a volume of poems, appeared since 1977, after which he served only as poet laureate of Ottawa from 1984 to 1987.

If, as Dabydeen first believed, this discrepancy was partly due to his residence in Ottawa, away from more cosmopolitan and stimulating literary and artistic influences of the big city atmosphere of Toronto, he at least deserves credit for perseverance. His career was sustained by seasonal teaching at the University of Ottawa, and working for federal and municipal governments centred in Ottawa; and it may not be misguided to detect in his writing a preference for the caution, reserve and balance of a town that serves as the nation's capital city.

The title story of *Multi-Ethnic Friends* dramatises meetings of the National Municipal Affairs Committee (NMAC) whose members are faced with the task of recommending: "action that will eliminate racial discrimination in the new nation now before us." [p. 51] The new nation, fashioned under patronage of Prime Minister Pierre Elliot Trudeau, in the 1970s, professes a new age ideology of multiculturalism. Members of the NMAC, many of them drawn from every race and colour, are agog with missionary passion, eager to debate issues and claims that may help to promote harmony among all ethnicities, religions and cultures. One committee member Lilian: "argues that schools must all adopt a comprehensive race-relations policy," and she follows up with magazines "to spread the message." [p. 56] But the narrator is skeptical, and asks: "To eliminate ... what in the North?" [p. 56] clearly implying, with his own brand of caution and reserve, the super-heated folly of mouthing such inane precepts and empty, impractical platitudes.

From the beginning, as with most Caribbean-Canadian authors, Dabydeen considers the plight of immigrants in Canada. In "Bearing Gifts" in *Multi-Ethnic Friends*, for instance, despite their general preoccupation with philosophical and political issues, Greek, Nigerian and Canadian university students are troubled by their sense of dislocation: "Where's real home?" [p. 88] Questions also arise about a sense of belonging, and the seemingly marginal role of immigrants as outsiders in Canada. Even a home-grown Canadian like Helene, from British Columbia, wonders: "about place, and about where's genuine home... Helene added that every province was her home, though each seemed like a separate country to her; it was what no outsider understood." [pp. 82-83] If this is not mysterious enough, a Greek student is asked:" "You don't belong here. [Canada} But where?" In the end, whether it is in Canada or elsewhere, the concept of "home" is so puzzling it appears partly mythical: "it was really about where one's forebears came from, if with gods and goddesses only."[p. 90] "Home," in other words, is just as elusive as ethnic or racial equality.

But rather than familiar themes such as ethnicity, colour, class, exile or home, what really separates Dabydeen from other Caribbean-Canadian authors is his perspective. For instance, his technique of magic realism lends a peculiar poise to his immigrant characters. In *Multi-Ethnic Friends.*, for instance, "The Starapple Canadian" dramatises the attraction of Guyanese toward Canada by means of whimsical images and conversations that capture aspects of Guyanese-Canadian relationships that might elude the reach of a more realistic narrative. The narrator, a Guyanese-Canadian immigrant on a visit home to his family in the rural, Corentyne district of Guyana, is named by an "eight-year-old girl with knotty hair" [p. 18] after a delicious, juicy and fleshy local fruit known as a starapple - a name that catches elements of fantasy and make-believe in the attitudes of Guyanese toward Canadians (and Americans) whom they automatically associate with Hollywood glamour and affluence.

The richness of "Starapple Canadian" is seen in multiple meanings derived from literary, religious and other references, and speech patterns, both Guyanese and Canadian, combined with a seemingly whimsical use of rhetorical, oral devices such as repetition of the informal "see" as in "the time of the horse's death, see" [p. 22] or

"It's not only Danny, see." [p. 26] Other stories employ inverted syntax "beguiling he sounded" [p. 41] and frequent rhetorical questions all of which create lightness of mood or playful unassertiveness.

What all this has to do with Ottawa may not be entirely clear, but the narrator in "Bearing Gifts" does mention: "government talk about ball-park figures, cost-benefit analysis, paradigm shifts. Buzz words or phrases ubiquitous, you see. 'It's what must be endured to save a country.'" [p. 84] Dabydeen's fiction is an undoubted mix of Guyana and Canada, not only in subject, but spirit. Had he remained in Guyana after 1970, it is unlikely he could have written the stories in *Multi-Ethnic Stories*. Forty-odd years of residence not only in Canada, but in Ottawa, have made a difference that now yields fiction with the lightness of Stephen Leacock's touch, the polemical energy of Margaret Atwood, and the deeply plumbed emotional resources of Alice Munro. Cyril Dabydeen has arrived.

"THE WAY THINGS WERE IN THE WORLD"

N.D. Williams
The Silence of Islands. pp.196.
Leeds, Peepal Tree Press Ltd. 1994.
ISBN 0-948833-46-7

The Silence of Islands is the first novel and second book of
Guyanese author N.D. Williams. Events unfold in "the city,"
New York, beginning with the arrival of Delia Mohammed,
a young Indian, Muslim woman and illegal immigrant or
"alien" from "the islands," presumably Trinidad, if we go by
her frequent reference to the popularity of Carnival in her
homeland. Delia first travelled by plane to Toronto along
with her black boy friend whose name "Trinidad" always,
disconcertingly, makes the reader wonder whether it's him or
his home island being mentioned.

Although the novel consists mainly of Delia's activities in
New York and her Caribbean homeland, it opens with a brief
"Prologue" by a middle aged Fillipino, Mr. Ni Win, who welcomes
Delia before he intervenes again, halfway through the novel, when
he reports that Delia is missing, and reveals the rest of her narrative
that he has rescued from notebooks she has left behind. Ni Win's
third intervention, in the last chapter of the novel, completes a
circular structure beginning with Delia's arrival, and ending
with her story after she disappears, including her account of the
death of her Haitian friend Danielle, which is reported in the first
chapter and fully described only at the very end.

Out of all this, Delia, a "frail wispy unsure person," [p. 91] emerges as pitifully vulnerable and victimised, her fragmentary biography riddled with mystery, perplexity, violence and fear. According to her biography, she and Trinidad work together in a bank at home, and leave under a cloud of suspicion over stolen money, although Delia doesn't even know about their alleged theft until her father visits while she lives alone in New York waiting for Trinidad to join her. When Trinidad eventually shows up, Delia gets a whiff of shady dealings, with the smell of marijuana in their room, and the discovery of a bag under her bed: "with someone's money, about an entire life savings." [p. 149] Delia is: "awash with fear and suspicion."[p. 149] The bag of money is: "like a saboteur's bomb," [p. 14] and the room: "like the place where some angry act of vengeance would be enacted one day." [p. 149] It is not only Delia, or aliens, or West Indian immigrants, or people in her neighbourhood, but New York, the US, and all of us who face this threat of vengeance. For the truth is that *The Silence of Islands* packs a prophetic punch through its portrayal of stark opposition between what used to be called the West and the rest of us, between developed or rich nations, and undeveloped or poor, Southern nations.

In the novel's portrait of New York itself, this contrast is seen in the difference between the: "ruin and desolation" [p. 20] of Delia's immigrant-infested neighbourhood with its: "throwaways, used-up persons, scratching out a bare existence," and not far away, standing proudly in regal affluence: "the towers of greed and profit". [p. 21] Also, the mere physical layout of life in New York is torture for Delia: "The doors to apartments, each with a number, made you feel alien, vulnerable, placeless." [p. 94] Delia is frightened by every thing from: "the snow-crusted pavements on which you must learn anew to walk" to the buildings themselves which: "tower like scaffolds over the condemned of the streets." [p. 101] These images may be threatening: they also convey brutal truths.

Truths are suggested in the novel's impressive array of literary references that includes English authors from Chaucer on. Shakespeare, for example, is quoted many times especially his *King Lear*, in which Cordelia is punished for her failure to articulate her love for her father as glibly as her hypocritical older sisters. Comparison between Cordelia and her namesake Delia, as innocent and vulnerable victims of an unequal and implacably cruel world order is the core of the novel, and its chief message is driven home. According to Williams, had Cordelia lived in a city today: "she might have fled even faster into the dungeon of her silence" [p. 50] for: "there's a meanness at the core, resentment like thick rind around the heart of a city," with its deceptive eagerness for saying: "I love you Dad. I love you Mom," [p. 50] as readily as Cordelia's sisters.

In explication of his title, when Williams writes: "Silence, not words, was our way of communing," [p. 133] we realise that "Silence" refers both to the powerlessness or victimisation of characters like Cordelia and Delia, or Southern nations in Asia, Africa, the Caribbean and Latin America, and to the tragic contrast between their vulnerable innocence and the coldly organised, soullessly routine amorality of a Northern city, which can carry out an abortion on Danielle in a: "tall building, all glass and stone and drawn blinds," with efficient, cynical and business-like routine: "Somewhere inside they stopped the beating heart of a foetus while on other floors they sold car insurance, or repaired computer units." [pp. 178-179]

At one level, while *The Silence of Islands* belongs to a genre of post-colonial writing that explores the mundane details of Caribbean, diasporic experience abroad, the hidden power of the novel's poetic diction, evident in quotations above, its seamless structure, suggestive literary references, and profound meditation on the psychological and philosophical implications of unequal, political relationships, lift Williams's novel to a level paralleled only by the best post-colonial literature, for example, the Sudanese author, Tayeb Salih's novel *Season of Migration to the North,* (1966) which searchingly probes issues of love/hate and silence that, inevitably, stem from unequal contact between strong and weak nations. It is why, in his final intervention, Ni Win confesses with abject, baffled resignation: "I became a man who could not change the way things were in the world. A man of silence." [p. 195]

WEST INDIAN CIVILISATION

N.D. Williams,
Julie Mango. pp.269.
Leeds, Peepal Tree Press, 2004.
ISBN 1-900715-77-5. First published by Xlibris Corporation
in U.S.A. 2000.

The nine stories in *Julie Mango,* N.D. Williams's fifth work of
fiction, roam from one Caribbean territory to the other, and
from these territories to popular destinations of Caribbean
migration such as Britain and the US. No doubt these stories
also stem directly from the experience of an author who was
born in Guyana (in 1942) and lived in various Caribbean
islands, during the 1960s and 70s, before settling in the US.
As well as physical dislocation, the stories project a prevailing
sense of inward disconnection in characters who appear mostly
as wayfaring wanderers, bereft of any solid notion either of
who they are, where they come from, or where they are going.

The title story "Julie Mango: Or, Yu see Har Dere?" is
the first in the volume. The fruit - Julie mango - which is
regarded as a delicacy in Jamaica, hints at the stunning, sexual
appeal of the story's heroine, Julie, a nurse who was born on a
Caribbean island that is as nameless as islands in other stories
in Williams's volume. So rampant is Julie's sexuality that it
inspires both her affair with an English doctor on her island,
and salacious gossip from fellow islanders; and all this we are
told by the narrator, a garrulous rum shop proprietor, who

acknowledges the orality of his island culture with disarmingly candid and conspiratorial charm: "Much gossip, scandal and intrigue prevail, and conversation is sometimes like an open sewer running down the middle of the street." [p. 11]

Julie ends her affair with her English lover when he fails to rescue her during a hurricane. She then goes off to England from where we get news of her consorting with male members of the aristocracy, before joining a photojournalist assigned to an African country, in the middle of a civil war. Julie's successful sexual seductiveness and appetite for reckless adventure seem boundless. Desirable and daring as she might be, however, the positive effect of these qualities is dispersed if not negated by her restless movement and general extravagance. The question mark in the title of her story surely arouses our puzzlement, doubt, perhaps even distress about her.

If Julie's conduct appears distressing, the relationship between the unnamed narrator of "Trinculo Walks the Dog" and his Caribbean homeland is no more comforting. His homeland can be readily identified as Guyana from descriptions such as: "a pocket-size republic," [p. 32] "shores washed by muddy waters of the Atlantic," [p. 32] and other geographical markers. The narrator has a Ph.D. from Cambridge University, while his father is a dentist in Guyana, and his brother a dental student in Canada; but eventually the entire family settle in Canada. Dispersal of the narrator's family illustrates a process of political corruption and national economic decline: "something rotten and deeply worrying, undermining the fabric of our family lives" [p. 35] that eventually drives Guyanese and other Caribbean people away from their homeland. Another story, "Your Slip is Showing Comrade," presents a similarly stark portrait of fear and corruption in Forbes Burnham's Guyana although, as already hinted, there is no explicit mention of names of politicians or Caribbean countries.

"Light of the World," perhaps the centre piece of *Julie Mango,* is a story that takes its title from a poem by Derek Walcott (in his 1987 collection *The Arkansas Testament*). In the poem, while riding on a taxi in the town of Castries, the St. Lucian birthplace of Walcott, the persona observes an old woman with two heavy baskets hobbling in desperation to catch the taxi, and pleading with the driver: "'Pas quittez moi a terre' / which means, in her patois 'Don't leave me stranded'/ which means, in her literal history and that of her people: / 'Don't leave me on earth, '" a quotation that serves as the first of two epigraphs to *Julie Mango.*

As the persona also observes, the old woman's sense of abandonment is part and parcel of Caribbean history: "Abandonment was something they [Caribbean people] had grown used to." [*Arkansas Testament* p. 50] At the same time, the persona is captivated by the beauty of a local, black, woman passenger who moves him to confess: "O Beauty, you are the light of the world;" [*Arkansas Testament* p.48] and the total effect of this woman's beauty, the desperate plight of the old woman, and the taxi driver's blaring music of Bob Marley, one of whose verses forms the second epitaph to *Julie Mango,* stirs up such turbulent feelings of "great love" and "pity" in the persona, that when he later leaves the taxi, he cannot help turning away to conceal his tears.

As mentioned in the beginning, feelings of disconnection, dislocation or abandonment appear in most stories in *Julie Mango.* For example, in "Monkey Wrenching Snaps," Hunter Michael Valcin, son of a Magistrate on a Caribbean island, teaches at a New York university, and compares his life to a spaceship built by NASA technicians who, like his teachers, have launched him: "spinning weightlessly around the planet, void of purpose, with no connection to mission control anywhere." [p. 125] Not that agonising over identity is new to Caribbean literature: it is probably the most enduring theme in the early work of Brathwaite and Walcott, Selvon and Naipaul, more than half a century ago, when independence was, foolishly, if understandably, anticipated with hope and promise.

Now this theme is updated in Williams's fiction, in a post-independence era, when anticipation has turned into lamentation, hope almost into total despair, and all is aimless, wayfaring wandering, through the imagination as well as in real life. Through his use of original, contemporary images, and remarkable, technical skills that dexterously shift gears from first to third person, or from one narrator to the other, Williams sheds new light on old themes, and updates us with alarming candour on the disturbed and disturbing condition of West Indian civilisation at the turn of the twenty-first century.

"EVEN WHEN WORDS FAIL, SEX CAN BE RELIED ON TO TELL THE TRUTH"

N.D. Williams
The Friendship of Shoes. pp.161.
XLibris Corporation, U.S.A. 2006.
ISBN 1-59926-041-7

The Friendship of Shoes, the author's eighth work of fiction, contains eleven stories by N.D.Williams who was born in Guyana, in 1942, and educated at the University of the West Indies in Mona, Jamaica. Most stories take place in New York city, and are related in the first person, usually by a black, male, West Indian immigrant or visitor, although female or Indian-West Indian narrators also occasionally appear. For instance, events in "Ms. Brody" are related by one of the pupils at St. Hilda's School for Girls on her Caribbean home island, even if the chief protagonist, the narrator's teacher – Ms. Brody – later visits New York, and decides to remain there. The author's collective portrait of a hodgepodge of Caribbean immigrants, in restless movement, in *Friendship*, reflects impressive familiarity both with pan-Caribbean traits or manners, and with diasporic West Indian experience in the US.

The opening story in *Friendship* -"Blog: or, What I Know About People"- portrays teachers and pupils, not in the Caribbean, but in the larger, multicultural context of a school of three and a half thousand students, in New York city, in the 1990s. On display are complicated relationships between local teachers such as Jewish Mrs. Schlesinger, and immigrant teachers like the Arab-American Mr Hamid, Ms. Amanda Kitchenamourty who was born in California, but whose father came from Sri Lanka in the 1980s, not to mention the unnamed black, Trinidadian narrator who looks like: "the [American] movie actor James Earl Jones ...tall, and bulky and brown-skinned." [p. 13] For all this multicultural melée, school activities in "Blog" flourish in a relatively calm atmosphere compared to another New York school in "The Cleaner" where students: "get arrested all the time," [p. 87] one teacher, Miss Spiny, was suspended because she struck a student with: "a sheet of loose leaf paper," [p. 85] and the principal, Mr. Knispel, is arrested for using his computer at home: "to set up meetings with girls just fourteen or fifteen years old." [p. 86]

Mr. Knispel's alleged offence, labelled as "a cybersex crime," [p. 86] exhibits both his story's contemporary currency, and the heightened sexual interest of most stories in *Friendship*. This is why "Blog" may be seen as deceptive, for although it appears calm or uncontroversial on the surface, sex is never very far from the mind of its narrator who not only describes himself as "womanless," but detects that "the moist blue" in a female teacher's eyes "spoke as clear as sky, *I would really like to f... you tonight.*" [p. 22] Even tight-laced Abigail Brody who spends a lifetime of unremitting toil instilling virtuous principles and high-minded ideals into her young, female charges at St Hilda's School for Girls, degenerates, by the end of her story, into someone to whom pure sensation and raw lust prove irresistible.

An important aspect of her story's dénouement is that Abigail Brody who is born in the West Indies is probably white or almost white. The author's astute reticence on this point hints at his protagonist's uncharacteristic gesture, toward the end of her visit to New York, when she becomes so besotted by one of the contestants in a Body Building contest: "this black god! The bulge of his manhood like a baby asleep in its pouch!" [p. 120] that, although her "black Adonis" doesn't win first prize, she decides that she: "was getting married to [him] a black body builder and never coming back to St. Hilda's." [p. 120] Nor is Ms. Brody guilty of perversity any more than Mr. Knispel in "The Cleaner," since their activities illustrate one of the author's epigraphs to his volume assigning sex a central, perhaps transgressive role in our lives: "Even when words fail, sex can be relied on to tell the truth," quoted from the South African novelist J.M. Coetzee.

A second epigraph, a Guyanese folk saying, "Moon a run, till sun ketch am," implies cyclic patterns that play as vital a role among planets as sex does in ordinary human lives; and both epigraphs connect with the title story of a woman in Guyana who reports killing her husband with his own cutlass, because he betrayed her with another woman. In somewhat bizarre fashion, her husband's apparently lifeless corpse then gives up the ghost only after his shoes are put on, invoking awareness, running through the very heart of Williams's fiction, of unmistakable connectedness universally, amidst flux and change, especially among Caribbean people whose lives, already broken by divisions from an history of slavery and indenture, now face continuing fragmentation through chronic dependence on immigration.

In the final story "Fly a Kite with us, Johann" the black Guyanese narrator who lives in New York city runs into a white girl, Julia, at a Manhattan music store where she has just bought a CD of Bach's "St. John's Passion." As their relationship deepens, Julia learns about the narrator's family, and his father's uncle - Mr. Ingram –who was a music composer since the 1930s and, now in old age, still lives in New York. Julia's imagination is fired by the idea of a great, unknown, black composer. She is also enthused with the idea of visiting Guyana after hearing about the popular Guyanese past-time of kite flying at Easter; and when she learns that a church choir sang at the funeral of Mr. Ingram's grandfather, years ago in Guyana, she instinctively jumps to the conclusion that the choir sang Bach's "St. John's Passion," because she insists: "everything in life is connected." [p. 161] Taken aback, the narrator is naturally sceptical; but, on reflection, he warms to Julia's view that: "it [her imagination] could move us in new directions. Hundreds of kites dancing in the sky, the steps of an old crumbling church, a tree-lined street, soaring voices lifting our spirits to the heavens... this would be no wild-goose chase in pursuit of happiness." [p. 161]

THE CARIBBEAN – HISTORIC BREEDING GROUND FOR REVOLUTION

Ken Puddicombe
Junta: The Coup Is On. pp.365.
MiddleRoad Publishers, 2014.
ISBN 878-14975-3558-9

If readers of *Racing With the Rain* (2012), the first novel of Guyanese-Canadian author Ken Puddicombe, remember ethnic rivalry, class prejudice and social injustice leading to violence and near anarchy, in Guyana, in the 1960s, they can expect a more finely etched portrait of the same combination in the author's second novel *Junta: The Coup is On.* Puddicombe's second novel is not a carbon copy of his first: while the action of *Racing* takes place in Guyana during the 1960s, the story of *Junta* unfolds, during 1979, in Saint Anglia, a fictional island in the Southern Caribbean sea; but in both novels deep-seated, ethnic division and endemic, social and political differences manure historic breeding grounds to make them more fruitful in exploitation and revolution.

Junta opens with a meeting between two chief characters, Marcus Jacobson, descendant of an old white, plantation-owning family in Saint Anglia, and Melanie Sanderson whose father, now retired, was a former Premier of the island. Marcus left Saint Anglia in 1956, at the age of seventeen, for studies in England, and returns now, in 1979, to become Professor of history in the local university. Melanie, whose father is white and mother black, is a student leader at the local university. According to Marcus's chauffeur, Wilson Kentish, a kind of wise fool, capable of some of the novel's shrewdest insights, Saint Anglia flourished during the régime of Melanie's father: "After Independence, though, the party kick out Sanderson, because he was white. He was good but they say you can't have a white man as Prime Minister when a black country is free... Then they bring in Manning, just because he was black. And that is when the corruption started." [p. 101]

This sequence of events leads to an army coup early in the novel, while the rest of the narrative relates public reactions to the coup, mixed with episodes of a seemingly romantic relationship between Marcus and Melanie. When Sandhurst-trained General Septimus Ignatious Marks formally announces reasons for his army's intervention, he blames: "growing communist insurrection" "bombs...property damaged, lives lost, people injured." [p. 120] He also states that the deposed (but democratically elected) government failed to preserve law and order, and: "pillaged the treasury and sucked it dry," [p. 121] – familiar charges in Caribbean countries, in the Cold War era.

From this summary alone, we sense beginnings of a political thriller as suspense builds between an army that seizes power by force, and a population that musters resistance through defiance from individuals like Melanie. Hence the need for a resolution between military dictatorship and democracy. To heighten the atmosphere of growing insecurity and danger, Puddicombe introduces regular bulletins on the approach of hurricane David as it devastates the already poverty-stricken islanders, made even more vulnerable by their pitiful political rumblings. It is another stroke of originality for Puddicombe, out of such raw material, to revive the genre of the political thriller which, though rare in West Indian literature, nowadays, recalls fiction, for instance, by the Jamaican John Hearne, in association with Morris Cargill, and novels by Puddicombe's compatriot Edgar Mittelholzer, in the 1950s and 60s.

What Puddicombe does is to inject seriousness into an exotic, Caribbean background formerly used largely as a holiday setting for scenes of adventure, romance and high jinks; in *Junta* there is nothing entertaining about destruction and damage engineered by an army through "Operation Undermine" in which gangs of thugs are led by Thomas Jefferson Freeman, a sinister, black American known as "Reverend" and linked to Jim Jones from the notorious "Jonestown" tragedy in Guyana. The damage caused by Reverend and his henchman Cockeye Charlie, and their thugs, is then blamed on (non-existent) communists who, we are told, can only be eradicated by a military coup.

This cunning justification of deception and wanton destruction does not pass unnoticed by responsible Santa Anglians such as Father Herbert de Groot, a white priest familiarly called Fr. Bert, who runs an orphanage and is dubbed: "the first socialist priest in the Caribbean." [p. 115] Another democrat is Clarence Baptiste who, after arriving from England at the age of six, has lived on the island all his life, and is now owner and Managing Editor of the Gleaner newspaper. Even more outspoken is Melanie who leads a protest march. It is Melanie's idealistic hostility to military dictatorship, together with her abortive, romantic entanglement with Marcus, that transform *Junta* from a merely entertaining adventure story of jostling for power to a more thoughtful and subtle political study.

Throughout the novel, Marcus, whose wife and daughter were sent away to Canada at the beginning, seems non-committal both about his feelings for Melanie, or about the fierce, democratic principles she voices in protest against the junta. Yet, when he says goodbye to Melanie at the airport, she admits that she will likely marry the new head of the army, and leader of the government - Glen Stevenson - who was her former lover. Feeling guilty that marriage will compromise her previously over-heated political principles, she also quickly asserts: "if Glen thinks he can use me to achieve his ends, I can do the same." [p. 364] Then she stares into her glass: "The ice cubes had disappeared. Life was just an endless journey down a circuitous path... Water to ice, and back to water again." [p. 364] This idea that change is impossible may be cynical or Machiavellian; but it is, perhaps, the novel's most realistic resolution to conflict between dictatorship and democracy in a Caribbean milieu.

"DEATH SHALL NOT FIND US THINKING THAT WE DIE"

Robert Lalljie (Ed).
A Bouquet of Guyanese Flowers: An Anthology of Guyanese Poems Covering Four Generations. pp 112.
Birmingham, R. Ferdinand Lalljie, Publishers, No Date.
ISBN 978-976-8159-21-2.

In *A Bouquet of Guyanese Flowers: An Anthology of Guyanese Poems Covering Four Generations,* forty-seven poems from twelve Guyanese authors are selected by Robert Lalljie, Guyanese actor, poet, broadcaster and publisher who, at a young age, moved to England where he grew up. During his mid-twenties British racism drove Lalljie back to Guyana, where he worked at the Guyana Sugar Corporation (GUYSUCO) and the Guyana Broadcasting Corporation (GBS), and acted in plays staged by the Guysuco Head Office Drama Group. He later returned to London where he still lives. His anthology includes work from A.J. Seymour (1914-1989) Martin Carter (1927-1997) Ivan Forrester (1929-2012) and Stanley Greaves (b.1934), plus other poets like Steve Persaud, Mahlon Herbert, and three female writers Janet Naidu, Pat Cameron and Brenda Richards.

Arthur James Seymour, well known as author, anthologist, and pioneering editor of the literary journal *Kyk-over-al* from 1945-1961, is also the first Guyanese poet to receive national acclaim. In "Auto/Bio" Seymour describes his lineage: "From St. Kitts Barbados / Miss Vires / Whose grandson fathered me. / And fierce or gentle slaves / Whose lives lean / Backward into sun-baked tribes... History / of rape and care," (pp.49-50) which acknowledges his mixed, Guyanese-Caribbean heritage of colonial dispossession, cruelty and slavery.

Seymour's poem "The Legend of Kaieteur" delves into the rich, mythic stock of Amerindian lore and legend in search of narratives of local history, tradition or belief that could ground the poet's own presence as a newcomer to the geographical space of Guyana. What better than an Amerindian legend about Guyana's geographical emblem, Kaieteur Falls, recognisable world-wide as one of the highest waterfalls in the world! "The Legend of Kaieteur" celebrates the mythic career of Kaie, chief of the Patamona people who reel from ravages by neighbours - the stronger, more warlike Caribs. Such is his people's plight that Kaie pleads for help directly from Makonaima, the Great Spirit, who gives him a sign, through the flight of birds, that He will guard Kaie's people, if sacrifice is made to Him.

In willing acceptance of his sacrificial role, Kaie readies himself in "a sacrificial bark" before plunging over the steep seven hundred and forty-odd foot drop of the falls: "Kaie then raised his tall / Huge bulk in the boat and towered over the fall / ... The boat rent all that musty veil in two,/... But Kaie's body never showed a trace/ He sat with Makonaima , before his face." [p. 45] Through an imaginative link forged between himself, a product of slavery /colonialism, and Kaie's ancient, Amerindian sacrifice, the poet's persona establishes an authentic, joint Guyanese identity in his new homeland.

Guyana's greatest poet, Martin Carter, first came into prominence during the 1950s when British Guiana's struggle against colonial rule had reached its highest pitch. As bard of the steadfastly anti-colonial People's Progressive Party (PPP), Carter laments the death of a fallen comrade in soaring political rhetoric: "Death will not find us thinking that we die," [p. 36] a line from his poem "Death of a Comrade" one of three selected in *Bouquet*. Even when this rhetoric is blunted by the brute force and clandestine treachery of British and American imperialism: "Men murder men as men must murder men / to build their shining governments of the damned," [p. 40] taken from "After One Year," there is unyielding defiance in : "Although you come in thousands from the sea / ... Although you point your gun straight at my heart / I clench my fist above my head: I sing my song of / Freedom," [p. 36] from "I Clench my Fist."

What comes through most strongly in Ivan Forrester's three poems in *Bouquet* is his Wordsworthian eloquence as a Nature poet. "Mazaruni" is a paean to the might and majesty of the Mazaruni river, whose titanic energy and vigour are simply unstoppable, as its waters plunge relentlessly forward: "Winding / Whirling / Dancing /... Never thwarted / Never contained / Never once prisoned" [p. 16] carrying all and everything, whether rocks or trees, man or beast, dead or alive, in one mighty heave toward: "The great Atlantic god who watched sightless / ... In oceans of boundless freedom." [p. 19]

In "Kamaria," a poem dedicated to Forrester, Stanley Greaves, also painter and sculptor, similarly pays homage to Nature lore in Guyana: "The forest is a secret blanket / but rivers know the way / past blue hypnotic fungus / sitting in the magic of / green twilight thoughts / that hide horizons forever." [p. 73] With a focus still on Guyana's land or produce, Brenda Richards celebrates Guyana's fruits in "The Guyana Fruit Vendor" while in "Guyana the Beautiful," she eulogises: "The Pakaraima Mountains [that] stand tall and proud / like a shrouded ghost behind a hazy cloud." [p. 63]

Pat Cameron's sly humour, playful rhythms and light-hearted atmosphere re-create the enchantment of a Guyanese childhood in poems such as "When I was Little" and "Wonderful Child Inside of Me." Of her three poems, in addition to documenting the physically back-breaking routine of Indian, peasant labour in "Selflessness," Janet Naidu confronts equally testing psychological problems of disconnection and alienation facing West Indian immigrants in the diaspora.

Of Lalljie's own four poems "I Envied no More" provides probably his best tailored, most coherent reflection on the challenging mystery of cosmic balance in a world of glaring inequality. Similarly, using the refrain "and love beckons all" in "Time and the Fortunes" Steve Persaud encompasses the multiplicity of human experience in a vision of almost mystic comprehension. Eusi Kwayana, continues his lifelong struggle against injustice in two poems that expose sexism and racism; and philosophical reflections in poems by Oscar Kilkenny and Mahlon Herbert further enhance the variety and excitement of Lalljie's inspired selections in *Bouquet*.

THE VOCATION OF WRITING FOR AN
INDIAN-CARIBBEAN AUTHOR

Sasenarine Persaud
A Writer Like You.
Toronto, TSAR Publications, 2002.
ISBN 1-894770-04-8

Two novels, a book of stories and nine volumes of poems announce Sasenarine Persaud as one of the more prolific Caribbean writers in the diaspora. Among younger, Guyanese authors, only Cyril Dabydeen, who began writing two decades before Persaud, has a longer list of publications. *A Writer Like You* is the last volume of a trilogy of poetry collections that include *The Hungry Sailor* (1992) and *A Surf of Sparrow's Songs* (1996).

A Writer Like You contains about one hundred poems which focus on the broad effects of immigration, especially on Caribbean, and particularly Indian-Caribbean people, living in contemporary North America. Persaud himself immigrated to Toronto in 1988 and stayed for six years before moving to Tampa, Florida. His poems have an air of documenting personal experience, which tends to increase the sense of authenticity in subjects like exile, homelessness and, the politics of Guyana, or the role of Hinduism in the lives of Indian-Caribbean immigrants. Most of all though, as we might guess from the title of the volume, Persaud is concerned with the vocation of writing for an Indian-Caribbean author who regards himself, self-deprecatingly, as a 'Coolie Poet" or "Coolie Writah".

Most poems in *A Writer Like You* are short lyrics, about one page or less in length, but a few like "Dharmakeepers" are several pages long. "Dharmakeepers" opens with a graphic description of Indian-Caribbean immigrants in New York as "twice shipwrecked Indians" [p. 9] who "hang red jhandi flags on bamboo poles in their front yards" in districts such as Richmond Hill, Queens, New York City. As the poet claims, the jhandi flags are "badges of courage and affirmation" [p. 19], but their misfit appearance in an unaccustomed milieu illustrates the outsider, marginalised status of those who put up the flags. Hence an ironic touch in describing such people as Dharmakeepers, an invented compound of "dharma" and "keepers" whose synthetic nature strikes a note of irony questioning if not deriding the role of such people as custodians of an essential feature of Hindu culture.

Intertextuality, something of a favourite technique with Persaud, is seen in his listing of references to writers and their works in order to enhance meaning, for instance, the reference to the Trinidadian novelist Sam /Selvon/ and his character Moses in "Dharmakeepers;" but the reference is only effective if the reader is familiar with the work of Selvon, which depicts similar marginalisation and alienation of West Indian immigrants in England in the 1950s.

Another reference to V.S. Naipaul and two characters from his novel *Guerrillas* may risk appearing as mere name-dropping. Whether fully successful or not, Persaud's intertextual references reflect wide reading, and combine with observations of contemporary people or events to reveal an alert and probing mind, constantly attuned to nuances of social and political change around him. Another long poem "No Elegy for Dr.J." pays sly tribute to Dr. Cheddi Jagan, former President of Guyana since, as the poem's title suggests, the tribute is mixed. Yet, mere mention of important issues which engaged Dr. Jagan as a politician hints at his stature. Persaud's main theme in this volume, the craft of writing as practised by Indian-Caribbean immigrants like himself, is seen in poems such as "Dr, Writer", or "Coolie Poet" or "Another Coolie Poet" and others which consider practical matters such as the necessity of earning a living in order to be able to write, and the possible advantage of a doctoral degree to one's writing career.

There is also some poignancy in his unrelenting preoccupation with the dilemma – one faced by all artists - of simultaneously achieving both artistic creation and physical survival. Poignancy is felt most intensely probably in "Mih Call Dhis Wan 'Coolie Writah'" in which a creole idiom is used by the persona to express determination, despite all linguistic, economic, educational or political obstacles, to succeed as a writer, even if it is merely as a [lowly] "coolie crabdog writah". [p. 43] Their sly pride, at least, in the artistic integrity of someone who settles for the lowest rank of writing, rather than not writing at all.

If Persaud's preoccupation with his writerly vocation or fate as an immigrant seems unrelenting, it is something of a relief to encounter poems which deal with less perfervid topics such as the celebration of Nature, pleasures of domestic and family life, or the comings and goings of everyday life. For example, in "Flight Arriving" [p. 48] the simple sensation of an aeroplane landing is re-created with admirable skill which gives the impression that, once freed from more compulsive preoccupations, Persaud can assume a more relaxed manner that displays his technical skills to better effect.

Altogether, Persaud's poems provide an illuminating commentary on the diasporic experience of Indian-Caribbeans in North America, in much the same way as Cyril Dabydeen has recorded the fortunes of the Caribbean diaspora in Canada, in prose as well as poetry. The sense of recording and documentation in Persaud's writing, comes through strongly in the title poem to his volume *A Writer Like You* in which he admits that Canada is a better place for aspiring writers than the US. There is sly poignancy again in the final lines of the poem: "Canada's so good to writers/ Man I tell yuh, If I had gone/ there instead I woulda've been/ a writer too – a writer like you." [p. 109] This catches the flavour of a new immigrant's often confused, self-mocking feelings of marginalisation, victimisation, powerlessness, and his/her will to overcome. So far as Indian-Guyanese immigrants are concerned, Persaud interprets these mixed, tentative and groping feelings with unsentimental accuracy.

"THE ONE UNENDING SORROW OF THE WORLD"

Mark McWatt
The Journey to Le Repentir: Poems in Four Narrative Sequences.
pp.146
Leeds, Peepal Tree Press Ltd. 2009.
ISBN 13 978 1845230814

Mark McWatt, Guyanese academic, literary critic and co-editor of the *Oxford Book of Caribbean Verse* (2005), is also a fiction writer and poet. *The Journey to Le Repentir: Poems in Four Narrative Sequences* is his third volume of poems, after *Interiors* (1989) and *The Language of Eldorado* (1994). In a succinct Introduction explaining that *Le Repentir* is divided into four sections, McWatt spells out subjects and themes, chief among which are two famous figures from Guyanese history: Sir Walter Raleigh, the Elizabethan explorer and coloniser whose *Discoverie of Guiana* (1596) is our first literary account of Guyana, and Pierre Louis De Saffon (1724-1784) who became a plantation owner in Guyana, toward the end of the eighteenth century, when Guyana was briefly in French hands.

"Mercator," the title of Part One of the volume, contains sixteen poems narrated partly from the perspective of an English sea captain, and partly from the point of view of a Guyanese persona in Guyana's North West district (today Region One), a region adjoining Venezuela, explored by Raleigh at the end of the sixteenth century. "Mercator" is also the Latin name of the renowned Flemish cartographer

Gerhard Kremer (1512-1594) whose publications, including maps, greatly facilitated voyages of explorers like Raleigh. In six poems in Part One, numbered from "Mercator I" to "Mercator VI," McWatt interprets the motives and reactions of his English sea captain, (based on Raleigh) from his explicitly admitted lust for gold to his confession of feelings of doubt and loneliness. Raleigh, after all, was drawn by the lure of Eldorado and the golden city of Manoa, supposedly hidden in the forests of Guyana; so it is no surprise that McWatt's fictional sea captain is driven by greed as well as illusion of civilising a savage land where: "mindless nature sprawled like a harlot" [p. 28] in order to bring it under: "the God-given authority of a mighty queen [Queen Elizabeth the First of England]" [p. 28]

Not all poems in Part One of *Le Repentir* are political. As McWatt writes in his Introduction, his poems have: "autobiographical significance" [p. 11] and produce: "glimpses of a fictional life which nevertheless correspond with – or suggest in some way – aspects of my own experience." [p. 11] The sea captain's imperialist adventures are interwoven with poems about an unnamed Guyanese boy, and his relationships either with his family or school friends, as he grows up and acquires natural (including sexual) awareness of the rural, colonial world around him in the 1950s.

In "Hello Marabunta," for instance, the boy hears his mother sobbing in bed alone at night, and discovers that: "it is not / always possible to name the hurt / that makes us weep." [p. 22] This is also part of a process of growing up, gaining experience, for instance, when the boy feels the same hurt on first leaving his familiar North-West, Guyanese surroundings for school in the capital city of Georgetown, or when his innocent curiosity about sex earns him two lashes at school, along with suspension for two days, and the indignity of his mother: "washing out my mouth with soap." [p. 30]

In "Drowned Lives" the boy feels genuine grief over death by drowning of a school friend, a girl: "so full before with the restless itch of life,"p.39) while the sea captain who observes a similar drowning is overcome by grief enough to doubt his mission of: "rape and conquest." [p. 40] Comparison between these reactions, nearly four centuries apart, along with contrast between the innocence of the boy's sexual awakening, and the crude, sexual imagery of the sea captain in "Mercator VI," lend coherence and continuity to Guyanese history; and this impression is enhanced by a more startling contrast between the sea captain's contemptuous reactions to Guyana's landscape, and the boy's affectionate identification with his homeland.

"Dark Consolation," second section of *Le Repentir*, looks at the poet's persona in adult life, while "The Museum of Love," the third section, takes in more middle–aged concerns. "Dark Consolation" celebrates Guyana's hinterland, and its so called Interior, with rivers and a forest that command total devotion. But in spite of similar precise and spare writing as in "Mercator," original images and an equally impressive range of figurative devices, the second and third sections of *Le Repentir* may not match the full fluency and power of its first.

Yet, "Le Repentir" - the fourth section of the volume - recaptures the full potency of the first, largely due to the poet's penchant for history, and insight into the elegiac nature of pain, brought on by ageing or loss. Four poems in this final section recall the life of Pierre de Saffon, whose accidental killing of his brother in a duel, forces him to flee from France to Guyana where, in torment from guilt and remorse, he names his two sugar plantations "Le Repentir" (repentance), and "La Penitence" (punishment.) There is even a personal connection to the poet himself through his grandmother, Henrietta (Hetta) Cendrecourt, who benefitted from a legacy left by de Saffon, and whose name appears in the title of "Approaching Le Repentir IV: Hetta."

Through this connection, the poem's fictional persona considers himself de Saffon's "secret legatee" who is: "hounded by guilt and a deeply buried / sadness ... just for who I am." [p. 130] He also feels a: "secret hurt" that defines him and his: "unimaginable love / not least for the land of / de Saffon's penitential places." [p. 130] This hurt also appears in "Approaching Le Repentir III: Atonement" where de Saffon admits to a: "pain no personal /wealth nor influence can assuage." [p. 124] Strange how these de Saffon poems recall "Hello Marabunta" and its persona who, despite his youth, summons enough maturity to realise that pain is often best borne quietly, and its causes sometimes left alone, joined: "to the one unending sorrow of the world." [p. 22]

"THEY ADORNED ME WITH JEWELS / FROM JUNKSHOP DISPOSALS"

Mahadai Das
A Leaf in his Ear: Collected Poems. pp.188.
Peepal Tree Press Ltd. 2010.
ISBN 9781900715591

Mahadai Das's *A Leaf in his Ear: Collected Poems* contains items from her three published volumes, plus a section, "Uncollected Poems" (1973-1994), that includes her unpublished poems. *Leaf* also includes a brief "Publisher's Note" from Jeremy Poynting, an informative Introduction by Denise DeCaires Narain Gurnah, an Index of first lines, and another brief note "About the Author." Das who was born in Eccles, East Bank Demerara, Guyana, in 1954, obtained a B.A. degree at the University of Guyana, another B.A. in Philosophy from Columbia University in the US, then an M.A. in Philosophy from the University of Chicago where, in 1987, she underwent heart surgery, and abandoned her attempt to complete the Ph.D.

As Poynting writes in his Note: "There is no way Mahadai Das's work can ever be anything other than an unfinished project."[p. 8] She did not complete revision of many of her uncollected poems before her death in 2003, and left little biographical evidence that corroborates links between her life and writing. One exception is that poems from her first volume *I Want to be a Poetess of my People* (1976, 1977) corroborate the political idealism and euphoria of her experience in the Guyana National Service, which Das joined in 1976. Das's poems also promote the concept of: "the new Guyana Man and Woman, oriented towards their role in nation building," as expressed in one of President Forbes Burnham's State Papers in 1973. The Guyana National Service was a theoretical project betraying hallmarks of ideological mimicry and coercion which, in hindsight, appear emblematic of the ersatz régime of Forbes Burnham which assumed total political power in Guyana, in 1968, through a fortuitous combination of electoral fraud and tacit blessing from the US government which had its own political objections to Burnham's opponent, Cheddi Jagan.

A poem like "Militant" from Das's first volume captures her feelings in the Guyana National Service: "I want my blood to churn/Change! Change! Change! / March! / We are the army, / We are the people, / We are Guyana marching for change." [p. 39] This declamatory outburst may now sound as mere bombast; but it matches the vision of the persona of another poem "Look in the Vision for Smiles of the Harvest" who exhorts fellow Guyanese to: "Think of the child of tomorrow passing through this now jungle/ Reaping the fruits of your hands, and sowing for tomorrow's children." [p. 31] Such huge nation-building expectations from projects of the Guyana National Service, conducted, military style, in the Guyanese forest, today seem exaggerated, impractical, even spurious: " My children, in universities, born and grown in the jungle/ Like a symbolic womb, cradling and nurturing the generations of yesterday's visions." [p. 34]

Predictably, this unrealistic optimism gives way to the opening image of a fallen star, stuck like a dagger in the persona's heart, in the title poem of Das's second volume *My Finer Steel Will Grow* (1982). The poem lists a catalogue of miseries in the life of its persona, a dog, although its penultimate line "My finer steel will grow" musters a semblance of unconvincing defiance. Other poems from her second volume also register the poet's reactions to corruption and injustice during Burnham's régime, after she had moved to the US for studies. It is not only from "For Walter Rodney and Other Victims" with lines like "remember a man gunned down/ his guts spilled their clandestine sin," [p. 54] but also from references to such grotesque distortions as "the tyrant's glee" [p. 52] and "the vengeance of heaven waits armed/ in the shadows," [p. 52] in "While the Sun is Trapped" that we sense Das's recoil into despairing disillusionment.

By the time of her third volume *Bones* (1988) the poet's despair and anguish are relieved only by occasional incidents of joy or celebration. Poems in *Bones* and "Uncollected Poems" are disfigured by reticent diction, disjunctive syntax, cryptic imagery and terse obliqueness, for instance, in "The Leaf in his Ear," which invokes a pervasive impression of studied incoherence, with thoughts and feelings so twisted as almost wilfully to resist comprehension, and turn Das into a female complement of Wilson Harris, whose fiction also meditates on psychic mysteries in the Guyanese soul. But while Harris's fiction may be complicated by extravagant philosophical speculation, Das's poetry seems more grounded in expressions of instinctive reaction to the trauma of her experience at home, during the Burnham era, and abroad, during her illness/misfortune.

In "Beast" images of kidnapping, dispossession and dismemberment conjure up confused reactions of fear, admiration and almost love. "Beast" is typical of poems in *Bones* blighted by upturned values, ruptured expectations and reversed roles. In such a world, the only glimpse of order, regularity or symmetry, as in "Sonnet to New Flowers," is the normal fourteen- line length of the sonnet form which is disrupted, nevertheless, by jagged, awkward, hyphenated adjectives like "iron-fisted" and "poor-inhabited" or scenes of bleak desolation in the US, where: "Hate stares in gunshot-interrupted/ Silence." [p. 74] "Resurrection" also paints a picture of oxymoronic reversal of contradictory expectations when the persona confesses: "In my burial robes, they adorned me/ With jewels from junkshop disposals/ And backyard sales." [p. 72]

As an Indian-Guyanese woman Das's poetry reaches its highest peak in "They came in Ships" or "Your Bleeding Hands Grasp the Roots of Rice," and other poems that reference Indian people, places or customs. Ethnic issues are one thing; but when combined with gender concerns, Das's poems soar even higher with an inspired and eloquent challenge against sexual discrimination in all forms, for example, in "For Anna Karenina" and "For Maria de Borges." For hers is the spontaneous eloquence of someone forced to assume care of nine younger siblings when she was only seventeen: it is why her protest against female victimisation rings so heart-wrenchingly, reminding us of her near contemporary Sylvia Plath, the American poet, who also died in tragic circumstances, while in full poetic flow, in 1963.

"GRATITUDE ARISES OUT OF LIFE'S GIFTS"

Janet Naidu.
Sacred Silence, pp.104.
Hertford, Hansib, 2009.
ISBN 978-1-906190-33-0

Janet Naidu emigrated from her Guyanese homeland to Canada in 1975. Like her previous poetry collections – *Winged Heart* (1999) and *Rainwater* (2005), *Sacred Silence* (2009) mainly considers themes of love and loss in the context of migration, and the struggle for fresh identity in a new land. But the three volumes are not identical: poems in the third volume appear more steeped in spiritual meditation than those in the first two.

Sacred Silence consists of fifty-nine poems divided into four sections. In several poems in the first section, "Fields to Seashore," the persona speaks from a vantage point in Canada and introduces us to remembered scenes of life in rural Guyana. In "Selflessness," for example, we see the rough and ready life of an Indian peasant family as the mother, "honouring her duty," [p. 30] gets up early in the morning to cook paratha and sada roti with "bare hands" [p. 30] while the father prepares for a long day of hard labour "on the backdam [plantation]." [p. 30] In "Cane Dust at my Feet," a woman sweeps away cane dust "on a clean mud floor," [p. 37] before setting off with a heavy basket of vegetables on her head to sell in the market.

These rustic, plantation folk scrape the barrel to survive; and their plight is heightened by the strangeness of their indentured background evoked, for instance, in "A Deeper Ocean" where the persona imagines a female ancestor newly arrived from India in: "red and gold bodice, / nose ring, foot ring and silver bangle," [p. 36] – dress which almost mocks the harshness and penury of living conditions in Guyana. Pin-pointing her own South Indian heritage, in "Movements," Naidu reflects on indentured Indians who travelled to the Caribbean from the South Indian port of Madras: "Departure and arrival/ fills me with endless yearning/ from the shores of Madras/ to the green fields of Demerara." [p. 40] The point is that the yearning stays with her even in Canada.

There is a slight change of pace in the second section of the volume, "Silk on the Clothesline," which switches to eleven poems on love. Yet it is more the loss of love rather than the happiness, satisfaction or joy it might bring. There is the possibility of happiness in some poems, for example, "We Meet by the Seadam," "Gentle Beginning" or "Beloved," but in most poems lovers seem temperamentally cautious, and speak as if they half-expect their love not to last. The impression they give is not of happiness or joy, but of a joint dividend of sadness and wisdom gained through love. Often love seems as much of a struggle as sheer survival proves for indentured labourers in the first section: "My Cold Encounter" could not provide colder images of snow and thick fog at night, followed only by: "fleeting love; " [p. 53] and although "Beloved" carries a glimpse of: "lingering in pure joy," [p. 59] it too repeats images of fading, transience or decline, for instance, either of: "autumn leaves in the wind" [p. 59] or of: "autumn leaves / now floating in the river." [p. 59]

The loss, transience and unsatisfied yearning that emerge from the first two sections of *Sacred Silence*, blend smoothly in the third "The Heart of Survival" which gropes for wisdom through spiritual meditation: "I thirst for wisdom - for something / glistening in the ocean / like morning sun / in timeless wonder." [p. 68] True to the real life, multicultural context of her Canadian workplace, the Liquor Control Board of Ontario, where Naidu promotes diversity and equity in employment, the poet draws on worldwide sources for sacred texts or concepts, whether Christian, Hindu or Buddhist, in her quest for wisdom. "Relinquishing" suggests an answer to her quest: "Time is all I see – an illusion / of wind and sun in the water / bringing a message already within. " [p. 72] This perception, that wisdom is an intuition that comes from within to satisfy her nympholepsy or yearning for the unattainable, is what Naidu's poems prescribe as the "sacred silence" of her title: a stillness inside her that may reveal answers, illumination.

Poems in the final section "Pond and Waterfall Singing Deep" wrap up the collection neatly. They reproduce much of the meditative and largely sorrowful reflection that reinforces a general tone of deep and sober contemplation running throughout the text. It is a tone of balanced awareness or calculated, controlled acceptance: "I wash my pain down the sidewalk / aware of my own mortality." [p. 97] Naidu's personae accept rather than grumble over or rail against the evanescence of love, or of life itself.

It is more than acceptance, as we see in the last poem of the volume "Contentment" which carries a revealing line: "Gratitude rises out of life's gifts." [p. 99] In addition, other lines mention "devotion" and the ringing of temple bells. Thus, for all the unsatisfied yearning we have seen in her poems, all the transience and evanescence, Naidu's prescription of gratitude within a structure of devotional (temple) ritual in "Contentment" clinches the idea of sacredness in her title; for despite human limitation, she seems to suggest, we should not simply be grateful but offer devotional (sacred) praise for what we have.

So far Naidu has established a name for herself among a growing number of female Indian-Caribbean writers who have emerged in the past couple of decades. She began writing in Guyana where, in the early 1970s, she joined a literary group that included Rooplall Monar who later became the supreme chronicler of Guyanese plantation society in fiction, and Mahadai Das, one of the most talented Indian-Guyanese women poets. Today, besides her own writing, as President of the Pakaraima Guyanese Canadian Writers and Artists Association, Naidu continues actively to promote Caribbean literature in Canada.

"AH LIVE FROM THEN TO NOW AN' DON' REMEMBER HOW"

Ian McDonald.
The Comfort of All Things. pp.81.
Georgetown, Guyana, Moray House Trust, 2012.
ISBN 978 976 8212-83-2

The Comfort of All Things is a collection of poems by Ian McDonald who was born in Trinidad, in 1933, graduated from Cambridge University and, since 1955, gave invaluable service to the sugar industry in Guyana. He also excelled at tennis, wrote one novel, edited the journal *Kyk-Over-Al*, and served for decades as a newspaper columnist. In 1970 he became a Fellow of the Royal Society of Literature and, in 1997, was awarded an Honorary Doctor of Literature degree by the University of the West Indies.

The title poem "The Comfort of All Things" in his fifth volume of poems indicates the comfort or satisfaction McDonald now feels at a stage of high maturity, closer to the end of his career. Many titles in the volume stress this idea of comfort or equanimity about life. Almost every poem sums up thoughts about mortality, for example: "the impermanence of what is gone and coming," [p. 49] in "Exploration of a Dream," or the last line of the same poem which perceives a dilemma in which: "we [fellow human beings] are phantoms moving toward a fire." [p. 49] But there is no accompanying panic or gloom, for instance, in "What it Was Like Once Forever" where, after celebrating: "The perfect day is upon me," the persona revels in the sheer pleasure of colourful, tropical vegetation, and the lively movement of animals around him, before enthusiastically concluding: "I give life a salute, the beauty it provides." [p. 62]

One illustration of a dilemma McDonald perceives and its inability to unsettle his equanimity appears in "Geometry of the Dying Mind" with the opening line: "These are bad days now," [p. 56] followed by images of fading possibilities, physical frailty or ageing: "mournful rain," "the cough deep in the chest,"and "unraked golden flowers going brown." [p. 56] But, paradoxically, the persona in the poem responds to these challenges with relief since: "In the fullness of life everything is good/ a wondrous maze of problems and of joys/ everlasting harvest of desires." [p. 56] In other words, far from being a lamentation or unsettling cry for help, the shared human dilemma of mortality or ageing becomes a realistic, even celebratory appraisal of the persona's stage of life when need for activity naturally dwindles: "Now the doing and the doing over / will not have to be done again." [p. 56]

Poems such as "Listen to the Wolves" adopt an apocalyptic tone with strenuous effort invested in resisting threat of rack and ruin: "Walls with strong foundations have been built/ against the tall seas that are coming/ the thunder of horses/ across the sunlit heavens/ avalanches of ice descending." [p. 46] In other poems, personae display more personal reactions to the transience of ageing or dying. The unnamed persona in "The Bone-Trip," a shoemaker who: "repaired boots for working men in Gentle street," [p. 41] does not mince words. For him the prospect of dying is hard: "The bone-trip is always hard." [p. 41] So it is not surprising that, one day, when his partner dies, the shoemaker reacts to his loss without grief, merely with respectful composure, as if death is just another routine item of everyday business: "Well, Buds gone to make his bone-trip now." [p. 41] The shoemaker's air of surface insouciance, as he: "wiped his sweaty face with rag/ went on nailing the rough, strong boots" [p. 41] conceals both inward strength and comfort /equanimity since Buds had merely reached another stage in his life.

The chief character described by the persona in "The Edge of Night" ran away from his drunken father and: "wandered far to other lonely lands," [p. 40] before becoming a "Watchman by the seawall koker" [p. 40] where he is regularly visited by the persona for over twenty years. He also served as a Museum guide who discovered the sculpture of a scorpion with a golden head for which he was awarded: "the keepsake plaque engraved in Latin script."[p. 40] The lowly watchman closely fits into an Epicurean universe as one who: "never built a home/ or had one woman or concerned himself with God." [p. 40] He is not even given a name, yet he utters one of the finest, most musical and meaningful lines, not only in McDonald's, but in West Indian poetry: "Ah live from then to now an' don' remember how;" [p. 40] in Epicurean terms he has attained the comfort of all things.

Like the watchman, none of us knows why we are here or where we are going, and none can explain how we survive. From *Mercy Ward* (1988) to his fifth volume, McDonald 's poems abound in themes of tough-minded persistence or survival. A typical survivor is Miaha an old, wizened aboriginal woman in the poem "Last of Her Race" from *Essequibo.* (1992) A similarly strong will to live is shown by Jaffo in *Jaffo the Calypsonian* where Jaffo, in hospital suffering from terminal throat cancer, steals spoons to defiantly bang out tunes on his bed posts.

But while themes of defiance exist throughout McDonald 's poems, those in *The Comfort of all Things* also express the more enlightened acceptance of a cycle of natural processes of which we are part. Poems in his fifth volume offer McDonald's most explicit assertion of a world view of Epicurean, stage/by/stage process, within an intricate but ordered pattern of change and renewal. It is a pattern that does not necessarily include systems of faith, or spiritual/supernatural beliefs on which most people rely. Sorrow, grief or regret also prove unnecessary. For the watchman all is simple wonder, fulfilment and an instinctive sense of gratitude for being included within a universal, self-sustaining and seemingly endless cycle of growth, transience, decline and regeneration. No wonder McDonald's fifth volume also includes his own poem - "De Rerum Natura"- title of probably the most celebrated poem on Epicurean philosophy, by the Roman poet Lucretius.

Part Three

"HE [BURNHAM] PUT FAT, BLACK PEOPLE TO RUN SUGAR AND RICE FACTORIES"

This essay examines fictional presentations of Guyana during the régime of Forbes Burnham, and focuses chiefly on work by Indian-Guyanese authors. Between 1957 and 1964, the People's Progressive Party (PPP), led by Indian-Guyanese Dr. Cheddi Jagan, formed the Government of Guyana. From 1964 to 1985, however, Guyana was ruled by African-Guyanese Forbes Burnham, either as Premier or President, and leader of the People's National Congress (PNC), as much an African-Guyanese party as the PPP was Indian-Guyanese. The PNC retained power for twenty-eight, continuous years by means of illegal procedures used repeatedly to win elections in 1968, 1973, 1980 and 1985, until American pressure enforced free and fair elections in 1992, and the PNC was defeated by a coalition of the PPP and a citizens' group named CIVIC.

Guyana ceased being a British colony in 1966, and the British were more or less out of the picture from the mid-1960s, so far as local affairs were concerned. For the first time, fortunes of Indian-Guyanese were in the hands of an independent Guyanese administration. Since Burnham was elected mainly by African-Guyanese, Indian-Guyanese no longer felt the solidarity they may have once shared with their African-Guyanese countrymen, as common colonial victims of the British; for they now perceived African-Guyanese as agents and collaborators of a ruling party that lorded it over them, in the same way as the British colonisers who immediately preceded them.

"My Girl, this Indianness" a story in Sasenarine Persaud's collection *Canada Geese and Apple Chatney*[1] claims that the intention of the 1964 coalition between the "Portuguese Party" – the United Force (UF) - and the PNC was to: "ensure that the PPP and Jagan stayed out of power." [pp. 33-34] According to Persaud, PNC rule was lawless and oppressive, for example, in being linked to the murder of an Irish Roman Catholic priest, Father Darke, an actual event in which the priest was killed by a "Black Jew" of the "House of Hebrews," an African-American group, led by a fugitive from American justice with known links to the Burnham Government.

Collusion between the Government and outright thugs also appears in another Persaud story "When Men Speak this Way" which reveals a general atmosphere of lawlessness: "Legality and the law were a joke, yet for the 'influential' and 'connected people' the law could be invoked with a vengeance." [pp. 52-53] This situation where, depending on race, the innocent are punished while the guilty get off scot free, compares closely with apartheid South African fiction, for example, as depicted in Alex La Guma's novel *A Walk in the Night.* [2] (1967)

In Persaud's stories, Indian-Guyanese feel disgruntled as they: "cursed the government for ruining our country, cursed our people [Indian—Guyanese] for being so docile and for participating in this destruction," [and submitting to] "economic ruin," "political-racial discrimination," [and] "blatantly rigged elections." [p. 54] Indian-Guyanese frustration stems from failed electoral strategies of the Opposition PPP which they support, but which are completely neutered by the government's practice of using illegal procedures to win elections. Hence the desperate resort of Indians to migrate from Guyana in droves.

References to emigration in many stories reinforce an impression that although, in time, the Burnham Government provoked Guyanese of all ethnic stripes to emigrate, Indian-

Guyanese had greatest cause to do so. When Persaud and other authors mention illegal Guyanese immigrants in foreign countries, for instance, chiefly Canada and the US, it is almost always in reference to Indian-Guyanese rather than African or other ethnic Guyanese.

The narrator in Oonya Kempadoo's novel *Buxton Spice* [3] is the child of an Indian father and a mixed blood woman living in Tamarind Grove, fictional name for Golden Grove, a village that is largely African-Guyanese. Kempadoo's portrait of villagers suggests that many of Burnham's policies, in particular banning importation of staple foods, and replacing them with local substitutes, create great hardship, especially for the poorest Guyanese. In an enterprising move, Kempadoo contrives a fictional portrait of Burnham visiting Tamarind Grove, and being questioned about his ban. He advises villagers to use local substitutes, for instance, to wash with salt instead of soap. As a fictional portrait, Burnham appears cynical, arrogant, detached and uninterested in the fate of ordinary Guyanese.

This fictional portrait fits a claim of the narrator's mother that Burnham: "cause de Race Riots. He make black people hate Indians. He take every-t'ing de Indians had an say is government own. He put fat black people to run the sugar an rice factories." [p. 53] The claim is plausible as an attempt by Burnham, on behalf of African-Guyanese, to redress what they perceived as an imbalance in wealth between Indian-Guyanese and themselves by the mid-twentieth century. Financial imbalance threatens the established dominance of African-Guyanese as the educated, urbanised, Westernised and professional middle class of Guyana. As already hinted, Indians arrived in Guyana more than two hundred years after Africans, and up to, at least, World War Two, were still a largely rural-based, peasant community, while African-Guyanese lived mostly in towns or villages and, as in most British Caribbean colonies, dominated the civic infrastructure of professions, teaching, civil service, army, police, even dock workers.

The illegal political ascendancy of Burnham and the PNC to power in Guyana, in the 1960s, is a direct result of African-Guyanese fear of losing their established social dominance. During this period of Cold War confrontation between the capitalist US and communist USSR, PNC ascendancy is also the result of fortuitous coincidence with the aims of American realpolitik, in the 1960s, in enforcing the Monroe doctrine of unchallenged US control throughout the Western hemisphere. This is why the US leaned on their British allies to disempower the allegedly communist PPP, led by Dr. Jagan, and install a PNC government in Guyana in 1964. This mixture of local and geopolitical motives promotes the racialised fear driving both main Guyanese ethnic groups in the 1960s and 70s.

In *Buxton Spice,* for instance, when the film projector breaks down in the middle of a show in their village cinema, the largely African patrons who automatically regard it as a racial affront, loudly protest by yelling: "ANSA! Fucking Coolie!" [p. 136] Ansa, the cinema owner, is described as: "an East Indian from somewhere near town and different – not a country coolie with coconut-oiled hair."[p. 135] In East Riumveldt too, when an incendiary glass bottle is thrown into the Mohammed family home, it causes the Indian Muslim owner to burglar proof his building, and instinctively blame Africans: "not a black man would mess with him again." [p. 45]

Ethnic polarisation goes hand in hand with systematic coercion of Indian-Guyanese. In *Buxton Spice*, the narrator attends a school where the headmaster Mr. Brown is mockingly given the nickname of "Burnham" because of his hero worship of the PNC leader: "As the PNC man, Headmaster Burnham took it as his personal duty to embarrass non-PNC teachers, mostly Indians, in front of us. There was a skinny, mousy maths teacher who he'd terrorize so much she shook when he was near her." [p. 154] "Mr. Burnham's" power and authority derives as much from his authority as headmaster, as from his dedicated collaboration with the Government and, as in Persaud's fiction, racist politics and coercion lead to emigration when the narrator's family pack their bags, at the end of *Buxton Spice*, and prepare to migrate.

Ethnicity in Guyana is not like race in the US where a numerically dominant (white) group holds power; nor entirely like apartheid South Africa, from 1948 to 1992, when a minority (white) group maintained power through enforcement of legalised racism. In Guyana, in the 1960s, Indian-Guyanese (51%) were the majority group compared with African-Guyanese (43%). In post-colonial Guyanese society, steeped for centuries in the racist, administrative patterns of British Caribbean colonies, including patterns of voting by race, class or colour, Indian-Guyanese were programmed, by their numerical majority, to win elections, as they did in 1957 and 1961, unless a tactic such as South African apartheid or institutionalized American racism were introduced. Instead, Burnham rigged voting procedures that produced victory for the PNC in four consecutive elections.

While the main events in *Canada Geese* and *Buxton Spice* occur explicitly in Guyana, those in the three novels to follow adopt imaginary locations, in order to mask specifically Guyanese implications. Despite its fictional location, the Guyanese implications in Nirmala Sewcharan's *Tomorrow is Another Day* [4] are easily detected, not only the landscape, names of people or places, but cultural practices, social peculiarities and the banned goods, food lines and smuggling caused by food shortages which, at the time, occurred only in Guyana among British Caribbean territories, and only under PNC rule. The atmosphere of heightened fear and tension, rigged elections, stage-managed rallies and kick-down-the-door bandits also remind us of Burnham's régime. Specific parallels are celebrated political manoeuvrings such as the crossing of the floor by PPP politicians like Vincent Teekah and Ranji Chandisingh who both joined the PNC.

In addition, the three fictional political parties in the novel – The Official Party, The United Party and the Workers Party – correspond closely in ideology and practice to the PNC, PPP and the Working People's Alliance (WPA) respectively in Guyana. Nor does the fact that Prime Minister Rouche is sick and absent for much of the time erase parallels between him and Burnham: he is the leader of a centrally managed, tightly controlled, dictatorial administration identical to Burnham's.

Tomorrow describes the régime of the Official Party exercising unfettered power, carefully calculating every move to ruthlessly eliminate enemies, imprisoning people without laying charges, and even committing murder. Jagru Persaud, the chief Indian protagonist in the novel, switches his membership from the United Party to the Official for what are claimed to be idealistic reasons. As Indian-Guyanese, he is a feather in the cap of an African-Guyanese, PNC government which flaunts him as their prized, token Indian-Guyanese, and living proof of the false, multiracial political image deceptively advertised by their party. Persaud is quickly given a car and appointed as Minister, but discovers the job is a mere sinecure: he has nothing to do. (Persaud matches his real-life model, Ralph Chandisingh, who defected from the PPP to the PNC.) But suspicion and disillusionment gradually set in before he is accused of sabotage, arrested, and briefly imprisoned. Persaud's career illustrates the dilemma of Indian-Guyanese who are politically marginalised whether or not they join the Official Party.

The portrait of another Indian-Guyanese politician, Lal Panday, is equally problematic. Panday is a weakling who hesitates to take political action, scarcely musters resources to support his family, and is eventually murdered. (Panday matches his real-life model, Vincent Teekah.) Panday's wife, like most female characters in the novel, is more resilient and resourceful, and devises ways and means of survival. Survival seems to be the main option for Indian-Guyanese characters in the novel, not only those with political ambitions, but ordinary folk who resort to smuggling goods and other alternative strategies.

If the Indian-Guyanese characters in *Tomorrow* squirm like flies trapped on sticky paper, non-Indians appear to prosper, certainly those who support the government. Meanwhile, Prime Minister Rouche, although absorbed and remote, emerges as cunning and hypocritical, fond of trumpeting empty rhetoric about his black skin, despite his mixed (African/ European) blood. He makes: "awesome speeches about the proud continent from which his ancestors had been uprooted, bound in chains, and dragged across an indifferent ocean into the horrors of slavery." [p. 50]

Rouche gives an impression of mere grandstanding, churning out fodder for political consumption, as when he refers, with feeling, to his "own people" [p. 50] while appealing to them: "in exclusive denial of the many other races which inhabited the land, including those whose forebears had come as indentured immigrants, driven by desperate poverty in India to sell their soul for five years and risk all for a chance of a better life." [p. 50] The parallel is unmistakable with Burnham who pursued pro-African policies that either excluded or marginalised the interests of Indian-Guyanese. But although he succeeds in subduing his political opponents, his régime fails because of endemic corruption leading to poverty and despair for most of the population, including his own supporters.

The action of Indian-Trinidadian Lakshmi Persaud's novel *For the Love of my Name* [5] is set on a fictional island called Maya, although its Guyanese context is revealed through the similarity between names of its characters and places with the social background and specific political events in Guyana. Events in the novel are recounted chiefly by Robert Augustus Devonish (Burnham) and his sister Marguerite, while politicians like Emmanuel Pottaro (Dr. Cheddi Jagan) and Lionel Gomes, (Peter D'Aguiar) along with other minor characters, correspond to particular individuals and happenings in Guyana during the Burnham era.

The distinction between city and country Mayans in *Love* reflects a division between African-Guyanese as mainly urban, and Indian-Guyanese as chiefly rural dwellers in mid twentieth century Guyana. Robert Devonish himself admits a need: "to demarcate our [African] urbanity from their [Indian] rusticity."[p. 129] Within the feudal ethics of Caribbean colonial societies, it was expected that African-Guyanese were better equipped to step into the shoes of British rulers, after Guyanese Independence in 1966, and Devonish makes no bones about his [African-Guyanese] supporters being: "the natural inheritors of the culture of [the British] Empire, its customs, tastes, religion and ways of thinking." [p. 131] Burnham's actions in making a bid for leadership of the original PPP which was multiracial in 1953 (when he was rebuffed), and again in 1955, when he was rebuffed once more, then forming his own African- Guyanese party, followed by his barefaced disenfranchisement of Indian-Guyanese through rigged elections from 1968 to 1985, betray a deep-seated African-Guyanese belief in their ethnic right to political domination over Indian-Guyanese.

Devonish cites the vision of his ancestors, emancipated Africans who, as early as 1903: "sought to terminate indentured immigration [of Indians] ...fearing their future influence on the island's development." [p. 129] This historic ethnic rivalry justifies him in trying: "to effectively disenfranchise the descendants of these indentured immigrants and so force them to leave." [p. 129] There is also a note of snobbery in his feeling of cultural superiority over Indians: "How then could one expect to share power with the sons of agricultural labourers, or worse, to find ourselves in a political situation where they [country Mayans] would be in power and we [city Mayans] in opposition for the foreseeable future? ... The political system then in place had to be changed." (p136)

Since Indian-Guyanese form a numerical majority of the population, Devonish is right to believe that city Mayans [African-Guyanese] would be in opposition for the foreseeable future. There is little doubt that this fear of political powerlessness is what, at least partly, inspires the cynical rationale of political survival in Burnham. That his rationale happens to coincide with a global, hegemonic policy of the Kennedy administration in the US which regarded Cheddi Jagan as a communist, and feared his creation of "a second Cuba" in their hemisphere is sheer luck.

Like previous authors in this essay, Lakshmi Persaud describes the Indian-Guyanese reaction to victimisation, resorting to emigration rather than direct physical resistance, as passive. One reason is the influence of the country Mayan leader - Emmanuel Pottaro. Devonish claims:" By personality and temperament Pottaro was a domestic cock while I [Devonish] have always been a prize fighter, with sharpened beak and claws, prepared for the kill." [p. 210] This contrast matches Dr. Jagan as ideologically pure or inflexible, if earnest and honourable, and Forbes Burnham as wily, wicked and ruthless. While Persaud's repudiation of Devonish is half-admiring, her pity for Pottaro is deeply patronising.

Persaud underestimates Pottaro's difficulties as an Indian-Caribbean politician. She admits that the Region – the English-speaking Caribbean – is predominantly African, which win little or no sympathy for country Mayans in the wider Caribbean. While Devonish can do no wrong in the eyes of commentators in the Region, Pottaro is suspiciously scrutinised for every word he utters. Devonish brazenly gloats over the solidarity he enjoys in the Region: "At no time have the Region's intellectuals accused me [Devonish] of ethnic prejudice, though it formed the very pivot of my economic policies. They were more than able to see race prejudice in Pottaro and his supporters... On the other hand they were silent or made excuses for my failings." [p. 108]

In the final novel, Harischandra Khemraj's *Cosmic Dance,*[6] the fictional country of Aritia possesses exactly the aura in Guyana already seen in previous texts during the 1970s and 80s: political repression, racial antagonism, corruption and desperation, although, in this case, the author tries to focus on the moral and psychological effects of these factors on Indian-Guyanese. As in *Tomorrow,* for example, the chief characters are Indian-Guyanese and African-Guyanese who are at daggers drawn so far as ethnic relations are concerned. Indian-Guyanese again appear to be the main political victims who survive by smuggling goods and selling them on the black market.

The narrator, an Indian-Guyanese doctor named Vayu Sampat, relates a childhood incident when he was in an Indian-owned cake shop with his best friend who happened to be African-Guyanese, and his friend's mother unexpectedly runs into them. Shocked to find her son in a cake shop when she thought he was in Sunday school, the mother addresses the narrator: "Get your coolie ass out of my way," before turning on her son: "So this...this creature is the nasty Coolie who's been leading you astray. Instead of going to Sunday school, you're wallowing in the filth of this... this loathesome looking pagan." [p. 146] Similar ethnic prejudice is reciprocated by Indian-Guyanese as well when an Indian-Guyanese woman is horrified that her husband receives blood from an African-Guyanese donor during life-saving surgery in hospital.

The central incident in the novel is the rape of a teenaged Indian-Guyanese girl, Mala, by Vernon Ashby, Chief Executive of one of the largest companies in the country, Binday Coconut Enterprises. Because of Ashby's power and authority, the crime seems all the more serious. Worse still, Ashby is African-Guyanese. Worst of all, Mala's father Samsundar Roy turns out to have arranged his daughter's rape, in return for promotion from Senior Field Foreman at Binday Coconut Enterprises to Assistant Field Superintendent. The incident reflects a degree of Indian-Guyanese demoralisation not found in the texts already examined. Roy's dehumanisation is the result of decades of political repression, leading Indian-Guyanese like him from one humiliating compromise to the other, until the narrator is wounded in a shooting incident, in which his best friend, Ramphal Chandra, a respected professor is killed, and both Roy and his daughter are murdered. In *Cosmic Dance*, Khemraj's main characters, Indian-Guyanese and African-Guyanese alike, are caught in a Kafkaesque world of moral inversion, in which values of right and wrong are dictated purely by a combination of expedience and an elemental need to survive.

At the end of the novel, when police investigate the deaths of Mala, Samsundar Roy and Ramphal Chandra, they replace the truth – that Ashby arranged the murders – with a more acceptable, but false version of events, namely, that Roy shoots Chandra, a lecherous professor who has been molesting his daughter; Mala hangs herself out of shame; and Roy is shot trying to escape. The policeman who suppresses the truth, himself Indian-Guyanese, recognises the perverse ethics of the political system in which he works; and as he informs the narrator, in a truthful version of events, the villain: "was not only Ashby - and possibly Samsundar – but a whole society which, if it accepted this version, would be indicting itself for venality and cowardice." [p. 258]

As we might expect, there are not as many fictional reports on the Burnham era by African-Guyanese as by Indian-Guyanese. Since Indian-Guyanese are perceived as chief victims during Burnham's régime their experience catches the attention of authors from their own ethnic group. It is generally true that Guyanese writers tend to consider living conditions or issues in which their own ethnic group is mainly invoved. But there are exceptions, for example, A.R. F. Webber's novel *Those That Be in Bondage: A Tale of Indian Indentures and Sunlit Western Waters* (1917) which portrays Indian sugar plantation workers, Mittelholzer's *Corentyne Thunder* (1941) which also focuses on the lives of Indian sugar, plantation workers , and Roy Heath's *The Shadow Bride* (1988) which is the best known, full-length fictional study of Indian-Guyanese experience that we so far have. Webber, Mittelholzer and Heath are from mixed blood, middle class stock, but similar examples of Indian-Guyanese fictional studies of African-Guyanese subjects are rare.

As seen earlier in Review #38 which discusses Heath's novel *The Ministry of Hope,* the author is the only non-Indian-Guyanese to produce a full-length fictional study of Burnham's régime. Heath's novel is steeped in an atmosphere where blackmailers and informers thrive, a local bank lends money to members of the ruling political party without expecting repayment, Government vehicles are unaccounted for, the Government auditor does not produce reports for years, Treasury accounts are years behind, and people indulge in corruption, lies and thuggery. However, unlike Indian-Guyanese fictional studies of the Burnham era, the action of *Ministry* shuns ethnic or political specificity: although it portrays the ruling régime as corrupt, neither its victimizers nor victims belong to a specific ethnic or political group.

The geographical and social environment of *Ministry* is recognized as Guyanese mainly because Kwaku, the hero, is known from previous fictional instalments of his career by the author. The novel's allegorical action is generalized, like Orwell's *Animal Farm,* where the animal characters are identified only by their political stripes, whereas the stripes in *Ministry* are moral rather than political. But the superior artistic level of Heath's novel cannot be disputed; his technical control of implied allegorical suggestiveness is in sharp contrast to the more explicit, allegorical technique used by Indian-Caribbean authors to display Burnham's political repression.

As already seen in Review #57 of the short fiction of African-Guyanese author, N.D. Williams, his story "Trinculo Walks the Dog," from his collection *Julie Mango,* portrays a middle class Guyanese protagonist (of unnamed ethnicity and nationality) who has a Ph.D. from Cambridge University, and whose father is a dentist, while his brother is a dental student in Canada. Although the specific time is not given, the story contains social details similar to those of the Burnham era, with the narrator's family being forced to migrate because of: "something rotten and deeply undermining the fabric of our family lives." [p. 35] In another N.D. Williams story, "Your Slip is Showing Comrade," is again pervaded by an atmosphere of fear and corruption typical of Burnham's régime, but as in *Ministry,* ethnic, national or political details are generalized.

In his non-fiction memoir *Path to Freedom,* by Conrad Taylor, an African-Guyanese who won a scholarship to West Point, the prestigious, US military college, the author returns to Guyana, only to come face to face with the Burnhamite repression of which his friends in Guyana had warned him. Interestingly, because Taylor's mother-in-law – Edmee Cummings – was one of Burnham's most trusted, PNC. activists, he is invited to a birthday party, attended by Burnham at Mrs. Cummings's house where he gets a rare, insider's view of the dictator. There is no bullying from Burnham: "no signs of authoritarianism" [p. 160] no resemblance to the:"power-hungry, egomaniacal politician." [p. 160] Instead, Burnham becomes: "almost humble, the folksy, engaging man of the people many Guyanese admired." [p. 164]

But Taylor also reports that Burnham feared the possibility of US action against his "dictatorial Government" [pp. 107-108] because he had collaborated with the Americans when he previously helped them to depose Dr. Jagan and: "feared a similar fate." [p. 108] Taylor's account shows the difference it could make to Guyana's future if other African-Guyanese , especially those who observed Burnham's dictatorship from inside the PNC, could reveal details of their experience in hope of deterring repetition of similar dictatorship in Guyana.

***

NOTES

1. Sasenarine Persaud, *Canada Geese and Apple Chatney* Toronto, TSAR, 1998.
2. Alex LaGuma, *A Walk in the Night*, London, Heinemann, 1967. First Published, Nigeria, 1962.
3. Oonya Kempadoo, *Buxton Spice*, London Phoenix house, 1998.
4. Nirmala Sewcharan,*Tomorrow is Another Day*,Leeds, Peepal Tree Press, 1994
5. Lakshmi Persaud, *For the Love of My Name*, Leeds, Peepal Tree Press, 2000.
6. Harischandra Khemraj, *Cosmic Dance*, Leeds, Peepal Tree Press, 1994.
7. Roy A.K. Heath, *The Shadow Bride*, London. William Collins Co. Ltd., 1988.

FEAR OF INDIAN-GUYANESE DOMINATION

Wilton Anderson "Jinks" Angoy (1907-2004) attended school in Guyana and Barbados, and worked as a civil servant in Guyana. In 1949 he attended a British Council Study Tour of Britain, and in 1953/54 took a course at Oxford University. He wrote an autobiography *Guyana Man: with Visions of Caribbean Integration.* (1990) His interview with Frank Birbalsingh was taped in Barbados on 30th October, 1996. F.B. speaks first.

FB: How did your career begin?
WA: I was born in New Amsterdam, Berbice, and went to Berbice High School. From 1926 to 1944 I worked in the Department of Customs in Georgetown. Then I moved to the Department of Labour.

FB: What was politics like during 1926 to 1944?
WA: In that colonial period, politicians had no power at all. There was a Legislative Council, but the expatriates and planters ran the country. There wasn't much development. It was just a matter of maintaining the roads and certain services.

FB: There wasn't much political expression?
WA: You had personalities, for example, A.R.F. Webber[1] who was editor of the Daily Chronicle, and Nelson Cannon.

FB: How did the political scene change after World War Two?
WA: As District Commissioner in 1952, I carried out the first

enumeration for the voters' list in the Rupununi. In that period Sir John Waddington and Dr Rita Hinden² visited Guyana to discuss the political situation. In 1952 the World Bank mission also came. I was appointed District Commissioner for East Berbice in 1956. This was Dr Jagan's stronghold and I served there from 1956 to 1960.

FB: What about the 1953 period and the suspension of the Constitution?
WA: Guyana had one of the most advanced Constitutions among Caribbean territories at the time, but Dr Jagan was taken with communism or socialism. In addition to that, the Burnham/Jagan partnership never worked from the very beginning.

FB: Why?
WA: Because Jagan would not take second place to Burnham, and Burnham wouldn't take second place to Jagan. It took two weeks before they could compromise on Jagan being the political leader of the People's Progressive Party, and Burnham being chairman. The split started from then.

FB: But Dr. Jagan won again in 1957?
WA: In 1957 I was returning officer in Dr Jagan's constituency. I cannot fault Dr Jagan on his sincerity. He has the country at heart. He is not a racialist. In the 1950s, Dr Jagan was so influential that it was said if he put up a broomstick as a candidate, people would vote for it. One of the most significant things was Brindley Benn winning a seat in the Essequibo islands: a black man winning his seat in an Indian community.

FB: In 1961 Dr Jagan was elected again. Then between 1961 and 1964 there were riots, the public service strike, and general social unrest, much of it engineered by outside forces such as

*American labour unions and the CIA. Do you see Dr Jagan
as the victim of a CIA conspiracy?*
WA: No, I'd don't see that at all. Dr Jagan was a victim of his
own circumstances. During the strike, I held a senior position.
I didn't want to go on strike, and my life was threatened by
fellow civil servants. So I went on the eighty-day strike. I
was told by my Minister when the strike was over that his
government was disappointed in me. I thought that was the
end, and decided to retire and come to Barbados to live. But
I gave Dr Jagan's government the most loyal support until I
retired.

*FB: Were the strikes in 1962 and 1963 not politically and
racially motivated to bring down the Jagan government?*
WA: No. It all started with Ishmael,[3] the head of the Manpower
Citizen's Association (MPCA). Then the civil service joined in.
We were the only civil service in the Caribbean to become a
member of the Trade Union Council. If the civil service didn't
join the union and go on strike, the whole thing would have
been over in two days. The Civil Service Association carried
the whole strike.

*FB: After Dr. Jagan lost power in 1964, how do you assess Mr
Burnham's performance in government from 1964 to 1985?*
WA: The straight fact is this: Burnham said we have to
live with the Indians. How do we live with Indians when
they were a numerical majority? He thought that by
establishing a Co-operative Republic and bringing people
of African origin into co-operatives, that they could match
the Indians in productivity. But the co-operative aspect
of it failed.

FB: Did he try to bring Indians and Africans together?
WA: There's no question about that. Jagan tried to cross

the ethnic barrier, and so did Burnham. Jagan took a lot of Africans into his cabinet, and Burnham took Indians into his cabinet. But it didn't work.

FB: What do you think of the 1968 elections when D'Aguiar was no longer with Burnham? As you know, there were charges that the elections were rigged.
WA: It was the overseas voting. How else was Burnham to counter the majority Indian vote?

FB: But during his twenty-one years in power Burnham is said to have reduced Guyana to an economic level which is second only Haiti in the Western world?
WA: That's fictitious. Burnham was anti-colonialist and anti-white. He removed all the white expatriates, and handed the economy to Indian-Guyanese on a platter. Probably he did not realise what he was doing. The expatriate firms formed a buffer between Indian-Guyanese and African-Guyanese, so once he removed Bookers, Sandbach Parker and other big expatriate investors, it meant that Indian-Guyanese would compete straight against African-Guyanese; and Indian-Guyanese had greater economic skills.

FB: So African-Guyanese let Burnham down in not being able to prosper from his policies?
WA: Not that they let him down. After abolition of slavery, as the Africans moved out of the sugar estates, they became demoralised. Indian-Guyanese are strong now in sugar and rice, and sugar and rice control the economy of the country. For instance, you will hardly find a black artisan, mason or shoemaker now. Every bit of industry is owned by the Indians. Their background in sugar and rice gave Indians an economic platform to move into business in Georgetown. Indian-Guyanese control every aspect of life in Guyana today.

FB: Are you saying that the economic enterprise of Indian-Guyanese suppresses African-Guyanese development, and therefore steps should be taken to limit it?

WA: Not limit but balance it. What is required now is for the Government to formulate a development programme which would open up the country to foreign investment, and provide employment for everyone. This is what foreign companies like Omai and Barama[4] have done: opened up the interior and provided employment. What is needed though is to provide economic opportunities for African-Guyanese in particular. Otherwise, it will seem that Indian-Guyanese want to take over Guyana.

FB: That has always been a fear among some people.

WA: It's a reality now.

FB: But Indian-Guyanese form a democratic majority of the population.

WA: What does democracy mean if the bacon is all on one side? It is marginalising the minority and, in time, it will mean liquidating the minority.

FB: You see that as part of Dr Jagan's program?

WA: It is not part of Dr Jagan's program. But there is great collaboration between Indians in Guyana and Indians in Trinidad.

FB: Are you implying that Indians in Guyana and Trinidad are cooperating in trying to achieve political control in Guyana and Trinidad?

WA: Political and economic.

FB: If Indians (or any other group) have political control of a territory in which they form a numerical majority, that doesn't

seem so bad? It would be worse if a minority group has control.
WA: But control by the majority in Guyana makes slaves of Africans who have contributed blood, sweat and tears to Guyana and the Caribbean. Why should Indians come as immigrants and have a greater claim to the resources of the country? It is a dangerous situation. It is bound to explode at some time, and it will involve the whole Caribbean.

FB: You are talking in terms of a racial war?
WA: Yes. A racial division. How far it will go I don't really know. If you are a rich man you should be able to live and let live. Although I am here in Barbados, I get news from Guyana all the time. It's the case now that Indian-Guyanese hate African-Guyanese. Blacks are tolerant and easy going. As long as they get sustenance they don't worry too much. But Indians from the lowest to the highest have one ambition: supremacy.

FB: Supremacy? You mean in the way the British had supremacy over us as colonial subjects?
WA: Dominance is a better word. My feeling is that Indians have a plan.

FB: To dominate?
WA: Yes.

FB: I think you said earlier that Jagan was not a racialist.
WA: Yes, but he has to answer to his constituency and do what his constituents say. Guyana needs people: immigration; but Indian- Guyanese don't want that. They are only giving lip service to regional integration.

FB: Because they want to preserve their numerical majority?
WA: That's it. You can stop there.

FB: Indian-Guyanese felt a sense of grievance between 1964 and 1992 when they had no political power at all.
WA: But they had economic power.

FB: Ashton Chase's book Guyana in Transit: Burnham's Role *described Burnham's government as locked into corruption at every level, from top to bottom. Government officers felt that they could go to their offices and do nothing. Their job was assured and no performance was necessary.*
WA: Burnham had to put in place people who were not qualified.

FB: But they were loyal.
WA: On the other hand, if you look at Dr. Jagan's government today, it has probably the worst corruption in history. It's not the government; it's the corrupt society. People falsify invoices and are not brought to trial. Bribery is rampant. There is no regard for law in the country.

FB: Isn't that an inheritance from Burnham's régime that Dr Jagan is trying to correct?
WA: No. That is the mentality. I think the Indian really wants to get everything.

FB: Once they were free from slavery, Africans became Westernised, educated and creolised. On the other hand, plantation living has remained with the Indians. They are slower in social development than Africans.
WA: That is it. The Indian has an objective. There are other sides of acquisitiveness. Indians are quick to learn. I remember as a boy, in the 1930s, all an Indian needed was for the traders selling a mill to give him some instructions. Then he would go to the bank and borrow money to set up a rice mill. Every month he would pay $100 until his debt was discharged. In competition with the Africans this is what stands out. Indians

are disciplined. If you want to see the real distribution of wealth in Guyana, travel from Georgetown to the Corentyne - the Indian stronghold. The Corentyne was so strong economically that there was one time, during the strike, [in 1962] when Indians were thinking of seceding from Guyana and holding on to the Corentyne. I have no feeling of a vendetta against the Indians. All I am concerned with is levelling the situation.

***

NOTES

1. A.R.F. Webber (1880-1932) was born in Tobago, but at the age of nineteen, moved to Guyana where he was active as a novelist, poet, historian, journalist, politician and businessman. Nelson Cannon was a local, white politician.
2. Sir John Waddington, Dr. Rita Hinden and Professor Vincent Harlow were members of a Commission appointed to make recommendations on B.G.'s political progress.
3. Richard Ishmael was principal and Founder of a high school, the Indian Education Trust College. He was also leader of the trade union Manpower Citizens' Association, (MPCA) and was active during a period of riots inspired by the US Central Intelligence Agency (CIA) in Guyana during the early 1960s.
4. Omai Gold Mines and Barama Timber Company were foreign companies operating in Guyana in the 1990s.

INDEX

St John's Passion, JS Bach 249-50
St Rose's High School 39-40
St Thomas and Guys Hospital 1
Salih, Tayeb 242
Salter, James 90
Sandbach Parker (formerly Jessel) 133-4, 298
Sanger-Davies VJ 173
Sankardayal, Clive 219
Savage, Sir Alfred 105, 107, 109
Scars of Bondage: A First Study of the Slave Colonial Experience of Africans in Guyana, Eusi and Tchaiko Kwayana XX, 63-5
Schomburgk, Sir Richard 24
Season of Migration to the North, Tayeb Salih 242
Seecharan, Clem 100, 115, 117-9, 125
Seecoomar, Judaman 143-6
Selvon, Samuel 229, 246, 260
Settlement of Indians in Guyana 1890-1930, The, Dale Bisnauth 71-4
Sewcharan, Nirmala 169, 285, 294
Seymour AJ 196, 255
Shadow Bride, The, Roy Heath 190, 292, 294
Shadows Move Amoung Them, Edgar Mittelholzer 158, 214
Shadows Round the Moon, Roy Heath 163-6
Shah, Ryhaan 91, 93-8
Shakespeare, William 118, 176, 197, 205-6, 214, 241
Shape-shifter, The, Pauline Melville 203
Sharples, Guy 196
Shinebourne, Janice (Jan Lowe) 82-3, 86
Short History of the Guyana Presbyterian Church, A, Dr Dale Bisnauth 71
Silence of the Islands, The, ND Williams 239-42
Singh
  Basil Aybarran (Barney) 227, 229-30
  Chaitram 147-52
  Dr JB 124